Essential Research Findings in Counselling and Psychotherapy

Praise for the book

'A remarkable summary of findings and their implications for practice as we enter the twenty-first century. Essential information to consider by professionals and students alike as they become more effective practitioners … This book is uncommon in its attempt to draw and highlight practice conclusions representing diverse and competing treatment methods and its openness to methods of investigating psychotherapy.'
Michael J. Lambert, PhD, Brigham Young University, UT

'A fantastic accomplishment. Mick Cooper brings together a vast amount of material in a relevant and interesting way.'
Professor John McLeod, Professor of Counselling, University of Abertay, Dundee

'The book's strengths are an inviting, personable style that draws the reader in and kindles thought, an objective perspective and a systematic review of research. I do not see any weaknesses.'
Arthur C. Bohart, California State University at Dominguez Hills, CA

'I generally do not become absorbed by texts about research, but this book was remarkably engaging – clear, concise, and handy as a reference guide.'
Kirk Schneider, psychologist and author of *Existential-Integrative Psychotherapy* and *Rediscovery of Awe*, CA

'Highly accessible, even for "statisticophobes". It is simple, without being simplistic, and brings quite complex concepts to a level that novices can grasp.'
Maureen O'Hara, Chair of Department of Psychology, National University, La Jolla, CA

'The publication of this book couldn't be more timely … Mick Cooper has a wonderful ability to write about complex things in a clear, accessible way. This is a comprehensive guide to what the evidence tells us so far – essential reading for practitioners, trainees and indeed clients themselves who want to understand more about the knowledge base of the powerful tool that therapy is.'
Laurie Clark, CEO of British Association for Counselling and Psychotherapy

Essential Research Findings in Counselling and Psychotherapy

The Facts are Friendly

Mick Cooper

British Association for
Counselling & Psychotherapy

Los Angeles • London • New Delhi • Singapore • Washington DC

First published 2008

SAGE Publications Ltd
1 Oliver's Yard
55 City Road
London EC1Y 1SP

SAGE Publications Inc.
2455 Teller Road
Thousand Oaks, California 91320

SAGE Publications India Pvt Ltd
B 1/I 1 Mohan Cooperative Industrial Area
Mathura Road
New Delhi 110 044

SAGE Publications Asia-Pacific Pte Ltd
33 Pekin Street #02-01
Far East Square
Singapore 048763

Library of Congress Control Number: 2008924198

British Library Cataloguing in Publication data

A catalogue record for this book is available from the British Library

ISBN 978-1-84787-042-1
ISBN 978-1-84787-043-8 (pbk)

Typeset by C & M Digitals Pvt Ltd, Chennai, India
Printed and bound in Great Britain by TJ International Ltd, Padstow, Cornwall
Printed on paper from sustainable resources

DEDICATION

For my princess, Maya, who wants to know everything.

Contents

Foreword

Psychotherapy had its humble beginnings as a 'new movement' at the beginning of the twentieth century and is now highly regarded as an indispensable form of treatment for a variety of mental health problems and personal crises, and remains a popular endeavour in which a growing number of professionals and paraprofessionals are actively involved. It is however a field characterised by considerable chaos, changing emphases, new developments, and considerable controversy. The number and types of psychotherapy has expanded, the practitioners of psychotherapy have increased in number and diversity along with training programmes. Psychology, social work, school psychology, nursing, pastoral counselling, marriage and family therapy, licensed professional counselling, substance abuse counselling, psychiatry, as well as a host of paraprofessionals participate in a variety of psychotherapeutic activities – all aimed at improving the mental health of patients. Yet programmes differ within and between themselves in the amount and intensity of didactic and supervised experience, but one cannot distinguish the training (or its quality) a particular provider has received by virtue of knowing the type of degree that has been attained. Since the various training programmes may emphasise different theoretical orientations and different practicum experiences, the diversity in training can be extensive. Even if training were more uniform, theories of change are somewhat independent of the actual activities that therapists engage in. It is also noteworthy that reimbursement systems have changed dramatically and emerged as a powerful force in theory, practice, and research.

In *Essential Research Findings in Counselling and Psychotherapy*, Mick Cooper has distilled and integrated findings from psychotherapy research (a vital and evolving enterprise), in order to supplement the theory-based activities of therapists, and provide a foundation for examining, exploring, and evaluating personal practices. While few psychotherapy research studies even attempt to examine the full range of consequences of entering treatment at a propitious moment in the life of a client who has a unique biological make-up, and is enmeshed in a family and social context, his book attempts to reduce the myriad of methods and results of psychotherapy research into a cohesive picture that has implications for practice – an ambitious undertaking. To this end, implications for practice' boxes are explicitly highlighted and distributed throughout the text, but with the hope that readers will find many more implications and catalysts for developing practice than those that are provided. Cooper also provides numerous opportunities to prompt clinicians to reflect upon the meaning of research findings for practice. This book is uncommon in its attempt to draw and highlight practice conclusions representing diverse and competing treatment methods (and modalities) and its openness to methods of investigating psychotherapy.

Cooper begins with a discussion of the limitations of empirical research in providing a basis for practice, as well as clarification of his preferences and belief system as they have influenced his review of research findings. He follows with a discussion of the overall outcomes of therapy then looks at the relationship between therapeutic outcomes and different factors within counselling and psychotherapy, including the contributions of therapists' orientation, client factors, therapist factors, relational factors, techniques, and practices. Psychotherapy of the near and distant future can be increasingly shaped by the results of psychotherapy research questions and findings. It is important that research has an important role in practice and *Essential Research Findings in Counselling and Psychotherapy* is an important contribution to this possibility. In Cooper's own words: 'So although the present book starts from the assumption that research findings are not a perfect or privileged source of information on how to practice counselling and psychotherapy, it does hold that they are one of several very valuable sources of information on therapy – and one that has tended to be overlooked by practitioners.' What is being advocated in this book, then, is not a 'research-directed' approach to therapy but a 'research-informed' one that relies on the integration of the best available research with clinical expertise in the context of the individual patient.

As a scholar of psychotherapy research I highly recommend this book as a remarkable summary of findings and their implications for practice as we enter the twenty-first century. Essential information to consider by professionals and students alike as they become more effective practitioners.

Michael J. Lambert, PhD

Brigham Young University

Foreword

The publication of this book couldn't be more timely, facing as we are in the counselling and psychotherapy profession what might be described as the evidence-based revolution. Interest in therapy has never been greater but with that comes the question 'Does it work? If I sign up for this therapy will I feel better and how long will it take?' Commissioners want to know the monetal value of counselling services: what is it worth in terms of savings to the public purse? The impact of the Improving Access to Psychological Therapies (IAPT) programme in the UK and the imminent regulation of the titles mean that the very survival of counselling and psychotherapy as we know it depends on us being able to develop robust evidence for psychological therapies across the board. Research has not traditionally been a significant part of counselling and psychotherapy training as it has in the psychology field; the British Association for Counselling and Psychotherapy (BACP) is working to change that and we funded the writing of this book as part of our very serious commitment to developing a research culture across the profession.

As an experienced teacher, researcher and practitioner of counselling and psychotherapy, Mick Cooper has a wonderful ability to write about complex things in a clear, accessible way. He is very aware of the limits of research and is cautious about encouraging practitioners to base their practice in any literal way on research findings. But as a practitioner–researcher he is also clearly excited by research and this passion comes across throughout the book. The facts may be friendly and in my opinion they are also fascinating. For example, anorexic clients weighed on average 40 kg before treatment and 48.2 kg after therapy. I was also interested to read that researchers show a marked tendency to find evidence to support their own orientation! The book will immerse you in the language of counselling and psychotherapy research such that you will be quite familiar by the end of it with terms like 'effect size' and 'meta-analysis'. You will also learn in three easy steps how to evaluate your own practice.

Of great value to practitioners and students I imagine will be the questions for reflection and discussion at the end of each chapter; such as 'How do you feel when you read about the relative efficacy of the different therapies?' It's interesting to monitor one's emotional reactions to some of the outcomes presented and reflect on why these might be so. This is a comprehensive guide to what the evidence tells us so far – essential reading for practitioners, trainees and indeed clients themselves who want to understand more about the knowledge base of the powerful tool that therapy is. And if empirical science does burst a few bubbles for us along the way, surely that is a good thing for ultimately it means being more real and more aware in the way we relate to clients.

Laurie Clarke, BACP Chief Executive

Acknowledgements

As always, I am enormously indebted to my partner, Helen Cruthers, whose love, support, friendship and generosity made the writing of this book possible.

This project was supported by funding from the British Association of Counselling and Psychotherapy (BACP), and I would like to thank Laurie Clarke and his team for all their help and encouragement in bringing the book to fruition. I am particularly grateful to Nancy Rowland, who supported this book from its very inception; Kaye Richards, who co-ordinated the reviewing and editorial process; and Angela Couchman and Suky Khele, for all their inspiration and encouragement.

Thanks to Alison Poyner, Michael Carmichael, Susannah Trefgarne, Alice Oven, Lucy Sinclair and other members of the Sage team for all their hard work on this book, and for once more making the editorial and production process such a pleasure.

Completing this book within a reasonable timescale would not have been possible without the help of Rachel Kelly in the Counselling Unit office, University of Strathclyde. Thanks also to Kathryn Cooper, Norma Craig and Heather Robertson for their input. I am indebted to David Alcock, Tom Malone, and other members of the university's library and learning services staff for all their help; and to academic colleagues for supporting my teaching leave: Lorna Carrick, Robert Elliott, Mike Hough, Tracey Sanders, Clive Rowlands and Iain Smith.

A number of colleagues provided invaluable feedback on early drafts of this book, and I am very thankful to them for all their time and effort: Mark Aveline, Christine Brown, Sarah Brown, Julia Buckroyd, Sue Cooper, Robert Elliott, Ewan Gillon, Alan Jamieson, Suzanne Keys, John McLeod, Dane Munro, Seb Randall, Kaye Richards, Nancy Rowland, Barbara Smith, Duncan Stoddart, Ladislav Timulak and Sarah Turner. Thanks also to Kate Anthony, Sophia Balamoutsou, Christian Gold, Craig Hutchison and David Tune for their suggestions and help; to Chris Evans for Figure 2.2; and to Michael Lambert and Laurie Clarke for their forewords.

Items from the Barrett-Lennard Relationship Inventory are reprinted, with thanks, with the permission of Godfrey Barrett-Lennard (see Chapter 6). Items from the

CORE-OM (Chapter 2) are reproduced with the permission of the CORE System Trust – special thanks to John Mellor-Clark at CORE for all his ongoing help and inspiration.

A number of people have been integral to my development as a therapist, teacher and writer over the years and I would like to take this opportunity to thank them for their mentoring and support: Christine Aubrey, David Bott, Philip Dodgson, Jessica Fox, Mary Manley, John McLeod, Dave Mearns, Lucia Moja-Strasser, Graham Molyneux, John Rowan, Pete Sanders and Peter Smith.

Finally, a special thanks to Maya, Ruby, Shula and Izzy, whose love, warmth and *chutzpah* makes it all feel worthwhile.

1

Introduction: the Challenge of Research

This chapter discusses:

- The value of applying research findings to practice.
- The limitations of applying research findings to practice.
- The aims of the book.
- The personal, theoretical and methodological perspective from which the book is written.
- What is in the book … and what is not.
- How the book is structured.

The Value of Research

Research findings can be like many things. They can be like dusty old library books hidden away, decomposing and seemingly irrelevant to everyday life. Or they can be like a mallet: something we get hit over the head with by people who want us to think like them. Research findings can also be like a deity: something we are in awe of and too afraid to question. This book hopes to convey another possibility – that research findings can be like good friends: something that can encourage, advise, stimulate and help us, but also something that we are not afraid to challenge and argue against.

Research

A systematic process of inquiry that leads to the development of new knowledge.

Empirical

Based on concrete experiences or observations, as opposed to purely theoretical conjecture.

So how can research findings be of help? For a start, they can give counsellors and psychotherapists (as well as clients) some very good ideas about where to start from in the absence of other information. Research can only ever tell us about the likelihood of certain things happening, but that knowledge can be enormously valuable if we have virtually nothing else to go on. So, for instance, if a therapist is meeting a depressed client for the first time, it can be very useful to know that, in general, positive outcomes with depressed clients are associated with empathic, caring and warm ways of relating (Castonguay et al., 2006). Subsequently, a therapist may discover that this particular client actually prefers a more distant form of encounter, but until the therapist has a clear sense of what that individual client wants, the research evidence can provide a valuable source of guidance on what the default therapeutic stance should be.

Second, and related to this, research findings can help practitioners to understand therapy from the *client's* perspective. Of course, trainee or practising therapists may feel that they already have a good insight into their clients' experiences – whether through theory, their own experiences in therapy or through listening to, and observing, their own clients – but the evidence indicates that is not always the case (and particularly in the early stages of therapy or when the therapeutic relationship is poor; Timulak, 2008a). For example:

- Therapists' ratings of the quality of the therapeutic relationship tend to show only moderate agreement with clients' ratings (e.g. Gurman, 1977; Tryon et al., 2007).
- In just 30 to 40 per cent of instances do therapists agree with clients on what was most significant in therapy sessions; with therapists tending to overestimate the importance of technical, as opposed to relational, aspects (Timulak, 2008a).
- Therapists are often poor at predicting the outcomes of therapy (Kadden et al., 1989), with one study finding that therapists correctly predicted just one out of forty-two clients who ultimately deteriorated (Lambert and Ogles, 1997).
- Client and therapist reports of the same episode of therapy often reveal striking differences in perception. For instance:

  Client: The counseling was worthwhile. It felt good … because it was the first time in years I could talk with someone about what's on my mind.
  Therapist: We were still in the beginning phases of treatment when she pulled out … I didn't feel that we were making progress. (Maluccio, 1979: 107–8)

- Counsellors and psychotherapists tend to overestimate their effectiveness relative to other therapists, with one study finding that 90 per cent of therapists put themselves in the top 25 per cent in terms of service delivery (Dew and Reimer, 2003 cited in Worthen and Lambert, 2007).

So although it can be important for trainee and practising therapists to trust their own intuitive sense of what clients are experiencing, it is also important for them to know that they can sometimes get it completely and utterly wrong, and empirical research findings can be a useful way of helping them to understand what their clients might be really going through. For even if their clients are telling them how good the therapeutic work has been or how much they value a particular intervention, the tendency for clients to 'defer' to their therapists (Rennie, 1998 see Box 7.2) means that an anonymous, independent examination can sometimes give a more accurate and reliable picture.

In this respect, the value of empirical research findings may not be so much in what they *teach* therapists, but more the way in which they can *challenge* therapists to reconsider their implicit assumptions and expectations (Cooper, 2004): shaking them out of rigid belief systems so that they can be more responsive to the actual client in front of them. Here is a personal example: as someone trained in existential psychotherapy (something I've defined as 'similar to person-centred therapy … only more miserable'; Cooper, 2003: 1), my tendency in initial sessions had always been to warn clients of the limits of therapeutic effectiveness. That is not to suggest that I would start off assessment sessions by saying: 'OK, so your life is meaningless, it has always been meaningless, you have no hope of change … and how can I help you?' but I did tend to adopt a rather dour stance, emphasising to clients that therapy was not a magic pill and highlighting the challenges that it was likely to involve. Then I came across a research chapter by Snyder and colleagues (1999) which showed, fairly conclusively, that the more clients hoped and believed that their therapy would work the more helpful it tended to be. How did I react? Well, initially I discounted it; but once I'd had a chance to digest it and consider it in the light of some supervisory and client feedback, I came to the conclusion that, perhaps, beginning an episode of therapy with all the things that might not help was possibly not the best starting point for clients. So what do I do now? Well, I don't tell clients everything is going to be fine the moment that they walk through the door; but I definitely spend less time taking them through all the limitations of the therapeutic enterprise; and if I think that therapy can help a client, I make sure that I tell them that.

Within the world of contemporary healthcare practices, there is another very good reason, albeit a more pragmatic one, why counsellors and psychotherapists should be aware of the research findings: to communicate with others about their work, and to help consumers understand the value of what it is that they do. Today, it is rarely enough to say to a commissioning agency, 'I really think you should employ me because *I* know that what I do is helpful.' And why should it be? Snake-oil salespeople would say exactly the same thing. Funding bodies, whether large-scale corporations or private individuals, are becoming increasingly critical consumers, and want concrete evidence with which to justify their expenditures; so with so much high-quality evidence demonstrating the value that therapy can have (see Chapter 2), it would seem entirely self-defeating for therapists not to have a good working knowledge of this material. As the research itself shows, counsellors and psychotherapists tend to underestimate the strong research support for certain positive therapy findings (Boisvert and Faust, 2006), so knowing what the research really says can help therapists feel more confident in promoting their work.

The Limitations of Research

The premise of this book, then, is that research findings can be like good friends but, as things stand today, it would seem as though many counsellors and psychotherapists are yet to get acquainted: research itself shows that many therapists have little interest in, or familiarity with, empirical research findings in their field (e.g., Boisvert and Faust, 2006). A study of American psychotherapists, for instance, found that only 4 per cent ranked research literature as the most useful source of information on how to practice; with 48 per cent giving top ranking to 'ongoing experiences with clients', 10 per cent ranking theoretical literature as the most useful source, and 8 per cent ranking their own experiences as clients most highly (Morrow-Bradley and Elliott, 1986).

No doubt, there are many good reasons why counsellors and psychotherapists should be wary of research findings. For a start, by its very nature, research talks in generalities rather than specifics. So, for instance, the research might show that depressed clients, *on average*, will exhibit fewer psychiatric symptoms after participating in short-term psychodynamic therapy (Leichsenring, 2001), but this does not mean that the one client in front of a therapist will *definitely* improve if he or she uses that therapeutic approach. The probability is that he or she will, but on the other hand he or she may not, and it is also possible that he or she will feel a lot worse if the therapist works in that way. In this respect, to base therapeutic practice wholly on empirical research findings – to the exclusion of other factors, such as the expressed preference of the client – would be profoundly unethical. Counselling and psychotherapy research findings can only ever tell us about what is most *likely* to happen – they cannot give us certainties.

Another limitation of research findings is that they will inevitably be influenced by the researchers' own assumptions and agendas (see Chapter 3). Take the following example: in a review of studies that compared the effectiveness of different anti-psychotic drugs, Heres and colleagues (2006) found that in 90 per cent of the studies the anti-psychotic drug that came out on top was the one manufactured by the drug company sponsoring the research. Hence, even when research is conducted in a highly rigorous way, biases still manage to creep in. This means that we should always read research findings in a critical way, paying attention to the background and context of whoever conducted the research and what their agendas might be.

Related to this is the fact that research findings are always arrived at through the use of some particular tool, measure or procedure, and these will inevitably influence the kinds of things that are 'found'. If psychological wellbeing is defined and measured in terms of a lack of 'mental illness', for instance, the kinds of therapies that are shown to be most effective may be very different to those if it is defined and measured in terms of a 'potential for growth'. Researchers can even come up with radically different conclusions with the same set of data if they use different tools of analysis (see, for instance, Elkin et al., 2006; Kim et al., 2006, Chapter 5). It is also important to bear in mind that research is always conducted with a particular sample of people, such that the generalisability of its findings will always be limited (see Chapter 3). We might know, for instance, that non-directive counselling is more effective than usual general practitioner (GP) care for a predominantly white, UK-based sample (King et al., 2000), but does that mean it will also be more effective for clients from black and minority ethnic backgrounds, or for clients in Japan? Again, the point is that research does not give us absolute truths, but one particular perspective on a phenomenon.

Sample

The collection of participants used in a study, from whom we want to make generalisations to a wider 'population'.

Even if it were possible for researchers and research tools to be entirely objective, value-free and comprehensive, we are still faced with the fact that the scientific method itself is not an assumption-free tool, but a particular way of understanding the world that is based on a specific set of assumptions (for instance, that events in the world are linked together by cause-and-effect relationships). So while, within the scientific framework, it may be possible to prove or disprove that certain things are true (though even that is questionable), it is never possible to prove that science itself is the 'truest' way of understanding the world.

RECOMMENDED READING

Slife, B.D. (2004) 'Theoretical challenges to therapy practice and research: the constraints of naturalism', in M.J. Lambert (ed.), *Bergin and Garfield's Handbook of Psychotherapy and Behavior Change* (5th edn). Chicago: John Wiley & Sons, pp. 44–83. In-depth and comprehensive critique of the assumptions behind traditional scientific research methods.

A Research-Informed Approach to Therapy

Given all these limitations, the basic premise of this book is that therapy should not be 'research-directed', but 'research-informed' (Westen et al., 2004). Here, research is seen as one very valuable source of information on how to practice counselling and psychotherapy, but it is not seen as a privileged or superior fount of knowledge – theory, personal experiences, supervisory input and many other factors are all seen as having a role to play too. Such a position may seem somewhat wishy-washy when compared with a harder-nosed, scientifically orientated approach, but it is worth noting that it is entirely consistent with the American Psychological Association's latest definition of 'evidence-based psychological practice': 'the integration of the best available research *with clinical expertise in the context of patient characteristics, culture, and preferences*' (APA, 2006: 273, italics added).

Aims

The principal aim of this book is to provide counsellors and psychotherapists with a user-friendly introduction to research findings in therapy. Accessibility is a key feature here: one of the main criticisms of therapy research is that it is seldom communicated in a 'clear and relevant fashion' (Morrow-Bradley and Elliott, 1986: 193). This book aims to be accessible to all, whatever their level of research expertise or professional training. Another key feature of the book is its orientation towards practice: the aim of the book is not just to help therapists reflect on their work, but to concretely and practically develop the therapy that they do. To this end, 'implications for practice' boxes are dispersed throughout the text, and it is my hope that practitioners will find many more implications for their work throughout the text.

The book also aims to help those in related fields – such as policy developers, service managers, social workers and general practitioners – to understand more about the impact of counselling and psychotherapy and the particular ways of working that may be most effective within specific contexts or with specific clients groups. It is also hoped that *users* (both actual and potential) of counselling and psychotherapy services will find this book a valuable resource: something that can help them to find the most appropriate therapist (see summary in Box 8.1), and to make the most of the counselling and psychotherapeutic services in which they might participate.

A third aim of this book is to act as a starting point for students or practitioners undertaking their own research in the counselling and psychotherapy field. Here, novice or experienced researchers can find out the kinds of questions that are being asked in particular areas of counselling and psychotherapy and the findings that have begun to emerge. To this end, recommendations for further reading are distributed throughout the book, and these are texts that I think researchers, or other interested readers, will find particularly useful or inspiring when wanting to follow up specific areas. The book also introduces readers to a number of key concepts in counselling and psychotherapy research. It should be emphasised, however, that the aim of this book is *not* to teach readers how to carry out their own research: for this, a number of excellent texts already exist, and I would particularly recommend McLeod's (2003) *Doing Counselling Research* (Sage, 2nd edn) and Barker, Pistrang and Elliott's (2002) *Research Methods in Clinical Psychology* (Wiley, 2nd edn).

Finally, and perhaps most importantly for me, what I hope this book can do is to convey something of my own passion and love for empirical inquiry. Without doubt, research findings can be dull, dreary and boring, but they also have the potential to be enormously stimulating, inspiring and challenging, and I would love for readers to experience something of that possibility when engaging with this text. My hope, when writing this book, was that it would be one of the first research texts that readers would want to keep by their bedside: that they will want to read and look forward to reading because they genuinely want to know what the research is saying.

Trying to Achieve Balance

In *Essential Research Findings in Counselling and Psychotherapy*, I have tried, as hard as possible, to produce a book that is a balanced and non-partisan evaluation of counselling and psychotherapy research findings. It should be emphasised, however, that such a task is by no means easy. Like many of us in the field, I *am* partisan and committed to a set of beliefs and assumptions about how counselling and psychotherapy does, and should, work.

To counteract these tendencies, I have tried to be as aware of my biases as possible, and to put them to one side whenever I notice them emerging. I have also tried to look for, and be open to, evidence which specifically counteracts my assumptions. In addition to this, the book has been reviewed by readers from a range of orientations to try to ensure that the material presented is relatively balanced. Nevertheless, it is important to acknowledge that this book does not, in any way, claim to be a definitive and objective presentation of the data. It is my, subjective, reading of the 'essential' research findings, and another reviewer, with other personal agendas and experiences, would almost certainly present it in a different way.

In trying to present a balanced overview of the field, one other thing that I can do is tell you, the reader, about my own particular perspective, so that you are more able to put my biases and assumptions to one side for yourself. In recent years I have come to see that the touchstone for my therapeutic work is a progressive political outlook (Cooper, 2006b). This means that I am particularly drawn towards those orientations, such as person-centred, existential and relational therapies (Cooper, 2003; Cooper et al., 2007; Mearns and Cooper, 2005), which I perceive as advocating an egalitarian, relatively democratic client–therapist relationship: in which clients are engaged with as intelligent, choice-making individuals who are trying, just as hard as their therapists, to do their best within their given circumstances. This means that I have a particular wariness towards those therapies – in particular, the more authoritarian forms of psychodynamic and cognitive-behavioural practice – which I perceive as promoting a relatively hierarchical client–therapist relationship: therapist as 'expert' and client as 'patient'. Having said all that, I am by no means a person-centred or existential purist, and feel strongly that an authentic expression of progressive values lies in an appreciation of the many different forms that therapy can take. Indeed, most recently, I have been working closely with John McLeod at the University of Abertay to develop a 'pluralistic' therapeutic framework (Cooper and McLeod, 2007), which starts from the assumption that different clients are likely to want different things from therapy at different points in time, and that there is no, one, 'right' way of working with clients. You may find, therefore, that this book is particularly challenging of therapeutic positions which suggest that one way of working is superior to every other, whether it is CBT or person-centred therapy.

This pluralistic bias, to some extent, also comes from my own experiences as a client. As someone who has been through some fairly severe episodes of psychological distress, I have experienced, and found helpful, a wide range of different therapies, including CBT, person-centred and psychodynamic; and I have also found anti-depressants an enormous help at a time of severe crisis. Concomitantly, I have come out of a few therapeutic relationships – two psychodynamic ones, in particular – feeling more traumatised than when I went in; and some of my experiences in existential, person-centred, cognitive and gestalt therapy have also been less than satisfying. In this respect, I really do believe that different therapies have lots to offer, and that what is generally most important is a therapist who is warm, respectful, non-defensive and willing to respond to a client's particular needs – though guidance, advice and structural interventions can also be very useful too.

Given that this book draws together research findings, it is also worth saying something about my biases in terms of what I consider valid methods of empirical inquiry. As might be expected from the above, I see different forms of research as having different contributions to make at different times, and do not feel that an 'either/or' split between quantitative and qualitative methods is either necessary or constructive.

Quantitative Research

Number-based research, generally incorporating statistical analysis.

Qualitative Research

Language-based research, in which experiences, perceptions, observations, etc., are not reduced to numerical form.

This preference for 'methodological pluralism' (see, for instance, Goss and Mearns, 1997) means that the present book draws on research findings from both the quantitative and qualitative realms. Quantitative findings are used to build up a picture of the typical outcomes of therapy and the kinds of factors that tend to be associated with positive changes; and, as with other reviews (e.g. Roth and Fonagy, 2005), there is a particular reliance on findings from studies with large numbers of participants, or where a large number of studies have been drawn together, because of the greater generalisability of such research. Also, the book draws primarily from those quantitative studies in which there is a high degree of methodological rigour and where efforts have been made to control bias, to minimise, as far as possible, the likelihood that the results are a product of the researchers' own prejudices (see 'hierarchy of evidence' in the Glossary for more details of how different sources of evidence tend to be weighted in this, and other, research reviews, e.g. Roth and Fonagy, 2005). As stated above, however, this book also draws, wherever possible, from qualitative research, and this is used to try to understand some of the more complex processes and outcomes in therapy, as well as some of the ways in which clients might specifically experience the therapeutic process.

Content

With respect to the content of this book, it might also be helpful to say a few words about statistics. Many people hate statistics, and I have tried, wherever possible, to report findings in a way that is accessible to even the most anxious statisticophobe. Having said that, there are some statistical concepts that are so useful for readers to know about that the book has not entirely dispensed with statistical terminology or analysis. This means that some of the writing (particularly the boxes in Chapter 2) might feel a bit tough going, but I would really encourage readers to stick with it and re-read sections, refer to the Glossary, 'Google' terms (the online encyclopaedia Wikipedia is a particularly useful and comprehensive source of information), or purchase a simple introductory text like Derek Rowntree's *Statistics Without Tears* (Penguin, 1991) to get a grasp of what is being discussed. I promise … it won't be for nothing: just understanding a few basic concepts like 'effect sizes' and 'significance' can make a world of difference to an understanding of counselling and psychotherapy research findings, and also to the confidence with which you will be able to communicate them to others.

In terms of the language used in this book, coming from a standpoint that wants to acknowledge the active role of service users, I have used the term 'client' throughout as opposed to 'patient'. I also tend to talk about clients 'participating' in therapy, rather than 'undergoing' it or having it done *to* them. I have tried to avoid the term 'treatment' because of its more medical connotations; and tend to write about psychological 'distress' rather than 'mental illness' or 'psychopathology' to avoid making judgements about what is or is not normal. The one exception to this is Box 3.1 on empirically supported treatments, where the research being discussed is very much framed within a medical outlook.

Given the lack of any reliable evidence indicating a difference between the practices of 'counselling' and 'psychotherapy' (Dunnett et al., 2007), I have tended to use the two terms interchangeably or used the generic terms 'therapy'. However, it should be noted that the vast majority of research findings discussed in this book are based on practices that are described as 'psychotherapy', so that the legitimacy of extrapolating from them to counselling could, conceivably, be challenged.

Finally, something about what is not in the book. A brief search on ISI Web of Knowledge (an internet journal search engine) reveals that around 60,000 academic papers have been published on counselling and psychotherapy research in the last thirty years. If each of these papers took one hour to read, a comprehensive reading of the literature would take about thirteen years. All that is a long way of saying that, inevitably, there are certain findings within the counselling and psychotherapy field that are not covered in this book. Most often this is because research in these areas is very limited, such that it is difficult to say anything with any degree of reliability. In other instances, however, I may have simply overlooked some important findings. If this is the case, I would be very happy to hear from readers about research that they think should be included for future editions (please email me via the publishers). Finally, for reasons of space I have focused primarily on the *outcomes* of *one-to-one*, *person-to-person* (i.e. not self-help) counselling and psychotherapy with *adults* (in the younger to middle-aged ranges). For research findings on aspects of counselling and psychotherapy not within this remit, see the suggestions for recommended reading below.

RECOMMENDED READING

The process of therapy

Tryon, G.S. (ed.) (2002) *Counselling Based on Process Research: Applying What We Know*. Boston: Allyn & Bacon.

Group therapy

Burlingame, G.M., MacKenzie, K.R. and Strauss, B. (2004) 'Small group treatment: evidence for effectiveness and mechanisms of change', in M.J. Lambert (ed.), *Bergin and Garfield's Handbook of Psychotherapy and Behavior Change* (5th edn). Chicago: John Wiley & Sons, pp. 647–96.

Family and couple therapy

Sprenkle, D.H. (ed.) (2002) *Effectiveness Research in Marriage and Family Therapy*. Alexandria, VA: American Association for Marriage and Family Therapy.

Self-help materials

den Boer, P., Wiersma, D. and van den Bosch, R. (2004) 'Why is self-help neglected in the treatment of emotional disorders? A meta-analysis', *Psychological Medicine*, 34 (6): 959–71.

Children and young people

Fonagy, P., Target, M., Cottrell, D., Phillips, J. and Kurtz, Z. (2002) *What Works for Whom? A Critical Review of Treatments for Children and Adolescence*. New York: Guilford Press.
Harris, B. and Pattison, S. (2004) *Research on Counselling Children and Young People: A Systematic Scoping Review*. Rugby: BACP.

Older adults

Hill, A. and Brettle, A. (2004) *Counselling Older People: A Systematic Review*. Rugby: BACP.

Research findings on counselling within specific contexts are also not covered here. For systematic reviews of research within such areas as primary care (Hill and Brettle, in press), further and higher education (Connell et al., 2006) and the workplace (McLeod, 2008) see the BACP publication pages at www.bacp.co.uk/publications/ index.html.

In terms of structure, the book begins with a discussion of the overall outcomes of therapy (Chapter 2). Subsequent chapters then look at the relationship between therapeutic outcomes and different factors within counselling and psychotherapy: the therapist's orientation (Chapter 3), client factors (Chapter 4), therapist factors (Chapter 5), relational factors (Chapter 6) and techniques (Chapter 7). The concluding chapter (Chapter 8) draws together the research findings and points towards ways of taking this work forward. Finally, for those interested in the evidence for specific therapeutic orientations, there is a review of the relevant research (Appendix 1). A Glossary of key terms is also presented at the end of this book.

Conclusion

For all of us, whether practitioners, researchers, students and/or clients, the challenge of research is by no means easy. It makes things complex, it can be hard work, and it can force us to reconsider our assumptions and most cherished beliefs. Carl Rogers (1961: 24), founder of the person-centred approach and one of the first psychotherapy researchers, wrote, 'in our early investigations I can well remember the anxiety of waiting to see how the findings came out. Suppose our hypotheses were *dis*-proved! Suppose we were mistaken in our views! Suppose our opinions were not justified!' However, he goes on to write:

> At such times, as I look back, it seems to me that I disregarded the facts as potential enemies, as possible bearers of disaster. I have perhaps been slow in coming to realize that the facts are *always* friendly. Every bit of evidence one can acquire, in any area, leads one that much closer to what is true. And being closer to the truth can never be a harmful or dangerous or unsatisfying thing. So while I still hate to readjust my thinking, still hate to give up old ways of perceiving and conceptualizing, yet at some deeper level I have, to a considerable degree, come to realize that these painful reorganizations are what is known as *learning*, and that though painful they always lead to a more satisfying because somewhat more accurate way of seeing life.

QUESTIONS FOR REFLECTION

1   What images or phrases does the word 'research' conjure up for you?

   • Write or draw these down, without trying to consciously filter them.
   • What does this tell you about how you might respond to counselling and psychotherapy research findings?

2   What do you consider the particular (i) strengths and (ii) limitations of research evidence as a basis on which to develop therapeutic practice?

3   To what extent would you trust research findings as against information from the following sources?

   • theoretical models
   • your own personal experiences as a therapist
   • your own personal experiences as a client
   • ethical and philosophical principles

4   Spend a few minutes listing the factors that you believe make therapy effective.

   • How would you feel, and what would you do, if you came across research that challenged these assumptions?
   • How open do you think you are to being challenged by research evidence?

Box 1.1   Research quiz

The following multiple-choice quiz offers readers an opportunity to reflect on the kinds of questions asked by counselling and psychotherapy researchers and to try to predict what they have found. Contrary to counselling and psychotherapy lore, there *are* right answers, but the quiz is not intended to be a test of readers' knowledge or ability; rather, its aim is to stimulate interest and discussion in the field.

   If used as part of a training programme, the quiz works well when undertaken in small groups of four or five. Groups should be given twenty minutes or so to try to come up with a *consensual* answer to each of the questions: i.e., students will need to discuss together which answers they think are right. With the input of a facilitator, the groups can then go through each of the answers (see page 190), discussing any issues, questions or surprises that emerge.

1   Compared with medical and surgical procedures, how would the effectiveness of counselling and psychotherapy, in general, be best described?
   (A)   It has a large positive effect.
   (B)   It has a small-to-medium positive effect.
   (C)   It has no effect.
   (D)   It has a small-to-medium negative effect.

2   Approximately how many sessions of therapy are needed to produce a 50 per cent rate of recovery among clients (i.e., about half of clients moving from a clinical, 'abnormal' level of psychological functioning to a non-clinical, 'normal' one)?
   (A)   1–5
   (B)   5–10
   (C)   10–20
   (D)   20–50

3   If therapists have personally experienced the same types of problems as their clients, are the outcomes of therapy, in general:
   (A)   Substantially enhanced?
   (B)   Slightly enhanced?
   (C)   Unaltered?
   (D)   Substantially worsened?

4   In a recent study, primary care patients for whom a brief therapeutic intervention was indicated were given the option of choosing between non-directive counselling and cognitive-behaviour therapy (CBT). In non-directive counselling, patients were told that the therapist would give them the opportunity to talk about what was troubling them so that they could explore their thoughts and feelings about it. In CBT, patients were told that the therapist would identify thoughts, feelings and behaviours that affected their mood and help them develop a more positive approach to them. Of those patients who specifically opted to choose one of these two therapies, what percentage chose the non-directive counselling and what percentage chose CBT?

(A)   10 per cent opted for non-directive counselling and 90 per cent opted for CBT.
(B)   40 per cent opted for non-directive counselling and 60 per cent opted for CBT.
(C)   60 per cent opted for non-directive counselling and 40 per cent opted for CBT.
(D)   90 per cent opted for non-directive counselling and 10 per cent opted for CBT.

5   In general, what is the relationship between clients' levels of psychological functioning and the amount that they tend to get out of therapy?
(A)   Clients who have poorer levels of psychological functioning tend to get the
most out of therapy.
(B)   Clients who have higher levels of psychological functioning tend to get the
most out of therapy.
(C)   Clients who have higher levels of psychological functioning tend to get the most
out of relational therapies (e.g., psychodynamic and humanistic approaches),
while those who have lower levels of psychological functioning tend to get the
most out of cognitive and behavioural therapies.
(D)   Clients' initial levels of psychological functioning are unrelated to how much
they get out of therapy.

6   Which of the following factors was described, in one of the most comprehensive reviews
of the research ever conducted, as 'the most important determinant of outcome'?
(A)   The quality of the therapeutic relationship.
(B)   The therapist's orientation.
(C)   The quality of the client's participation in therapy.
(D)   The quality of the therapist's interpretations.

7   Which one of the following statements is true?
(A)   More 'resistant' clients (i.e., those with greater tendencies to oppose their ther-
apists) tend to do better in non-directive therapies, while less resistant clients
tend to do better in directive therapies.
(B)   Less resistant clients tend to do better in non-directive therapies, while more
resistant clients tend to do better in directive therapies.
(C)   The vast majority of clients do better in more directive therapies.
(D)   The vast majority of clients do better in less directive therapies.

8   Which of the following events did clients, in one study, most frequently describe as
important in forming and strengthening a positive therapeutic relationship with their
therapists?
(A)   Technical activity (e.g., The therapist got me to make a list of my goals).
(B)   Self-disclosure (e.g., The therapist's business card said he/she was a trauma
survivor like me).
(C)   Emphasising client expertness (e.g., The therapist said, 'You know yourself
best').
(D)   Active listening (e.g., The therapist remembered and repeated back to me
things I had said in previous sessions).

(Continued)

(Continued)

9   For which of the following forms of psychological distress does psychotherapy appear to be most *cost*-effective?
    (A)   Severe psychological distress (e.g., schizophrenia).
    (B)   Moderate psychological distress (e.g., moderate depression).
    (C)   Mild psychological distress (e.g., mild generalised anxiety disorder).
    (D)   None: it is never cost-effective.

10 Which one of the following statements is true?
    (A)   On average, clients of female therapists tend do *much better* than clients of male therapists.
    (B)   On average, clients of female therapists tend do *a bit better* than clients of male therapists.
    (C)   On average, clients of male therapists tend do *a bit better* than clients of female therapists.
    (D)   On average, female clients tend to do better with female therapists and male clients tend to do better with male therapists.

RECOMMENDED READING

Lebow, J. (2006) *Research for the Psychotherapist: From Science to Practice*. London: Routledge. Hugely readable collection of essays on psychotherapy research findings, controversies, and implications for practice.

2

The Outcomes of Counselling and Psychotherapy

This chapter discusses:

- The evidence that counselling and psychotherapy can have a beneficial effect.
- The amount of change that therapy can bring about.
- The percentage of clients who improve in therapy.
- Whether or not some people deteriorate in therapy.
- Whether or not therapy brings about change in 'real world' settings.
- The relationship between how much people change and how much therapy they have.
- The long-term effects of therapy.
- The relative effectiveness of therapy versus medication.
- The cost-effectiveness of therapy.
- How researchers study, and report, therapeutic outcomes.

Does therapy help? Findings from thousands of studies over the last half century give an unequivocal answer to this question: yes (Lambert and Ogles, 2004). How can researchers be so sure? At its most basic, what researchers have done is to compare clients' levels of wellbeing before and after therapy on some indicator of psychological distress: for instance, number of hours slept per night or number of days panic-free. What they find, again and again, is that clients are better off after therapy than before it. For example: prior to a course of family therapy, clients with anorexia nervosa weighed, on average, 40 kg. After twelve months of therapy they weighed, on average, 48.2 kg (Eisler et al., 2000).

Findings from such studies show that participation in counselling and psychotherapy is associated with positive changes in behaviour or external characteristics. However, what many researchers are also interested in is changes in clients' *subjective* experiences: for instance, do clients *feel* less depressed after therapy? To assess this, researchers tend to use a range of different psychological questionnaires, which ask clients to rate how they are feeling before and after therapy on a variety of items (often about thirty). Some of these questionnaires are 'global' measures of psychological distress (i.e. they measure levels of distress in general) and others are measures of more specific psychological difficulties, such as depression or anxiety. Below are some items (i.e. statements that clients rate) from one of the most popular UK-based measure of global psychological distress, The Clinical Outcome in Routine Evaluation Outcome Measure (CORE-OM, see www.coreims.co.uk):

- 'I have felt terribly alone and isolated.'
- 'I have felt panic or terror.'
- 'I have felt despairing or hopeless.'

With this measure, clients are asked to rate how frequently they have experienced these thoughts or feelings over the past week on a 0 to 4 scale, with 4 meaning that they have experienced these feelings 'most or all of the time' and 0 meaning that they have experienced these feelings 'not at all'. The scores for each of the items can then be averaged, so that it is possible to compare pre-therapy scores with post-therapy scores, both for individual clients and for clients overall.

Studies that use such an approach consistently show that clients, on average, rate themselves as less psychologically distressed after therapy as compared with before it. Stiles et al. (2006), for instance, found that average CORE-OM scores for 1,309 clients seen in primary and secondary care settings went down from 1.74 pre-therapy to 0.85 post-therapy (higher CORE-OM scores indicate more psychological distress).

The 'Efficacy' of Counselling and Psychotherapy

But do such findings show that therapy, in itself, has helped people? The answer here is no, and the reason for this is that, with pre- and post-therapy measures alone, we cannot be sure that the counselling or psychotherapy was *actually* responsible for the changes that came about. For instance, it might be that psychological problems simply tend to go away over time (what Eysenck, 1957, referred to as 'spontaneous remission'), so that average improvements from pre- to post-therapy are not, actually, anything to do with participating in counselling or psychotherapy, but something that would just tend to happen anyway.

Because of this possibility, to show that psychological therapies are 'efficacious' – that is, that they bring about a desired effect – it is necessary to compare changes in clients who have undergone therapy with changes in a similar group of individuals who have *not* undergone therapy: what is called a 'control' group. This could be people who are *waiting* for therapy or people who are receiving treatment as usual from their doctors. If, in this comparison, the people who have therapy change more than a similar group of people who do not have therapy (see Box 2.1), *then* we can be fairly certain that the therapy, and no other factor, is responsible for the changes.

Efficacy

The potential to bring about a desired effect.

Experimental group

Individuals who participate in the procedure being tested.

Control group

A group of individuals with characteristics similar to those in the experimental group but who do not participate in the procedure being tested.

Box 2.1   Randomisation and randomised controlled trials (RCTs)

To ensure that individuals in both the control and experimental groups are as similar as possible, researchers will normally attempt to *randomly* allocate participants to the different conditions. Although this means that some differences will inevitably exist between the two groups, randomisation is generally seen, within the social sciences, as the best means of ensuring that the differences between the groups are kept to a minimum. A study which uses such a procedure to compare the effectiveness of different interventions is called a randomised controlled trial (RCT), and is considered by many people the 'gold standard' of research.

So, once they have controlled for other factors, what do researchers find? Pretty much the same thing, albeit to a slightly lesser degree (see, for instance, Lipsey and Wilson, 1993). That is, as compared to individuals who do not receive any therapy, clients who *do* receive therapy tend to improve more over time (Lambert and Ogles, 2004), and to an extent that is almost certainly *not* due to chance (a 'significant' difference, see Box 2.2). A typical example of this comes from a study by King and colleagues (2000), which compared, among other things, the efficacy of up to twelve weeks of non-directive counselling with usual general practitioner (GP) care for adults who were experiencing depression. Figure 2.1 presents participants' scores on the 'Beck Depression Inventory' (the 'BDI': a common measure of depression, with higher scores meaning more depressive symptoms) at assessment and at four months follow-up. This graph shows that, at assessment, both groups had about the same levels of depression (as one would expect if participants had been randomly distributed across the two conditions). After four months, however, those who received counselling experienced a greater decrease in their depression ratings than those who had received GP care as usual (a drop of 13.9 points compared with a drop of 9.3 points). Given that these two groups were virtually identical in every other respect, we can be relatively certain that this change was due to participation in the non-directive counselling.

Box 2.2   Are differences 'significant'?

Almost inevitably, the average amount of change in an experimental and a control group will not be the same. What are the chances, for instance, that clients participating in non-directive counselling and those receiving usual GP care will both improve, on average, by 3.123 points on an outcome measure? For this reason, counselling and psychotherapy researchers must not only ask if the experimental group has improved more (or less) than the control group, but also whether the difference is 'significant': i.e., is it meaningful and important rather than simply a consequence of chance variations?

To calculate this, researchers use a range of social science statistical procedures known as 'inferential' tests. Essentially, these indicate how likely it is that there are actually no real differences between the effectiveness of the two procedures (i.e., that people will do just as well in usual GP care as in non-directive counselling) and that the results of the study are actually just a product of chance. This is known as the 'p-value' (probability-value), and is a figure which ranges from 1 to 0, with lower scores indicating a lower probability that the experimental results are a product of random variations. What social science researchers then do is to adopt a cut-off point, often $p = 0.05$ (i.e., 1 in 20), and say that, if the p-value for a particular set of findings is less than the cut-off probability (for instance, if it is a probability of 1 in 30 or 1 in 10,000), then they will *reject* the hypothesis that the results just came about by chance. Rather, they will say that the differences between the conditions are '*significant*'.

With respect to findings in the counselling and psychotherapy field, what studies show is that the differences in improvement between therapy and control groups – whether pre-therapy, no-therapy or placebo – *are* nearly always significant. In other words, the likelihood that they have just come about by chance is very small, and nearly always less than 1 in 20. For instance, in my counselling in schools research, the likelihood that the reduction in Young Person's CORE scores ('YP-CORE', a measure of psychological distress for young people) from pre- to post-therapy was due to chance was about 0.0000000000000000000002 or more than one in a billion billion billion – i.e., not very likely at all (Cooper, 2006a). However, in some instances, research findings are *not* significant (for instance, if their p-value was 1 in 4), and this means the hypothesis that the different procedures are equivalent in effectiveness *cannot* be rejected. This does not mean that they have been shown to be the same, only that, at the present time, there is insufficient evidence to rule out the possibility that the findings are due to chance variations alone.

Figure 2.1   Assessment and four-month follow-up BDI scores for participants undergoing non-directive therapy or usual GP care (King et al., 2000)

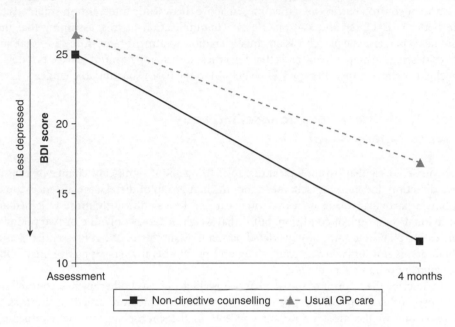

For someone who was highly sceptical about the value of counselling and psychotherapy, however, such findings would still not be entirely convincing. True, psychological therapy does seem to be responsible for bringing about positive change, but how do we know that this is really due to the 'active ingredients' of the therapy, and not simply the fact that someone *expects* to be changed or improved by it? After all, we know from medical research that pills or treatments with no inherent pharmacological properties can bring about substantial symptomatic improvements if people believe that they are going to be helped: the so-called 'placebo' effect. To examine this issue, researchers have not only compared changes in therapy with changes in non-therapeutic control groups, but also with changes in placebo conditions: generally some kind of supportive, listening-based befriending, which clients are encouraged to perceive as a genuine therapeutic treatment (e.g. Foa et al., 1991).

Placebo

A procedure that, while remaining credible to the participant, lacks the supposedly effective ingredients.

So what happens here? Well, the research shows that such minimal, placebo interventions do *actually* bring about quite positive results as compared with an entirely no-treatment control; but, at the same time, an active therapeutic intervention still tends to do better (e.g. Lipsey and Wilson, 1993). The implication of this, assuming that the clients *do* perceive the placebo as an equally credible treatment (an assumption that has its critics, e.g., Wampold, 2001), is that the efficacy of therapy cannot just be put down to clients believing that therapy will be helpful to them or expecting to change.

How *Much* Effect Does Counselling and Psychotherapy Have?

Of course, to say that psychological therapies bring about significant change in a positive direction does not, in itself, mean too much. A group of dieters, for instance, could follow a particular eating plan over one year and lose significantly more weight than individuals in a control condition, but if that weight loss was only one or two pounds, the eating plan would not be considered particularly successful. What is essential to ask, therefore, is not just *whether* counselling and psychotherapy has a positive effect, but *how much* positive effect it has.

To describe the amount of impact that counselling and psychotherapy has, counselling and psychotherapy researchers generally use a statistical measure called an 'effect size'. This is one of the most important concepts in the counselling and psychotherapy research field and it is really worth spending a few minutes getting to grips with it. An effect size is simply an expression of the strength of the relationship between two variables (a 'variable' being anything that can take on different values, such as the amount of chocolate people eat or the amount of weight they put on). A large effect size means that the two things are strongly linked (i.e. the more chocolate people eat, the more weight they put on), while a small or non-existent effect size means that the two things are only weakly linked or not linked at all (i.e. there is no relationship between eating chocolate and putting on weight).

Effect size (ES)

The strength of relationship between two variables.

Variable

Something that can take on different numerical values.

Effect sizes can be expressed in a variety of ways (see Box 2.3), but the most commonly used one in the counselling and psychotherapy research field is called 'Cohen's *d*' (indeed, sometimes the two terms are used synonymously, and for the purposes of this book 'effect size' refers to Cohen's *d* unless otherwise stated). Within the behavioural sciences, a *d* of 0.2 is considered a 'small' effect, a *d* of 0.5 is considered a 'medium' effect, and a *d* of 0.8 is considered a 'large' effect. Table 2.1 gives examples of small, medium and large effects from the medical and social science field.

Box 2.3   Effect size statistics

Cohen's *d*

Cohen's *d* expresses the amount of difference *between* two groups on some variable (for instance, the average difference in CORE-OM scores between experimental and control groups) relative to the amount of 'background' variation *within* the groups (i.e., how much CORE-OM scores vary, in general, for both experimental and control participants). Taking this latter variation into account is important in knowing how large an effect really is, because a difference of five points between groups on a measure means very different things if people usually vary by just one or two points, compared with normal variations of hundreds of points. Within the behavioural sciences, a *d* of:

- 0.2 = 'small'
- 0.5 = 'medium'
- 0.8 = 'large'

Note, a larger Cohen's *d* is more likely to indicate a *significant* difference (see Box 2.2), but the two terms are not entirely synonymous: factors like sample size make it possible to have large effect sizes that are not significant and small ones that are.

Correlation

Correlations are another way of expressing effect sizes, and are particularly appropriate when looking at the relationship between two 'continuous' variables (i.e., variables that can take on many different values, such as levels of congruence and therapeutic outcomes). Correlations are expressed as a number from 1 to −1, with a correlation of 1 meaning that two variables are entirely interlinked (i.e., higher levels of congruence always gives better outcomes), a correlation of −1 meaning that the two variables are entirely interlinked but in an opposite direction (i.e., higher levels of congruence always gives poorer outcomes), and a correlation of 0 meaning that the two variables are not related at all.

So what is the effect size of counselling and psychotherapy? Fortunately, researchers are in an excellent position to answer this question, because a standardised measure of the size of a relationship like Cohen's *d* allows researchers to combine findings of tens, hundreds or even thousands of studies, even where different measures and instruments have been used. This is known as a 'meta-analysis', and because it draws from an extensive body of data, can be considered one of the most reliable sources of information (see, for instance, Roth and Fonagy, 2005).

Table 2.1 Examples of effect sizes (from Meyer, Finn et al., 2001)

Small

Ever smoking and subsequent incidence of lung cancer within 25 years
Impact of media violence on subsequent naturally occurring interpersonal aggression

Medium

Sleeping pills and short-term improvements in chronic insomnia
Gender and self-reported assertiveness

Large

Increasing age and declining speed of information processing in adults
Gender and arm strength for adults

Over the last thirty years, hundreds of meta-analyses have been conducted on the efficacy of psychotherapy – both specific interventions (e.g. Matt and Navarro, 1997) and psychotherapy as a whole (e.g. Shapiro and Shapiro, 1982) – and what the summaries of these meta-analyses suggest is that the average effect size for counselling and psychotherapeutic practices, compared with a no-treatment control, is somewhere around 0.75 to 0.85 (Lambert and Ogles, 2004; Wampold, 2001). In other words, *counselling and psychotherapy has a large effect*, and substantially larger than many medical or surgical procedures, which have an average overall effect size of 0.5 (Caspi, 2004 cited in Carr, 2007).

Meta-analysis

A statistical procedure which brings together findings from similar studies to estimate overall effects.

Another way of conceptualising what a Cohen's *d* of 0.8 means is by converting it into percentages. More specifically, a Cohen's *d* of 0.8 means that around 79 *per cent* of clients who have had therapy do better than the average person who has not had therapy. This is illustrated in Figure 2.2, where the solid line indicates the extent to which people who participate in therapy improve (the further to the right, the more improvement), and the dashed line indicates the extent to which people who do not have therapy improve. In this diagram, the vertical line in the centre of the control group indicates the amount of improvement for the average person not in therapy, with the shaded area to the right of it indicating the 79 per cent of those participating in therapy who improve more than that.

Alternatively, consider an average person – let's call him Frank – going to his doctor with depression, and being encouraged to wait and see how things improve. Now imagine

Figure 2.2 Percentage of individuals in therapy who do better than the average control

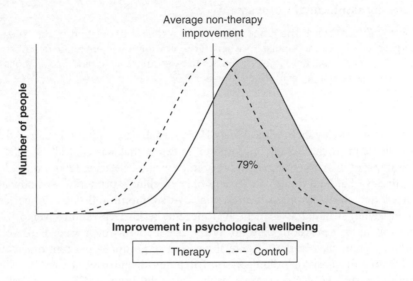

Frank two months down the line: possibly feeling a little better, but still relatively depressed. And now imagine another ten people going to their doctor, but this time being referred to therapy. So what the research is saying is that, in two months' time, approximately eight of these people will be feeling better than Frank, while two of them will be feeling worse.

Clinical Change

An effect size is a useful means of indicating how much change counselling and psychotherapy bring about. However, what it does not tell us is how many people in counselling and psychotherapy achieve their *desired* outcome: in particular, to be free of severe psychological distress (Jacobson and Truax, 1991). This distinction is important because, even if effect sizes are very large, if people are coming into therapy with extremely high levels of psychological distress, then they may still be leaving it with higher than desired levels of distress (and hence the successfulness of counselling and psychotherapy could be called into question). For this reason, improvements associated with counselling and psychotherapy can also be expressed in terms of 'clinically significant improvement'. This is the number of clients who have moved from levels of 'abnormally' high psychological distress – as defined by diagnostic criteria or by heightened scores on a measure of psychological disorder – to levels that are within a 'normal' range.

Clinically significant improvement

Movement from within the range of scores for a clinical population to the range of scores for a non-clinical population; when this clinical improvement is also described as 'reliable', it means that it is large enough not to be attributable to random variations on the measure (i.e. a significant change, see Box 2.2).

Summarising twenty-eight clinical trials, Hansen et al. (2002) found that around *60 per cent* of clients in psychotherapy improved to an extent that was clinically significant. A good example of this comes from a study by Simpson and colleagues (2000) which looked at the efficacy of around four to six sessions of counselling – primarily psychodynamic – with depressed clients in primary care settings. At six-month follow-up, 72 per cent of the clients who, at initial assessment, had met the Beck's Depression Inventory (BDI) criteria for 'mild depression' were no longer classifiable as depressed. However, it is important to note that, in the 'GP care alone' control group, 54 per cent of clients *also* moved from a diagnosis of 'mild depression' to a non-diagnosable status. Overall, then, this indicates that 18 per cent more people clinically improved with counselling as compared with GP care alone.

Change in the Real World: the Effectiveness of Therapy

Up to this point, most of the findings we have looked at have come from highly controlled experimental studies in which closely monitored therapists carry out manualised therapeutic practices (see Chapter 7) with clients who tend to fall neatly into one, clearly definable diagnostic category. Such a closely controlled approach is helpful in establishing the efficacy of counselling and psychotherapy (i.e. whether or not it has the potential to make a difference), but some researchers have argued that the kind of therapy carried out in these studies bears little relationship to the real world of therapeutic practice (e.g. Westen et al., 2004), where minimally monitored practitioners carry out an idiosyncratic mixture of therapeutic strategies, with clients who generally experience a diverse range of psychological difficulties. As well as knowing, then, what difference therapy *can* make (its 'efficacy'), it is also important to establish what *actual* difference it makes (its 'effectiveness').

Effectiveness

The extent to which an intervention, when used under ordinary circumstances, brings about a desired effect.

Studies of therapy in 'clinically representative' (i.e. real-world) conditions generally indicate that it is highly effective. For instance, within a UK primary care setting, Stiles and colleagues (2008) found that around 58 per cent of counselling and psychotherapy clients achieved reliable and clinical improvement, with effect sizes from pre- to post-therapy of around 1.35. And, indeed, in an extensive meta-analysis, Shadish and colleagues (2000) found that therapy in real-world conditions was no less effective than it is under more controlled conditions. This suggests that the findings discussed earlier in this chapter can be legitimately extrapolated to everyday therapeutic practice.

Clients' self-reports of how helpful they find therapy also point towards its real-world effectiveness. In a 1995 survey of over 4,000 former clients, for instance, America's foremost independent consumer magazine found that most clients had experienced counselling or psychotherapy as beneficial, even when the problems that had brought them into it were quite severe. The report states: 'Of those who started out "very poor," 54 per cent said treatment "made things a lot better," while another one-third said it helped their problems to some extent' (Consumer Reports, 1995: 735). In another survey, around nine out of ten former clients said that therapy had helped them in one or more ways (Feifel and Eells, 1963).

RECOMMENDED READING

Consumer Reports (1995) 'Mental health: Does therapy help?' *Consumer Reports*, 734–9. Results from the largest survey yet of people's experiences of therapy and its perceived effectiveness.

Shadish, W.R., Matt, G.E., Navarro, A.M. and Phillips, G. (2000) 'The effects of psychological therapies under clinically representative conditions: a meta-analysis', *Psychological Bulletin*, 126 (4): 512–29. Statistically complex, but the most comprehensive survey of the 'real-world' data available.

Do Some People Get Worse in Therapy?

While most people improve as a consequence of counselling and psychotherapy, there is a significant minority who do not, and the evidence indicates that therapists tend to underestimate this possibility (Boisvert and Faust, 2006). Research suggests that around 5 to 10 per cent of clients deteriorate in therapy – rising to 10 to 15 per cent in substance abuse work (Lilienfeld, 2007) – and this compares with deterioration rates of less than 5 per cent in no-therapy controls (Lambert and Ogles, 2004; Levy et al., 1996). A recent study also found that around 20 per cent of clients indicated that there was something in their therapy that was harmful or problematic (Levy et al., 1996); and there is also evidence to suggest that around half of clients will ultimately drop out of therapy (see Box 2.4). More compelling evidence of counselling and psychotherapy's potential to damage clients comes from first-person accounts of deeply destructive therapeutic encounters (e.g. Bates, 2006; Sands, 2000). In a recent collection of essays entitled *Shouldn't I be Feeling Better by Now?* (Bates, 2006), for instance, clients describe feeling humiliated, abandoned, manipulated, traumatised and emotionally abused by their therapists, and coming away from their psychotherapy sessions feeling far worse than they went in. As Lambert and Ogles (2004: 157–8) conclude from the data: 'psychotherapy can and does harm a portion of those it is intended to help'.

Box 2.4   The process of therapy: drop-out

A client can be defined as dropping out when they fail to attend a last scheduled visit, or when they withdraw from therapy before the therapist thinks advisable (Pekarik, 1992). Defined in these ways, research indicates that about half of all clients drop out (46.86% on average, Wierzbicki and Pekarik, 1993), with 20–57 per cent of outpatients (i.e. non-hospitalised clients) in mental health agencies dropping out after a first session (Brogan et al., 1999).

Research indicates that therapists may interpret drop-out as a personal failure or a rejection of them by the client (Brogan et al., 1999). And, indeed, clients who drop out – particularly in the first few sessions – *do* tend to have poorer outcomes and are less satisfied with therapy than those who do not (Wierzbicki and Pekarik, 1993). However, research also indicates that only around one-third of clients drop out of therapy because they are dissatisfied with their therapist or with the progress they are making; with a further third dropping out because they feel that their problems are sufficiently ameliorated, and a final third dropping out because of environmental constraints, such as a lack of finances or time (Pekarik, 1992).

Moderately higher rates of drop-out have been found in clients with lower socio-economic status, lower levels of education, and black and minority ethnic status, with some indications that this is due to different expectations concerning the nature and duration of therapy (see Chapter 4; Wierzbicki and Pekarik, 1993). There are also some indications that female clients and clients working with less experienced therapists are more likely to drop out (Wierzbicki and Pekarik, 1993). Lower levels of engagement in therapy (i.e. returning after an initial interview) are also associated with clients who:

- have longer waiting times from intake interview to being offered a first session
- have not had prior experiences of therapy
- are less ready to change
- are less satisfied with their initial intake interviews
- are provided with less clarity, perspective and information on their concerns at their initial intake interview
- have an intake interviewer with poorer communication skills.
(Tryon, 2002; Tryon and Winograd, 2002)

How Much Therapy Do Clients Need? The 'Dose–Effect' Relationship

In both the clinical laboratory and the real world, then, most clients seem to get better with counselling or psychotherapy, but how much therapy are we talking about?

Obviously, to say that most clients get better after two sessions of therapy is very different from saying that most clients get better after ten years of it.

Although researchers cannot predict exactly how much therapy each individual client will need to improve, what they can do is to calculate how much therapy is needed for a certain percentage of clients to demonstrate clinical improvement, and the percentage normally used here is 50, or half of the client group. As in other fields of science, this is known as the 'median effective dose,' or 'ED50' (Kopta et al., 1994). Studies of this type suggest that the number of therapy sessions required before 50 per cent of clients meet the criteria for recovery is somewhere between ten and twenty (Hansen et al., 2002), while fifty-eight or so sessions are required for 75 per cent of clients to clinically improve (the 'ED75'). However, these figures vary considerably depending on the kinds of problems and symptoms being looked at (Kopta et al., 1994). While the ED50 for 'crying easily', for instance, is five sessions, the ED50 for 'having trouble falling asleep' is more than 100 sessions (Kopta et al., 1994); and while the ED50 for treatments of anxiety and depression is around eight to thirteen sessions, the ED50 for clients categorised as 'borderline-psychotic' is between thirteen and fifty-two sessions (Howard et al., 1986). As might be expected, then, change on acute and symptomatic problems tends to happen more quickly than change on characterological and personality-based problems (e.g. Kopta et al., 1994).

ED50

The amount of something that is required to produce the desired effect in 50 per cent of the population.

Research into the 'dose–effect' relationship makes it clear that the more therapy clients have, the better they tend to get, and this has been shown in both the efficacy (e.g. Howard et al., 1986) and the effectiveness (e.g. Consumer Reports, 1995; Shadish et al., 2000) research. It would not be true to say, however, that there is a direct relationship between the number of sessions and the degree of improvement. Rather, what the research tends to show is a 'law of diminishing returns' – otherwise known as a 'negatively accelerating curve' (Kopta et al., 1994) – which means that, as clients have more and more sessions, so the added benefit of each session becomes less and less. This can be seen in Figure 2.3, which uses data from a number of different psychotherapy studies to plot the average numbers of clients improving for different amounts of psychotherapy (Howard et al., 1986). As can be seen in this graph, even before the first session, around one in seven clients have improved, and by session two, around a third of the clients have demonstrated improvement. As the number of sessions increases, however, so the degree of improvement decreases, so that the amount of improvement between sessions 53 to 104 is about the same as the amount of improvement between sessions two and four. It is important to note, however, that this graph is a depiction of *average* changes in therapy, with individual clients likely to show much more uneven patterns of growth (see Box 2.5).

Figure 2.3 Mean estimates of percentage of clients improved per sessions of therapy (from Howard et al., 1986)

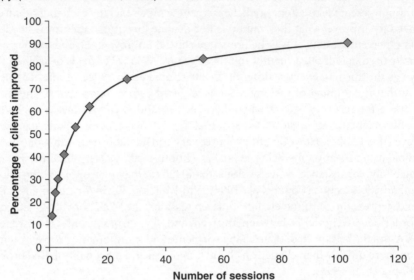

Box 2.5   The process of counselling and psychotherapy: sudden gains

Within the counselling and psychotherapy research field, an interesting recent discovery is that around 40 per cent of clients have more than half of their total symptom improvement concentrated in one between-session interval (Tang et al., 2007). These 'sudden gains' were first noted in CBT for depression (Tang and DeRubeis, 1999), but have since been found in a range of other therapies (e.g. Andrusyna et al., 2006); and appear to be sustained, with clients who experience sudden gains having considerably better outcomes than clients who do not (Tang et al., 2007). It is not clear what brings sudden gains about, although in CBT they seem to be preceded by sessions in which there are substantial cognitive changes (Tang and DeRubeis, 1999), and in psychodynamic therapy by a greater number of accurate interpretations and a better therapeutic relationship (Andrusyna et al., 2006). Qualitative accounts by clients also indicate that therapeutic change is often experienced as taking place suddenly: like 'a light going on', 'a load being lifted' or 'putting a shilling in the meter' (Carey et al., 2007).

Findings on the dose–effect relationship have important implications for the debate around short-term versus long-term therapy. On the one hand, it is clear that clients who participate in long-term therapy will tend to do better than clients who participate in short-term therapy. Indeed, while many counselling and psychotherapy services offer clients six sessions or less, evidence from the dose–effect research indicates that fewer than 50 per cent of clients can be expected to achieve substantial clinical benefit from such a provision (Hansen et al., 2002; Lambert and Ogles, 2004). At the same time, the law of diminishing returns means that short-term therapies can be viewed as relatively more effective than long-term ones: for instance, clients who have eight sessions of therapy will do more than half as well as clients who have sixteen sessions (Barkham et al., 1996). Indeed, in contexts where resources are strictly limited (say sixty hours of therapy), providing more clients with fewer sessions (say, ten clients with six sessions each) is likely to produce greater overall benefits than providing fewer clients with more sessions (say, two clients with thirty sessions each). Also, there is some evidence to suggest that change occurs more rapidly when tighter time limits are imposed (Barkham et al., 1996). Barkham and colleagues, for instance, found that clients who had completed an eight-week course of therapy averaged greater symptom reduction than those who were half-way through a sixteen-week programme.

RECOMMENDED READING

Hansen, N.B., Lambert, M.J. and Forman, E.M. (2002) 'The psychotherapy dose-response effect and its implications for treatment delivery services', *Clinical Psychology – Science and Practice*, 9 (3): 329–43. Excellent summary of the relationship between number of sessions and degree of improvement.

What Happens After Therapy?

Follow-up

Assessment or examination of a client at some point after the termination of therapy to monitor the efficacy of earlier treatment.

It is one thing for clients to feel better after ten or twenty weeks of therapy, but if they start to feel worse again once therapy is over, the positive impact of counselling and psychotherapy is relatively limited. A critical question, then, is: what happens when the therapy ends? Do clients rapidly deteriorate, are their gains maintained, or do they just keep on getting better and better? Here, findings from the empirical research are fairly clear: clients, on average, do not tend to improve once the therapy is over (a hypothesised 'sleeper effect'), but equally they do *not* tend to deteriorate rapidly (Lambert and Ogles, 2004; Nicholson and Berman, 1983). Rather, therapy gains tend to be maintained at 'follow-up' (i.e. at some point after the therapy has ended, often six months or one year), though there is some evidence of a decrease in improvement as time goes on (Nicholson and Berman, 1983). In one of the largest meta-analyses of the data, for instance, Nicholson and Berman found an effect size against a no-therapy control of 0.68 at the end of therapy, dropping down to 0.55 at an average eight months after therapy had ended (remember, an effect size of 0.8 means a large effect and 0.5 means a medium effect). This trend was evident across a range of different therapies, although there were some indications that certain social problems, such as assertiveness and public speaking, seemed to continue improving post-therapy; while phobias and somatic problems tended to get worse once the therapy had ended (Nicholson and Berman, 1983). In general, what the research also shows is that how well clients are doing at follow-up is strongly predicted by how well they are doing at the end of therapy (see Box 2.6).

Box 2.6   The process of therapy: improvement predicts improvement, deterioration predicts deterioration

Research on the long-term outcomes of counselling and psychotherapy suggest that clients who do well at the end of therapy tend to do well at follow-up, while those who make few gains during therapy tend to show little improvement further down the line (Nicholson and Berman, 1983). This is consistent with the research which indicates that clients who do well at the start of therapy tend to keep on doing well, while those who show an initial poor response to therapy are more likely to deteriorate (Lambert, 2007). There is little research evidence to support the assumption, then, that 'clients need to get worse before they get better'. Rather, if a client's symptoms are getting worse, this is a strong predictor that they will continue to get worse or drop out of therapy (Lambert, 2007), and is something that may be important to address: for instance, through trying to improve the therapeutic relationship, changing intervention strategies, helping the client to strengthen their social supports, or considering onward referral (Lambert, 2007; see Chapter 7).

One of the limitations of this research, however, is that most of the studies only follow up clients for a year or so after therapy, and there is very little information on what happens to clients eighteen months or more after termination. There are good methodological reasons for this (research participants tend to disappear), and also ethical ones (it would be unethical to withhold therapy from control participants for such a long time), but it does mean that our understanding of the long-term effects of counselling and psychotherapy is relatively limited. However, while there is no reason to believe that the effects of counselling and psychotherapy rapidly drop off after eighteen months or so, some researchers, such as Westen et al. (2004), have suggested that the long-term success rates of counselling and psychotherapy may be relatively modest. In a meta-analysis of controlled clinical trials for such disorders as depression and panic, for instance, they calculated that, by two years post-therapy, roughly 50 per cent of clients had sought further therapy; and that, of those treated for depression, only one-third had improved and remained improved over those two years. Another study found that, ten to sixteen years after participating in therapy for a specific phobia, around three-quarters of clients had again experienced clinically significant impairment or marked distress (Lipsitz et al., 1999). On the other hand, Fava and colleagues (2001) found that the long-term outcomes of behavioural therapy for panic disorder were generally well-maintained, with around 62 per cent of clients remaining free of the problem after ten years.

RECOMMENDED READING

Nicholson, R.A. and Berman, J.S. (1983) 'Is follow-up necessary in evaluating psychotherapy?' *Psychological Bulletin*, 93 (2): 261–78.

Therapy Versus Medication

In terms of how counselling and psychotherapy compare with pharmacological treatments, findings are relatively encouraging for the psychological therapies field. While there are some studies which suggest that drugs produce a faster initial response (e.g. Keller et al., 2000), by the end of treatment psychological therapies are usually as efficacious as pharmacological therapies (e.g. Chilvers et al., 2001) and sometimes more so (e.g. Gloaguen et al., 1998). Furthermore, once therapy comes to an end, the evidence suggests that many psychological therapies have a more enduring effect (e.g. Gould et al., 1995). A comparison of the efficacy of cognitive therapy against medication for depressed clients (De Maat et al., 2006), for instance, found that around 57 per cent of patients relapsed after drug treatments, compared with 27 per cent for psychotherapy. However, some studies do suggest that clients with more severe or 'endogenous' depression (i.e. depression that seems to have internal, biological causes) respond more positively to medication than to psychological therapies (Lambert and Ogles, 2004). It is also important to note that some of these findings come from studies conducted prior to the arrival of more recent anti-depressants, such as fluoxetine (Prozac©) (Lambert and Ogles, 2004), with the result that the relative efficacy of psychological therapies against contemporary pharmacological treatments is not clear.

Relapse

A term drawn from the medical field, indicating a return to ill-health following a period of improvement.

Another interesting question is the relative willingness of individuals to participate in verbal or pharmacological therapies. Here, again, the evidence tends to favour the psychological approaches (e.g. Iacoviello et al., 2007). Of 220 clients with mild to moderate depression who expressed a preference between counselling and anti-depressant drugs, for instance, 64 per cent chose the talking therapy while 36 per cent opted for the pharmacological treatment (Chilvers et al., 2001). Drop-out rates also tend to be higher in pharmacological treatments as compared with talking therapies (e.g. De Maat et al., 2006). In their meta-analysis of studies with panic-disordered clients, Gould and colleagues (1995) found that around 20 per cent of individuals dropped out of drug therapies, compared with just 5 per cent for CBT.

Finally, there is the question of how psychological therapy compares with psychological therapy *plus* medication. Findings here are relatively mixed. In some instances, combined treatments tend to do better than therapy alone (e.g. Bacaltchuk et al., 2001). However, in many studies, adding drugs treatments to a psychological therapy seems to do little to improve the efficacy of the latter (e.g. Gould et al., 1995), except in some cases of more severe or endogenous depression (Lambert and Ogles, 2004). However, it should also be noted that there is no strong evidence to suggest that pharmacological treatments *reduce* the efficacy of psychological therapies.

IMPLICATIONS FOR PRACTICE

There is no evidence to support the practice of encouraging – or requiring – clients to discontinue pharmacological treatments while participating in psychological therapies.

Cost-Effectiveness

Is counselling and psychotherapy worth it? To address this question, researchers have tended to compare the cost of the talking therapies with the cost of those interventions – such as medication or hospitalisation – that are necessary if clients do not use counselling or psychotherapy services. Research, here, indicates that psychotherapy can make a substantial reduction to the utilisation of medical care (Chiles et al., 1999; Mumford et al., 1984), including a reduction in inpatient stays of about 1.5 days per client from a control group average of 8.7 days (Mumford et al., 1984). Given, then, that a day in hospital can cost several times as much as an hour of individual therapy (Gabbard et al., 1997) (see Table 2.2 for relative costs of counselling), one might predict that a course of therapy could have considerable economic advantage over treatment as usual; and, indeed, this seems to be the case. In their meta-analysis of the most rigorous studies in the field, for instance, Gabbard and colleagues (1997) found that around 90 per cent of studies showed psychotherapy to be economically beneficial, with savings of as much as $10,000 (approximately £5,000) per individual per year over a no-therapy control.

Table 2.2   Unit costs of counselling (as of 1997–98) compared with other services and treatments in the UK (adapted from Simpson et al., 2000)

Inpatient stay	£211 per inpatient day
Community psychiatrist	£207 per hour of patient contact
Psychiatric outpatients	£97 per attendance
Social worker	£83 per hour of face-to-face contact
Psychologist	£56 per hour of patient contact
Health visitor	£52 per hour of client contact
Physiotherapist	£31 per hour of client contact
Counsellor	£27 per hour of client contact
GP consultation	£10 per contact
Home help	£8.50 per hour of face-to-face contact
Diazepam (Valium®)	Approx. £0.10 per tablet

Inpatient

A patient who resides at the institute in which he or she is being treated.

Outpatient

A patient who does not reside at the institute in which he or she is being treated.

Given that the greatest costs for those who do not receive psychotherapy tend to be in the form of increased hospitalisation (Mumford et al., 1984), cost-savings in inpatient settings tends to be greater than in outpatient settings ($d = 0.53$ and 0.23, respectively, Chiles et al., 1999). Along these lines, cost-savings are also particularly high when behavioural and psycho-educational procedures (see Chapter 3) are used in medical settings: for instance, relaxation training for patients awaiting surgery (Chiles et al., 1999). Because of the savings from reduced hospitalisation, counselling and psychotherapy seem to be most effective with older clients (Chiles et al., 1999; Mumford et al., 1984), and also those who experience the highest levels of psychological distress, such as people with schizophrenia (Gabbard et al., 1997). For those psychological difficulties such as affective disorders, on the other hand, where hospitalisation is a less likely outcome, psychotherapy and counselling appear to be about 'cost-neutral' (Gabbard et al., 1997; Simpson et al., 2000). An example of this comes from the study by King and colleagues (2000), which compared the efficacy of primary care counselling with GP treatment as usual, and also with CBT, for clients with depression and mixed anxiety and depression. In the year after recruitment to the study, participants in the treatment as usual condition, as compared with those in the two therapeutic conditions, did go to their GPs more (around nine contacts per year compared with seven), were prescribed more anti-depressants, and did receive more psychiatric referrals, but overall costs – for both the individual, the health service, and society in general – were about the same as for the therapeutic conditions (around £1,200 per client per year).

Findings such as these, however, only take into account the direct costs of psychological 'illness', and do not consider the wider, less tangible costs of mental distress on a country's social and economic wellbeing. In contrast, the *Layard Report* (Layard, 2004), one of the most influential policy documents in recent years in the UK mental health field, has suggested that mental illness costs the UK some 2 per cent of its gross domestic product (GDP), or around 25 billion pounds per year. This is made up, firstly, of around 4 billion pounds lost through time off work as a consequence of depression, anxiety and stress. Then, there is around 9 billion pounds lost because of the reduced employment of those with mental health problems. Added to this is 4 billion pounds or so lost because of the need for carers for the mentally ill. Finally, there is the 8 billion pounds or so that is spent on public services devoted to mental health, which includes around 1 billion pounds spent on GPs, drugs and social services; and around 5 billion pounds which goes towards mental health trusts (Layard, 2004). Based on such figures, the *Layard Report* calculates that, over a two-and-a-half year period, an expenditure of £1,000 on sixteen sessions of cognitive-behavioural therapy (CBT) or ongoing drug treatments could save around £3,000 in wider economic costs, or approximately £2,000 per individual. Furthermore, it is important to note that such calculations do not take into account the benefit for the individual or society in terms of increased happiness or social wellbeing. Indeed, if the 'human cost' of mental illness – in terms of personal suffering, distress and disability – is taken into account and translated into monetary terms, it has been estimated that the economic cost of mental illness may be as much as 41.8 billion pounds per year for England alone (Sainsbury Centre for Mental Health, 2006), and around 8.6 billion pounds for Scotland (Scottish Association for Mental Health, 2006).

RECOMMENDED READING

Gabbard, G.O., Lazar, S.G., Hornberger, J. and Spiegel, D. (1997) 'The economic impact of psychotherapy: A review', *American Journal of Psychiatry*, 154 (2): 147–55.
Layard, R. (2004) *Mental Health: Britain's Biggest Social Problem*. London: Department of Health.

Summary of Key Findings

- There is unequivocal evidence that, on average, psychological therapies have a positive effect on people's mental health and wellbeing.
- Overall, the average impact of counselling and psychotherapy is large, with a mean effect size of around 0.8.
- Almost eight out of ten individuals who participate in counselling or psychotherapy improve to a greater extent than the average person who does not participate in therapy.

- Overall, around 60 per cent of clients who are diagnosable with a clinical disorder at the commencement of therapy will be diagnosis-free by the end of it.
- Around ten to twenty sessions of therapy are required for 50 per cent of clients to show clinical improvement.
- The more therapy clients have, the more they tend to improve; but the amount of improvement they experience tends to decrease over time.
- Approximately 5–10 per cent of clients deteriorate as a result of therapy.
- Improvements in mental health tend to be maintained one or two years after therapy has ended, but the longer-term impact of psychological interventions is less clear.
- Talking therapies are generally as effective as pharmacological treatments for psychological distress, and seem to have lower relapse and drop-out rates.
- Counselling and psychotherapy are relatively cost-effective forms of mental health treatment – particularly for more psychologically distressed individuals – with an economic advantage above and beyond their contribution to psychological health and wellbeing.

RECOMMENDED READING

Carr, A. (2007) *The Effectiveness of Psychotherapy: A Review of Research.* Dublin: Irish Council for Psychotherapy. Chapter 2 gives an excellent summary of outcome findings in the field.

Lambert, M.J. and Ogles, B.M. (2004) 'The efficacy and effectiveness of psychotherapy', in M.J. Lambert (ed.), *Bergin and Garfield's Handbook of Psychotherapy and Behavior Change* (5th edn). Chicago: John Wiley & Sons, pp. 139–93. Definitive, detailed summary of counselling and psychotherapy outcome research.

QUESTIONS FOR REFLECTION

1   How do you *feel* when you read about the findings on the efficacy and effectiveness of counselling and psychotherapy? Pleased? Disappointed? Irritated? Intrigued? What might this say about your own beliefs, expectations and assumptions?
2   Do any of these findings *surprise* you? What surprises you most and what does this say about your expectations?
3   How do these findings match your own experiences of receiving or providing therapy?
4   What can you take from these findings into your own work?

3

Does Orientation Matter? The Great Psychotherapy Debate

This chapter discusses:

- The 'differential effectiveness' perspective: that some therapies are more efficacious for some forms of psychological distress than others.
- The particular types of therapy that have been shown to be efficacious for particular forms of psychological distress.
- Evidence against, and criticisms of, the differential effectiveness position.
- Evidence to support the 'dodo bird' hypothesis: that most therapies are about equivalent in their efficacy.
- Evidence against, and criticisms of, the dodo bird position.
- Ways of trying to reconcile the differential effectiveness position and the dodo bird position.

Of all the questions in the field of counselling and psychotherapy research, probably the most fiercely contested one is that of the relative efficacy and effectiveness of the different therapeutic orientations. On the one hand, there are those researchers, mainly of a cognitive-behavioural orientation, who argue that some therapies – mainly cognitive-behavioural ones – are more efficacious for certain forms of psychological distress than others (e.g. Chambless, 2002; Hunsley and Di Giulio, 2002). On the other hand, there are those researchers, mainly from non-CBT backgrounds, who argue that the different therapies are about equal in their overall efficacy (e.g. Asay and Lambert, 1999; Hubble et al., 1999; Wampold, 2001) and that it is other factors, such as the quality of the therapeutic relationship, that really make the difference to outcomes. What does the research *actually* say? Here, how one 'cuts the cake' – i.e. how one asks the questions and reads the evidence – makes all the difference to the answers one gets.

This chapter reviews the evidence regarding the 'Does orientation matter?' debate, and also presents a summary of the therapeutic practices that have been shown to be efficacious for specific psychological problems (Box 3.1). Readers who are interested in the evidence base for specific psychological orientations should refer to the Appendix.

Differential Effectiveness: Some Therapies are Better for Some Forms of Psychological Distress than Others

Which is the most appropriate form of psychological therapy to offer an individual? One way of answering this question is to identify the particular problem that an individual has, and then to look at which forms of therapy have been found to be efficacious for this problem. In other words, just as you might ask, 'Which drugs are effective in the treatment of diabetes?' so you might ask, 'Which psychological therapies are effective in the treatment of depression?' Such a line of questioning has been advanced by advocates of 'empirically supported treatments' (ESTs) (e.g. Chambless and Hollon, 1998), a movement which has its roots in the concept of 'evidence-based medicine': that current best evidence (and not mysticism, commercialism or political interests) should be used in making decisions about the care of individual clients (Chambless and Ollendick, 2001).

Today, many policy-making, governmental and funding bodies world-wide – for instance, the UK's National Institute of Health and Clinical Excellence (NICE) – adopt such an approach in determining which psychological therapies should be recommended, funded or implemented for the treatment of particular forms of psychological distress. After all, just as you would not give people with diabetes a medicine that had not been tested and proven to be effective, so, from this perspective, you should not give people with depression psychological treatments that are of no proven value.

Empirically supported treatments (ESTs)

(Also know as 'empirically supported therapies', 'empirically supported interventions', or 'empirically *validated* therapies/treatments/interventions'). Therapeutic practices that have been shown, through rigorous experimental studies, to be efficacious with a particular group of clients.

For supporters of this perspective, 'proven' means that the therapeutic approach has been shown to work at the highest possible level of rigour. In the US-based guidelines for empirically supported treatments (Chambless and Hollon, 1998), for instance, a therapy can only be deemed 'efficacious' if it has been shown to be more beneficial than no treatment (or equivalent to an already proven treatment) in at least two independent studies: studies which are normally expected to be randomised controlled trials, using therapeutic practices that are conducted according to a manual (see Chapter 7), and with clients who meet standardised diagnostic criteria. If only one study exists, or all studies have been conducted by the same research team, then the therapy is deemed '*possibly* efficacious'. If it has been found to be superior to a placebo, non-specific treatment, or rival intervention, it is categorised as 'efficacious *and specific*'.

Viewed in this way, there is much more evidence for some psychological orientations than for others. In particular, while cognitive, behavioural and cognitive-behavioural therapies have been shown to be efficacious with a wide range of psychological difficulties, other orientations, such as psychodynamic therapy, have been shown to be efficacious for only a few; and many, such as existential therapy, have not been shown to be efficacious for any (see Box 3.1).

Box 3.1   Empirically supported treatments

This box presents a review of the therapies that are of proven, or probable, efficacy for specific forms of psychological distress (according to the empirically supported treatments criteria – which are the subject of fierce controversy – see below). Descriptions of the therapies and diagnostic categories are given in the Glossary.

Mood disorders

Depression
As one of the most intensively researched forms of psychological distress, several different therapies have been shown to be efficacious with depression (National Institute for Health and Clinical Excellence, 2007b). For people with mild to moderate difficulties, a number of brief interventions, such as *non-directive counselling* and *problem-solving therapy* have been found to be helpful (National Institute for Health and Clinical Excellence, 2007b); and there is also evidence for the efficacy of *psychodynamic therapy* (Leichsenring, 2001), *process-experiential therapy* (Watson et al., 2003), *behavioural marital therapy* (where the depression is linked to relationship distress) (Baucom et al., 1998) and particularly *interpersonal therapy* (Elkin et al., 1989). The therapeutic approach most clearly demonstrated to be efficacious with depression, however, is *cognitive-behavioural therapy*, with around fifty high-quality trials showing that cognitive therapy has a large average effect size against controls or placebo groups ($d = 0.82$); remission rates of around 50 per cent; and an efficacy equivalent to anti-depressants, with lower relapse rates (Gloaguen et al., 1998; Hollon and Beck, 2004). *Mindfulness-based cognitive therapy* has also shown impressive results in reducing rates of relapse in depression (Ma and Teasdale, 2004). Amount of evidence, however, should not be confused with evidence of superiority (see below), and experimental studies which have directly compared CBT against other bona fide therapies have generally found them to be of about equivalent efficacy (e.g. Watson et al., 2003).

Bipolar disorder
Cognitive-behavioural techniques, *family-oriented interventions* and *psycho-education*, as adjunctive treatments to medication and as part of multimodal treatment programmes, have shown some ability to reduce relapse rates and to improve quality of life (Gutierrez and Scott, 2004; Roth and Fonagy, 2005).

Anxiety disorders

Across the anxiety disorders, evidence for the efficacy of CBT techniques – in particular, *exposure* – is especially strong (Ogles et al., 1999), with only limited evidence for most other psychological practices.

Specific phobias
Specific phobias (such as fears of snakes or flying) have been shown to be highly responsive to *cognitive-behavioural treatments* – one of the 'success stories' in the field of psychiatric treatment (Choy et al., 2007) – with clinically significant improvements in 70–85 per cent of clients (Roth and Fonagy, 2005) that are maintained at follow-up (Choy et al., 2007), at least in the short to medium term (Lipsitz et al., 1999). Evidence is particularly robust for *in vivo exposure,* with an average of just five hours of therapy needed to bring about clinical improvements in three-quarters of clients (Emmelkemp, 2004). However, some studies suggest that *introceptive exposure* and *virtual reality exposure* may be equally effective (Choy et al., 2007; Emmelkemp, 2004). *Cognitive therapy* has also been shown to be as effective as *in vivo* exposure for claustrophobia (Choy et al., 2007), and there is also evidence for its efficacy with hypochondriasis (Hollon and Beck, 2004), but evidence for its value with other phobias is more limited (Choy et al., 2007). Blood injury phobias are characterised by a specific physiological response, and have been shown to be particularly responsive to *applied muscle tension* (Roth and Fonagy, 2005).

Social phobia
As with specific phobias, *CBT* has been shown to be highly effective with socially phobic individuals, with as many as 85 per cent of participants making clinically significant gains that are maintained at follow-up (Hope et al., 1995). *In vivo exposure*, delivered both individually and in groups, is most strongly supported by the research, with evidence that exposure alone is as effective as combined cognitive-behavioural treatments (Hope et al., 1995; Scholing and Emmelkemp, 1996). *Social skills training* (Wlazlo et al., 1990) and *internet-delivered CBT* (Carlbring et al., 2007) have also been shown to be effective with social phobia, and at levels that are generally equivalent to other forms of CBT.

Panic disorder (with or without agoraphobia)
Cognitive-behavioural therapies, such as *panic control treatment,* have been shown to be highly efficacious with panic disorder, with as many as 85 per cent of clients panic-free by the end of therapy (Roth and Fonagy, 2005), gains maintained at long-term follow-up (for instance, after seven years, 68 per cent of clients were still in remission; Emmelkemp, 2004), and lower relapse rates than medication (Hollon and Beck, 2004). *Exposure-based* interventions have been shown to be particularly effective in the management of agoraphobic symptoms; though there is some evidence to suggest that *cognitively oriented treatments* may be superior to relaxation-based methods (Clark et al., 1994). *Bibliotherapy* based on CBT principles is also recommended as a treatment (National Institute for Health and Clinical Excellence, 2007a).

(Continued)

(Continued)

Generalised anxiety disorder

Generalised anxiety disorder has been shown to respond well to *CBT* treatments, although recovery rates (around 57 per cent) and effect sizes ($d \approx 0.7$ against controls) are less impressive than for simple phobias, social phobia and panic disorder (Emmelkemp, 2004; Gould et al., 1997). *Cognitive* and *behavioural* practices appear to be about equivalent in efficacy, with good results for relaxation training programmes such as *anxiety management* and *applied relaxation* (Öst and Breitholtz, 2000; Siev and Chambless, 2007). *Bibliotherapy* based on CBT principles is also recommended as a treatment (National Institute for Health and Clinical Excellence, 2007a).

Obsessive–compulsive disorder

Although among the most difficult problems to treat (Emmelkemp, 2004), obsessive–compulsive disorder has been shown to respond well to CBT, with equivalent or superior success rates to the most effective anti-depressants (Roth and Fonagy, 2005; van Balkom et al., 1994) and as many as 70-80 per cent of clients remaining improved up to six years after therapy (Emmelkemp, 2004). Evidence is greatest for *exposure and response prevention* treatments (Abramowitz, 1996), with indications that they are most effective when there is complete abstention from compulsive rituals and when the exposure is supervised by a therapist (as opposed to being self-directed) (Abramowitz, 1996). In instances where exposure and response prevention and behavioural interventions may be less successful – for instance, in managing mental ruminations – *cognitive* techniques may be of benefit.

Post-traumatic stress disorder (PTSD)

Cognitive-behavioural therapies – generally incorporating some form of *imaginal exposure* and *relaxation* techniques – have been shown to be effective with PTSD, with clinical improvement rates of around 50 per cent (maintained at follow-up) for clients who have been traumatised by such events as rape, assault and war (Bradley et al., 2005; Emmelkemp, 2004; Sherman, 1998). There is also some evidence to indicate that CBT may be effective for PTSD and other psychological problems for torture survivors (Campbell, 2007). Eye movement desensitisation and reprocessing (EMDR) has also been shown to be effective in the treatment of PTSD, with rates of improvement and average effect sizes ($d = 1.25$ against wait-list control) similar to CBT (Bradley et al., 2005); and there is also some research to suggest that *structured psychodynamic treatments* and *experiential therapies* may be efficacious (e.g. Paivio and Nieuwenhuis, 2001). Research indicates, however, that single-session *debriefing* shortly after traumatic events does not reduce the risk of developing PTSD, and may have adverse effects in the long term (Bisson et al., 1997). Based on such research, the authors of a recent 'Cochrane review' state: 'The practice of compulsory debriefing should cease pending further evidence' (Rose et al., 2006: 10).

Eating disorders

Anorexia nervosa

A handful of studies indicate that *cognitive-analytic therapy* (CAT), *psychodynamic psychotherapy* and particularly *family therapy* can be efficacious in the treatment of anorexia in adolescents and young adults, though gains appear to be relatively modest

(Dare et al., 2001; Eisler et al., 2000; Hay et al., 2007; Treasure et al., 1995). Inpatient treatments do not appear to be superior to outpatient treatments (Roth and Fonagy, 2005; Treasure et al., 1995), though gains seem to be greatest when the eating disorder is tackled at an early stage (Le Grange and Lock, 2005). Conventional CBT has not shown any great benefit in the treatment of anorexia with younger clients (Hollon and Beck, 2004); and, indeed, like interpersonal therapy, has been found to be less effective than non-specific supportive clinical management (McIntosh et al., 2005). However, there are some indications that CBT may be moderately efficacious with older adults (Serfaty et al., 1999).

Bulimia nervosa
In contrast to anorexia, a substantial body of evidence indicates that psychological therapies, specifically *CBT*, are efficacious in the treatment of bulimia, with around 30–60 per cent of clients fully abstaining from binge and purging behaviours by the end of treatment (Hollon and Beck, 2004). CBT has outcomes that are superior to, and more enduring than, drug treatments, with lower drop-out rates (Bacaltchuk et al., 2007; Hollon and Beck, 2004), though there are some indications that the effects of CBT 'decline substantially' at follow-up (Roth and Fonagy, 2005). *Interpersonal therapy* (IPT) has been shown to have some success with bulimia, particularly in the long term (Fairburn et al., 1993).

Obesity
Although many obese individuals will lose weight in standard behavioural (e.g. physical exercise) programmes, research indicates that most will regain the weight lost within a few years of treatment termination (Hollon and Beck, 2004). Extending such behavioural programmes with CBT techniques such as *problem-solving therapy* has led to improved maintenance of weight loss. *Hypnosis with CBT* may also be an efficacious treatment for obesity (Chambless and Ollendick, 2001; Kirsch et al., 1995).

Substance dependence and abuse

A range of psychological therapies have been found to be moderately effective in the treatment of substance abuse problems, though relapse rates are relatively high, with no clear indications of superiority for any one orientation (Roth and Fonagy, 2005).

Alcohol
Motivational interviewing/motivational enhancement therapy, twelve-step programmes and *CBT* have all been shown to be about equally helpful for alcohol-related problems (Project MATCH Research Group, 1997); as have specifically behavioural interventions, such as *relapse prevention, social skills training* and *cue exposure* (Miller et al., 2002; Roth and Fonagy, 2005; Walters, 2000). During the year after therapy, about one in four clients will remain continuously abstinent, with another 1 in 10 using alcohol moderately and without problems, and reduced alcohol consumption in the remaining clients of about 87 per cent (Miller et al., 2001). In many instances, brief therapies seem to be as effective as more extended treatments (Moyer et al., 2002): for instance, the Project MATCH (1997) study found that four sessions of motivational enhancement therapy were equivalent to twelve sessions of CBT or twelve-step facilitation.

(Continued)

(Continued)

Cocaine
Cognitive-behavioural therapies such as *relapse prevention* have been shown to be helpful in the treatment of cocaine-related problems, as has *twelve-step facilitation* (Roth and Fonagy, 2005). Individual drug *counselling* is also of demonstrable efficacy, with a recent large-scale study finding higher rates of continual abstinence over a three-month period for this approach (38 per cent) than CBT (23 per cent), psychodynamic psychotherapy (18 per cent), or group counselling (27 per cent) (Crits-Christoph et al., 1999). A meta-analysis of the overall efficacy of drug abuse treatment programmes for cocaine, heroin and other drug use against controls found effect sizes in the small range: 0.3 for drug use and 0.13 for crime (Prendergast et al., 2002).

Opiates
As with cocaine dependency, *contingency management* and *community reinforcement approaches* have been shown to improve outcomes in the treatment of opiate-related problems (Roth and Fonagy, 2005), and there is evidence to indicate that *dialectical behaviour therapy* is of value for opiate-dependent women who meet the criteria for borderline personality disorder (Linehan et al., 2002). *Supportive-expressive psychotherapy* and *counselling* have also been shown to be of benefit for methadone-maintained individuals (Woody et al., 1995). However, there is inadequate evidence to prove the effectiveness of psychological interventions *alone* for the treatment of opiate dependency (Mayet et al., 2004).

Cannabis
A small number of studies indicate that both *CBT* and *motivational enhancement therapy* can reduce severity of dependency on cannabis as well as rates of use (around seven days of use per month compared with seventeen days for a delayed-treatment control group) (Denis et al., 2004; Emmelkemp, 2004).

Sexual dysfunctions

Male
For erectile problems, behaviourally based techniques such as *systematic desensitisation* and *sensate focus exercises* have been shown to be effective (at about equivalent levels), with around two-thirds of men satisfied with treatment at follow-up, though relapse rates appear to be high (Emmelkemp, 2004; Mohr and Beutler, 1990). However, much of this research was conducted pre-Viagra®, and it is not clear how psychological treatments compare with modern pharmacological ones (Emmelkemp, 2004). For premature ejaculation, behaviourally based approaches such as Masters and Johnson's *squeeze technique* show around 50 per cent improvement rates, though relapse rates are again quite marked (Roth and Fonagy, 2005).

Female
For women who experience inhibited orgasm, sexual technique training (such as *masturbation training* and the *coital alignment technique*), as well as *communication training,*

have demonstrated moderate levels of success. For instance, at six months follow-up, 37 per cent of women who participated in psychological therapy could reach orgasm during coitus more than half of the time, compared with none of the women prior to therapy (Roth and Fonagy, 2005). There is some evidence that vaginismus responds well to *exposure-based* behavioural techniques, with up to 90 per cent success rates (McGuire and Hawton, 2001).

Personality disorders

Despite the widespread belief that personality disorders are intractable to psychological therapies (Perry et al., 1999), a meta-analysis of fifteen studies using a range of approaches showed a large overall effect size from pre-therapy to follow-up ($d = 1.11$, versus 0.25 in controls), with around 50 per cent of clients recovered after seventy-eight sessions (Perry et al., 1999). *Cognitive-behavioural therapy* and *psychodynamic therapy* (conducted in both outpatient and partial hospitalisation settings), the two main approaches used in these studies, appear about equal in their efficacy (Leichsenring and Leibing, 2003). Overall, patients diagnosed with cluster C personality disorders (anxious or fearful types, see Table 4.1) tend to improve most, with clients diagnosed with schizotypal personality disorder the least, and clients diagnosed with borderline personality disorder (BPD) somewhere in between (Ogrodniczuk and Piper, 2001; Perry et al., 1999). Much of the recent research in this area, however, has focused on treatments for borderline personality disorder, and *psychodynamically oriented partial hospitalisation* programmes have shown particularly impressive results, with reduced use of medication at eighteen months follow-up (27.3 per cent versus 73.7 per cent in controls), reduced numbers of average outpatient visits (0.7 versus 4.3) and lower rates of depression (59 per cent versus 12.5 per cent below the clinical cut-off) (Bateman and Fonagy, 2001). *Dialectical behaviour therapy* has also been shown to have some positive impact on clients diagnosed with BPD, reducing rates of self-harming and parasuicidal behaviours (Binks et al., 2006).

Schizophrenia

While there is no reliable evidence to indicate that psychological therapies can 'cure' schizophrenia, it has been shown to reduce some of the stresses associated with the condition and improve quality of life (Dickerson, 2000). Evidence is strongest for *family-based* interventions and *CBT* approaches, such as *coping strategy enhancement therapy* (Pilling et al., 2002). Tarrier and colleagues (1993), for instance, showed that CBT reduced symptoms of schizophrenia by half or more in 60 per cent of the coping skills group, compared with 25 per cent in a generic problem-solving condition. There is also evidence to suggest that CBT may improve levels of insight, adherence to drug treatments, and reduce relapse rates (National Collaborating Centre for Mental Health, 2003). As a specific variant of CBT, *social skills training* has also been shown to improve social functioning in people with schizophrenia (Emmelkemp, 2004; National Collaborating Centre for Mental Health, 2003). Longer-term CBT (greater than three months) appears to be particularly effective as compared with shorter-term approaches (National

(Continued)

(Continued)

Collaborating Centre for Mental Health, 2003). *Family interventions*, primarily of a CBT-form, have been shown to be particularly effective at reducing relapse rates in people with schizophrenia (12.8 per cent absolute reduction, Pilling et al., 2002), and there is also evidence that they can increase adherence to drug treatments and reduce the 'burden of care' among carers (National Collaborating Centre for Mental Health, 2003). Evidence is strongest for the use of psychological therapies with persisting psychotic symptoms as opposed to acute symptoms (National Collaborating Centre for Mental Health, 2003), and seems to be of greater benefit with 'positive symptoms' (i.e. heightened levels of thoughts, emotions or behaviours, such as delusions) as compared with 'negative' ones (i.e. loss or absence of normal traits or abilities, such as blunted affect) (Dickerson and Lehman, 2006).

Miscellaneous problems

Health-related difficulties
Cognitive-behavioural therapies have been shown to be efficacious in the treatment of headaches, chronic back pain, rheumatic disease pain and smoking cessation; with evidence that they may also be efficacious for such conditions as irritable-bowel syndrome (IBS), heterogeneous chronic pain, chemotherapy side effects, chronic fatigue, pre-menstrual syndrome, and pain associated with such diseases as cancer and sickle-cell disorder (Chambless and Ollendick, 2001; Compas et al., 1998; Department of Health, 2001). There is also some evidence that *psychodynamic therapy* and *hypnotherapy* are effective in the treatment of IBS; and that *family and marital therapies* (Department of Health, 2001) and *experiential therapies* (Elliott, Greenberg et al., 2004) may be helpful in the treatment of a range of health-related difficulties.

Relational distress
Behavioural marital therapy has been shown to be efficacious with marital and relationship difficulties, and there is also evidence that *systemic therapies, insight-oriented therapies, cognitive therapies*, and *emotion-focused couples therapy* are efficacious in this area (Chambless and Ollendick, 2001).

Deliberate self-harm
Although the evidence is very limited, there are some indications that *problem-solving therapy* and *dialectical behaviour therapy*, both forms of CBT, can reduce rates of deliberate self-harm (Hawton et al., 1999).

Anger
Cognitive-behavioural treatments such as relaxation training, behavioural skills training, cognitive restructuring and self-instructional training have been shown to be effective with a range of anger problems, with a moderate to large average effect size against controls ($d = 0.71$) (DiGiuseppe and Tafrate, 2003). There is also some evidence to indicate that *experiential group therapies* can significantly reduce experiences and expressions of aggression (DiGiuseppe and Tafrate, 2003; Elliott, Greenberg et al., 2004). Treatments for

perpetrators of domestic violence have yet to be shown to be efficacious in experimental studies (Babcock et al., 2004; Smedslund and Ringdal, 2004), although there are some indications that both the *Duluth model* and CBT can lead to small reductions in re-offending, with some evidence of superior effectiveness for the former (Babcock et al., 2004).

Pathological gambling
Cognitive-behavioural treatments have been shown to reduce both desire to gamble and amount of gambling, with large effect sizes at post-treatment ($d = 1.41–1.78$ versus wait-list controls (Pallesen et al., 2005)), and around 86 per cent of treated participants no longer considered pathological gamblers by end of therapy (Sylvain et al., 1997).

Complicated grief
Psychological interventions for grief, *per se*, have become a controversial topic in recent years, with meta-analyses indicating only small effect sizes of around 0.1 to 0.4 against controls (Allumbaugh and Hoyt, 1999; Kato and Mann, 1999). However, for clients experiencing more 'complicated' or 'pathological' forms of grief, CBT programmes – and particularly *exposure* therapy – have been shown to be more effective than an alternative treatment control (Boelen et al., 2007; Shear et al., 2005).

Recommended reading

Roth, A. and Fonagy, P. (2005) *What Works for Whom? A Critical Review of Psychotherapy Research* (New York: Guilford Press). A monumental, enormously comprehensive and detailed review of empirically supported therapies for particular forms of psychological distress – essential reading for those working with clients with specific psychiatric diagnoses. An alternative, more US-oriented compilation is Nathan and Gorman's (2007) *A Guide to Treatments that Work*.

Challenges to the Differential Effectiveness Position

For practitioners of a non-CBT orientation, Box 3.1 can make for challenging reading. And, indeed, many researchers and practitioners in the field have vehemently questioned such an understanding of the research findings – as well as the assumptions behind, and evidence for, the differential effectiveness position.

Do Discrete Forms of Psychological Distress Exist?

First, as we have seen, the concept of empirically supported treatments is based on the assumption that discrete forms of psychological 'illness' exist, but is this actually the case? Is there, for instance, a specific illness called 'panic disorder', which can be reliably discriminated from 'generalised anxiety disorder' or 'social phobia'? Many authorities in the field do not think so. Duncan and colleagues (2004: xii), for instance, write: 'Factually, it is quite uncertain that the cluster of symptoms that we bind together under discrete diagnostic labels really represent discrete conditions or disease processes at all.' In support of their critique, they point to the fact that even specially trained clinicians will differ quite markedly in their diagnoses of the same client. Moreover, research shows that around 50–90 per cent of individuals who meet the criteria for one 'mental disorder' also meet the criteria for one or more additional 'disorders' (what is known as 'comorbidity', Westen et al., 2004), indicating that there is a great deal of overlap among the different forms of mental 'illness'. Furthermore, around one-third to one-half of clients who seek mental health treatment do not meet the criteria for any disorder (Westen et al., 2004) – again questioning the validity of basing treatment choices around a diagnostic system.

Comorbidity

Diagnosis of more than one form of severe psychological distress in an individual at the same time.

RECOMMENDED READING

Duncan, B.L., Miller, S.D. and Sparks, J.A. (2004) *The Heroic Client*. San Francisco: Jossey-Bass. See chapter 2, 'The myth of the medical model'.

How Generalisable are Empirically Supported Treatments?

A second problem with the empirically supported treatments approach is that the research on which it is based comes from particular samples of participants, and extreme care must be taken in generalising out from this sample to the population as a whole (see Chapter 1). In particular, given that the vast majority of experimentally controlled studies have been conducted with clients of a predominantly European ethnic origin, there is no certainty that therapies shown to be efficacious with this group will also be efficacious with clients from other ethnic backgrounds. Furthermore, given that particular groups of clients tend to be systematically excluded from randomised controlled trials – such as people with comorbid diagnoses, on medication, or at high risk of suicide (e.g. Watson et al., 2003) – there is a serious question of how generalisable efficacy findings can be to such groups.

A Lack of Evidence is not the Same as Counter-Evidence

It is also essential to point out that, in the vast majority of instances, the absence of a therapy on the empirically supported treatments list does not mean that it has been shown to be ineffective; only that it has yet to be tested. This is something that advocates of an empirically supported approach accept (e.g. Chambless et al., 1996), and they invite non-CBT therapies to prove their clinical worth. However, if the primary determinant of whether or not a therapy is empirically supported is whether or not it had been adequately evaluated, it could be argued that a list of empirically supported treatments tells us next to nothing about the relative worth of different therapies. Rather, all it tells us is whether 'anyone has been motivated (and funded) to test it and whether it is readily testable in a brief manner' (Westen et al., 2004: 640). In this respect, it could be argued that the principal reason that there is so much more evidence for CBT is because, as a brief structured therapy, it lends itself much more easily to testing; and because many of its developers are based in academic institutions where research is encouraged and supported.

Researcher Allegiance Effects

In response to such criticisms, advocates of a differential effectiveness position might argue that some studies *do* show a superiority of cognitive and behavioural methods over other forms of treatment, in particular, 'non-directive' or 'supportive' 'counselling' or 'psychotherapy'. For instance, a study by Foa and colleagues (1991) found that CBT was more effective than 'supportive counselling' for post-traumatic stress in women who had recently been raped; and such findings are regularly included in government summaries of the evidence and guidelines on best practice (e.g. National Institute for Health and Clinical Excellence, 2007c). Here, however, another major problem with the evidence base emerges: that researchers show a marked tendency to find evidence which supports their own orientation. This is known within the counselling and psychotherapy research field as the 'research allegiance effect' (Luborsky et al., 1999), and can be considered one instance of the more general phenomenon of 'experimenter-expectancy' effects – 'The influence of the experimenter's expectations regarding the outcome of an experiment' (Christensen, 1997: 249) – the impact of which has been demonstrated in hundreds of psychological studies (Rosenthal and Rosnow, 1991). In a classic review of twenty-nine comparative psychotherapy studies, Luborsky and colleagues (1999) found that researchers' allegiances accounted for over two-thirds of the variance found in outcomes. In other words, researchers who were allied to behavioural rather than psychodynamic approaches to therapy (as defined by themselves, their colleagues, or as indicated in their papers) tended to find that behavioural approaches were more effective than psychodynamic ones, while researchers allied with the psychodynamic approaches tended to find the opposite. Indeed, on the basis of Luborsky et al.'s data, Westen and colleagues (2004) calculate that, in more than nine out of ten instances, the results of a comparative trial can be predicted by knowing the researchers' allegiances alone. Luborsky et al. (1999: 102) also found that 'there are no articles in the entire literature published by a first author who is a founder of a treatment, where the results are counter to that author's allegiance'. Hence, while researchers may claim that they are carrying out their investigations in a neutral and objective manner, the data strongly challenges this assumption (and, indeed, also shows that researchers tend to underestimate their biases; Luborsky et al., 1999). Given, then, that much of the empirical support for cognitive and behavioural therapies comes from cognitively and behaviourally aligned researchers, some fundamental questions are raised about its validity.

Researcher allegiance effects

The tendency for researchers to 'find' results that support their own beliefs, expectations or preferences.

Here, it is important to emphasise that there is no suggestion that researchers will deliberately attempt to manipulate their findings or the ways that their studies are conducted. Right from the start, advocates of empirically supported treatments have attempted to include a range of perspectives in their work (Task Force on Promotion and Dissemination of Psychological Procedures, 1995); and some of the leading authorities in this field, such as Professor of Psychoanalysis Peter Fonagy (Roth and Fonagy, 2005), are not of a cognitive-behavioural orientation. Nevertheless, there are a number of ways in which biases may unintentionally slip into even the most rigorously controlled research. For instance, researchers may tend not to put into print those findings that disconfirm their hypotheses (the 'file drawer problem'); or they may analyse their data in ways that maximise the apparent differences between approaches: in particular, by failing to consider the variations across individual therapists (see Wampold, 2001). Implicit biases may also arise because of the measures that are used to assess therapeutic outcomes. These may tend to favour one approach over another by being more sensitive to changes brought about by that particular way of working. One of the most commonly used outcome measures, for instance, the Beck Depression Inventory (BDI), was developed by the founder of cognitive therapy, Aaron Beck (Beck et al., 1979), and is particularly sensitive to changes in cognitive style (Wampold, 2001).

What is more, where researchers have allegiances to one particular approach, the control 'therapies' that are developed to test these approaches against often bear little relationship to those approaches as actually practised in the field, and cannot really be considered therapeutic at all (Wampold, 2001). (Shapiro and Shapiro, 1982, refer to these approaches as 'straw men'.) In the Foa et al. (1991) study of post-traumatic stress disorder (PTSD) in women who had been raped, for instance, 'therapists' in the 'supportive counselling' condition were instructed that, if their clients started to talk about their assault, they should redirect them to focus on current daily problems. Clearly, such practice cannot be considered an adequate representation of a bona fide form of therapy. In many studies (e.g. Boelen et al., 2007), it should also be noted that the developers of the manuals for the control treatments are advocates of the experimental interventions. Hence, while the researchers may have made every effort to create a coherent and practical approach, it is difficult to believe that they will have worked to maximise the effectiveness of the non-experimental 'treatment'.

Another important criticism of comparative outcome trials is that, in most instances, the control 'therapies' are delivered by practitioners who are neither fully trained in, nor committed to, the control approach; but are either implicitly or explicitly aligned with the experimental approach. In some instances, this may be the researchers themselves (e.g. Greenberg and Watson, 1998); in others, trainees or practitioners who may work for, or be trained or supervised by, the developers or advocates of the experimental condition (e.g. Boelen et al., 2007). There are numerous ways in which such practitioners may then inadvertently tend towards validating the experimental hypotheses; out of such desires as to be positively evaluated by the researchers (Christensen, 1997), or to contribute to the development of 'scientific knowledge' (Orne, 1962). Most importantly, perhaps, where researchers or allied practitioners believe that one way of working is more effective than another, it is almost certain that this conviction will, in some way, be implicitly transmitted to their clients – for instance through their body language or tone of voice – and, as we shall see in Chapter 4, clients' beliefs in the efficacy of their therapy would appear to be a crucial factor in determining its effectiveness. Indeed, given the level of bias that can emerge in medical trials using the most rigorous 'double-blind' designs (i.e. studies in which neither the researcher nor the participant know which condition the participant has been allocated to, see Heres et al., 2006, chap. 1), one might wonder what hope there is for studies in which researchers and therapists (and possibly even clients) are aware of the condition that the client has been allocated to, and in which the level of contact between practitioners and participants means a much greater opportunity for influence to take place.

RECOMMENDED READING

Westen, D., Novotny, C.A. and Thompson-Brenner, H. (2004) 'The empirical status of empirically supported psychotherapies: assumptions, findings, and reporting in controlled clinical trials', *Psychological Bulletin*, 130 (4): 631–3. Excellent, in-depth comprehensive critique of reliance on randomised controlled trials as the basis for psychological practice.

Equivalent Effectiveness: the 'Dodo Bird' Verdict

Given these potentialities for bias, one of the most surprising findings to come out of the comparative research literature may be just how effective control 'therapies', like the placebo conditions discussed in Chapter 2, can be. In Haddock et al.'s (2006) study of first-episode psychosis, for instance, participants under 21 years of age actually did significantly *better* in the 'supportive counselling' condition than in the CBT condition over three months; and in many other instances, clients in the control condition have fared as well, or almost as well, as those in the experimental treatment (e.g. Birmaher et al., 2000; Blowers et al., 1987; McIntosh et al., 2005).

This leads us on to one of the best-established findings in the counselling and psychotherapy research field: that if one looks at the data on the *comparative* efficacy of different therapies (either across studies or within the same study), rather than the data on which specific therapies have been shown to be efficacious with specific psychological problems, there is an overwhelming body of evidence to suggest that there is little difference in how efficacious different psychological therapies are (see, for instance, Luborsky et al., 2002; Wampold, 2001) (even though it is evident that the therapists are doing quite different things, see Box 3.2). This is particularly the case when all therapies being compared are bona fide ones (Wampold et al., 1997). Drawing together the findings from seventeen meta-analyses of comparative studies, for instance, Luborsky et al. calculate that the average difference between therapeutic approaches was an effect size of 0.2, a figure almost identical to that arrived at by Wampold and colleagues (1997) and Grissom (1996) in their meta-meta-analyses of the data. An effect size of 0.2, as we saw in Chapter 2, can be considered 'small', 'negligible' (Smith and Glass, 1977) or 'trivial' (Elliott, 2007); and means that around 42 per cent of clients in the 'inferior' treatment will actually do better than the average client in the 'superior' treatment (Luborsky et al., 2002; Wampold, 2001). This difference is further reduced when such factors as researcher allegiance effects are taken into account (Luborsky et al., 2002; Wampold, 2001) – Luborsky and colleagues suggest to an effect size of 0.14, Wampold suggests to zero. It should also be noted that this effect size of 0.2 is an average of *all* differences that have been found across therapies, whether it is, for example, a superiority of CBT over psychodynamic therapies or a superiority of psychodynamic therapies over CBT. However, where differences do emerge, they *do* tend to favour cognitive and behavioural approaches (Lambert and Ogles, 2004), though this is not always the case: humanistic approaches, for instance, have shown some superiority in the fields of play therapy (Bratton et al., 2005) and music therapy (Gold et al., 2004).

Box 3.2   The process of therapy: do different therapists actually do different things?

One explanation for the dodo bird finding might be that different practitioners, although calling themselves different types of therapists, actually do similar things. Research findings, however, do not tend to support this hypothesis. A study comparing the process of interpersonal therapy and CBT, for instance, found that the items rated as most characteristic of interpersonal therapy (for instance, 'patient's interpersonal relationships are a major theme') were very different to those rated as most characteristic of CBT (for instance, 'therapist actively exerts control over the interaction,' Ablon and Jones, 1999). Compared with psychodynamic therapists, CBT therapists have also been found to make around 50 per cent more utterances (Stiles et al., 1998), and have been shown to focus less on emotions, and concentrate more on what might be effective for the future rather than what has not worked in the past (Goldfried et al., 1997). In general, then, research findings suggest that the outcomes of therapy are very similar even though the practices can be quite different.

Figure 3.1 Assessment and four-month follow up BDI scores for participants undergoing non-directive therapy and cognitive-behavioural theory (King et al., 2000)

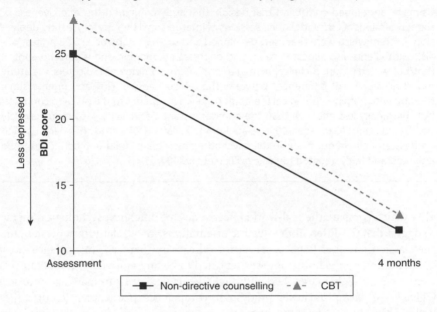

Bona fide therapy

A therapeutic practice delivered in 'good faith': i.e. one that the practitioner is trained in and committed to, and is based on sound psychological principles.

A classic example of equivalence in outcomes across therapies can be found in the study by King and colleagues (2000), introduced in Chapter 2, in which non-directive counselling (as practised by bona fide, accredited counsellors) was compared with CBT (as delivered by qualified psychologists) and treatment as usual. Figure 3.1 displays the results for both therapies at four months, and shows an almost identical reduction in levels of depression across the two therapies. This is very similar to the results of the National Institute of Mental Health's Treatment of Depression Collaborative Research Program (see Box 3.3).

Box 3.3   The National Institute of Mental Health Treatment of Depression Collaborative Research Program (NIMH TDCRP)

Undertaken in the US in the late 1980s, the NIMH TDCRP (Elkin et al., 1989) is considered to be 'the most methodologically sophisticated study ever done' (Duncan et al., 2004: 26).

(Continued)

(Continued)

Using a randomised controlled trial design, the study compared the effectiveness of sixteen sessions of CBT and sixteen sessions of interpersonal therapy for treating depression (both of which were practised, developed and supervised by bona fide professionals), with clients also allocated to an anti-depressant condition and a placebo control (both of which included 'clinical management'). Across a range of indicators, the study found no significant differences between the effectiveness of CBT and interpersonal therapy, with both psychological therapies somewhat superior to the placebo condition but marginally less effective than the anti-depressant, particularly with more severely depressed clients (Elkin et al., 1995). Data from the NIMH TDCRP study has been used to address a wealth of questions in the psychotherapy research field, and continues to be analysed and hotly debated today (e.g. Elkin et al., 2006).

Studies which compare the real-world effectiveness of different psychological therapies also suggest that the different therapeutic orientations are of relatively equivalent merit. In the classic Consumer Reports survey introduced in Chapter 2, for instance, no specific orientation of psychotherapy was reported to be any more helpful than any other for any problem (Seligman, 1995), although clients who went to marriage counsellors did give their therapists lower grades for competence (Consumer Reports, 1995). Equally, in the Stiles et al. (2006) study of primary and secondary care therapies (introduced in Chapter 2), CBT, person-centred therapy and psychodynamic therapy all brought about relatively similar reductions in levels of CORE-OM scores from pre- to post-therapy (8.9, 8.7 and 7.7 respectively). Percentages of clients experiencing reliable and clinically significant improvement across the three conditions were also not significantly different (62 per cent, 57.6 per cent and 48.1 per cent, respectively). A replication of this study with a larger sample found almost identical results (Stiles et al., 2008).

Within the counselling and psychotherapy research literature, this finding of equivalence across the different therapies has come to be known as the 'dodo bird' verdict (Luborsky et al., 1975; Rosenzweig, 1936). This is after the dodo bird in *Alice in Wonderland* who, after judging a race around a lake, declares that 'everyone has won and so all must have prizes'. The validity of this verdict is also apparent when one looks at the evidence in support of the different therapeutic orientations, as presented in the Appendix to this book. Here, it would appear that most therapies seem to be effective with most things they have been tested for, with little evidence that any one approach is much more effective than any other.

The dodo bird verdict

The assertion that different bona fide therapies are about equivalent in their efficacy and effectiveness.

Within the field of counselling and psychotherapy research, the dodo bird verdict has been heralded by advocates of a 'common factors' approach to counselling and psychotherapy (e.g. Hubble et al., 1999). Introduced by Saul Rosenzweig (1936) in the 1930s, the common factors model holds that the primary determinants of therapeutic change are a set of *non-specific* factors common to all therapies (for instance, the quality of the therapeutic relationship) as opposed to the *specific* techniques and practices of a particular therapeutic approach (for instance, transference interpretations). Common factors models are important to the counselling and psychotherapy research field because they are one, very credible way of accounting for the dodo bird finding: different therapies are about equivalent in their efficacy because they all share the same key ingredients, albeit not the same specific techniques.

Non-specific/common factors

Aspects of the therapeutic process that are common to most therapeutic relationships.

Specific/model factors

Well-defined actions on the part of the therapist that are associated with a particular therapeutic orientation.

RECOMMENDED READING

Wampold, B.E. (2001) *The Great Psychotherapy Debate: Models, Methods and Findings*. Mahwah, NJ: Erlbaum. Definitive critique of the differential effectiveness position: some tough statistics, but essential reading for anyone interested in the dodo bird debate.

Hubble, M., Duncan, B.L. and Miller, S.D. (1999) *The Heart and Soul of Change: What Works in Therapy*. Washington, DC: American Psychological Association. Excellent collection of chapters summarising the quantitative and qualitative research in support of a range of common factors: see, in particular, Asay and Lambert's chapter for an overview of the evidence.

Dead as a Dodo?

The dodo bird verdict and the common factors approach, however, are not without their critics, and there are those in the empirically supported treatments world who have warned practitioners to 'beware the dodo bird and shun over-generalisations' (Chambless, 2002), or who have declared the dodo bird to be an 'urban legend' rather than an empirically supported fact (e.g. Hunsley and Di Giulio, 2002). This critique draws on a number of arguments and empirical findings, most notably:

1 Meta-analytically 'mushing' together data from thousands of different studies with hundreds of different client groups is inevitably going to occlude any meaningful differences between therapies (Eysenck, 1978, referred to it as 'an exercise in mega-silliness'), and cannot be taken as proof that a particular therapy is not superior for a particular problem (Siev and Chambless, 2007). Does it really make sense to say that everything is as good as everything for everything? Even if, for instance, we wanted to argue that person-centred therapy is as effective as teaching the squeeze technique for sexual dysfunctions, would we really want to argue this the other way around for the treatment of depression? For Chambless and colleagues (Chambless, 2002; Chambless and Ollendick, 2001; Siev and Chambless, 2007), what the research indicates is that some forms of psychological distress, like depression or generalised anxiety disorder, respond well to a wide range of psychological therapies; while others, like panic disorder, respond most positively to one specific form of treatment. So to simply assert that 'All therapies are as good as each other' is to make a statement that is as bland, over-generalised and unhelpful as saying 'surgery works' or 'antibiotics are effective' (Chambless, 2002). It also serves to stultify the field of counselling and psychotherapy research rather than helping it to advance and develop more effective therapies for particular forms of psychological distress.

2 The dodo bird verdict ignores the fact that different clients may benefit from very different types of therapy (Beutler, Engle et al., 1991). Addis and Jacobson (1996: 1417) write: 'equivalent average effectiveness for each treatment does not necessarily imply that different treatments will be equally effective for all clients'. With the dodo bird verdict, there is also the danger that the vastly complex and unique change processes that individual clients may go through are overlooked, such that 'more precise hypotheses about how patient change may be set in motion' (Jones et al., 1988: 54) become obscured.

3 Many meta-analyses *do* show meaningful differences between different therapies (e.g. Reid, 1997), with CBT generally coming out on top (e.g. Shapiro and Shapiro, 1982). Furthermore, even if it is accepted that the average difference in outcomes between CBT and other approaches is an effect size of about 0.2, this is far from negligible, and means that about 94 out of every 1,000 clients will do better in the superior condition: a difference that is anything but 'trivial' for the 94 individuals involved (Hunsley and Di Giulio, 2002).

4 Although a *lack* of evidence does not mean that there is evidence *against* a particular form of therapy, it does mean 'exactly what it says on the tin': that there is *no* evidence to demonstrate that particular form of therapy is efficacious with a particular psychological problem. Given, then, that there may be treatments which *have* been shown to be efficacious with that difficulty, 'responsible practice requires using treatments for which efficacy has been demonstrated' (Chambless, 2002: 15) until such time as there is good evidence to show that another form of therapy is just as effective.

5 Researcher allegiance effects *may* have some impact on counselling and psychotherapy research results, but they cannot fully account for the findings of meta-analytical studies. For instance, cognitive therapy still demonstrates superior efficacy over other psychotherapies for depression when allegiance effects are controlled for (effect size = 0.17, Gaffan et al., 1995). It is also claimed that allegiance effects have markedly decreased in recent years, to the point where they no longer correlate with outcomes (Gaffan et al., 1995). Moreover, even if allegiance effects do correlate with outcomes, this does not prove that

the former has determined the latter (see Box 4.1). Indeed, it might be that researchers who have found a particular therapy to be efficacious then become more committed to it. Finally, 'credibility checks' in many randomised controlled trials suggest that clients perceive control 'therapies' as no less bona fide than the experimental treatments.

6   The fact that some approaches are more researched and that there is more funding for research into certain therapies than others is not just a consequence of bias or chance (Chambless, 2002). It arises because there is strong preliminary data suggesting that a treatment is likely to be efficacious.

RECOMMENDED READING

Hunsley, J. and Di Giulio, G. (2002) 'Dodo bird, phoenix, or urban legend?' *The Scientific Review of Mental Health Practices*, 1 (1): 11–22. Vigorous critique of the dodo bird position.

Towards Common Ground

This debate between the differential effectiveness and dodo bird positions could go on and on, with claims and counter-claims, all held to be firmly rooted in the empirical data. So how do we make sense of the findings, and move forward in a way that is of benefit to researchers and therapists – and, most importantly, to clients? For increasing numbers of researchers in the field (e.g. Castonguay and Beutler, 2006b; Ilardi and Craighead, 1994), an important starting point is to try to avoid absolutist, all-or-nothing thinking and instead to start from the premise that *both* common factors *and* orientation-specific factors are likely to have the potential to contribute to psychological change.

Such a standpoint is consistent with a wealth of psychological findings. It would explain, for instance, why most therapies tend to be about as effective as each other for some forms of psychological distress, but why other forms of psychological distress (in particular, anxiety disorders) may be more responsive to some practices than others. It would also explain why, as we will see in Chapters 4–7, that both common factors *and* the use of specific techniques and practices are associated with positive therapeutic outcomes. Studies that ask clients what they found helpful in therapy also consistently show that clients value a wide variety of factors, some of which are common across the therapies, and others of which are unique to particular ways of working (see Timulak, 2007 for an excellent summary). In a fascinating study of clients' perspectives on change processes in cognitive therapy, for instance, Clarke and colleagues (2004) found that clients highlighted the value both of common therapeutic factors (such as being listened to and feeling more comfortable with self), and factors that were specific to the cognitive approach (such as keeping thought diaries and listing their core beliefs).

If both common and specific factors are held to be important, a key question emerges as to the amount that each contributes to the process of therapeutic change. Lambert

Figure 3.2 'Lambert's pie': estimates of percentage improvement in psychotherapy clients as a function of therapeutic factors (from Asay and Lambert, 1999)

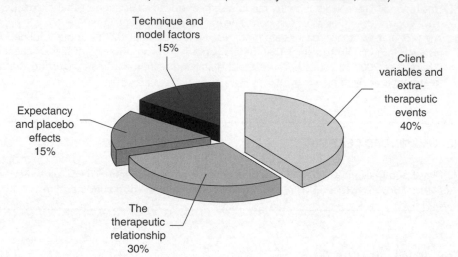

Technique and model factors 15%

Client variables and extra-therapeutic events 40%

Expectancy and placebo effects 15%

The therapeutic relationship 30%

(Asay and Lambert, 1999; Lambert, 1992), drawing on years of experience as one of the world's leading psychotherapy researchers, estimated that non-specific factors – in particular, client factors, relationship variables and expectancy/hope – account for about 85 per cent of the variance in therapeutic outcomes, with 15 per cent of the variance attributable to the therapist's specific techniques or model (see Figure 3.2).

Principles of Therapeutic Change

'Lambert's pie' (Asay and Lambert, 1999) provides a useful starting point to consider the relative contributions of specific and non-specific factors (though remember that it is an estimate), but one of its limitations is that it assumes that these proportions will be relatively similar across different forms of psychological distress. As Chambless and Ollendick (2001) have pointed out, however, this might not necessarily be the case. Also, it tells us very little about the specific factors that might contribute to therapeutic change. In these respects, a very interesting recent development has been the work of a joint American Psychological Association/Society for Psychotherapy Research Task Force, which has attempted to identify the key *principles* of change (both specific and non-specific) for clients with particular forms of psychological distress (Castonguay and Beutler, 2006b). By 'principles of change', what the Task Force means are client factors, therapist factors, relationship factors and technique factors that are associated with positive therapeutic outcomes. Here, what is particularly important to note is that the Task Force did not focus on the efficacy of therapeutic practices at the 'brand name', global level, but at the more specific level of particular ways of working (for instance, developing a strong therapeutic alliance, challenging cognitive appraisals, self-disclosing) (Beutler and Castonguay, 2006). In this respect, the Task Force attempted to step beyond the 'horserace' (Shoham-Salomon and Hannah, 1991: 218) approach of asking 'Which therapy is best?' and instead focus on practices and principles that may be utilisable by all (Beutler and Castonguay, 2006).

RECOMMENDED READING

Castonguay, L.G. and Beutler, L.E. (eds) (2006b) *Principles of Therapeutic Change that Work*. New York: Oxford University Press. Essential reading for counsellors and psychotherapists, drawing together a wealth of research findings to identify key principles of therapeutic change for clients with depression, anxiety disorders, personality disorders and substance use disorders.

Aptitude-Treatment Interactions

One of the limitations of a 'principles of change' approach, however, is that it still tends to start from the assumption that clients with similar diagnoses need similar things. But is this necessarily the case? For instance, it may be that one depressed client will find advice and guidance helpful, while another may benefit from a more non-directive way of working. Kiesler (1966) refers to the assumption that all clients need similar things as the 'patient uniformity myth', and argues that it is indelibly impressed on the field of clinical research; and, indeed, it is: for the whole point of experimental research trials is to arrive at generalities, and diversity among respondents is simply considered 'random variance' (Shoham-Salomon and Hannah, 1991).

In an attempt to take individual differences more fully into account, a number of researchers in the psychotherapy field (including those developing 'principles of therapeutic change', see above) have begun to explore 'aptitude-treatment interactions' (ATIs). This is a concept borrowed from the field of education (Elkin et al., 1999), and starts from the premise that 'patients with certain characteristics will do better in one treatment than another and that the reverse will be true for patients without those characteristics or with other contrasting characteristics' (Elkin et al., 1999: 438). From this standpoint, then, the question is not so much 'Which therapy is most effective?' or even 'What are the key principles of therapeutic change for particular groups of clients?' but 'What kinds of client characteristics will make one way of working more effective than another?' For instance, it might be that clients who are more extroverted will do better in directive therapies as compared with non-directive therapies, or that clients who have experienced emotional neglect do particularly well with an interpretative approach, as compared with clients who have had relatively benign childhoods.

Aptitude-treatment interaction (ATI) paradigm

The assumption that clients with particular qualities and characteristics will do better in some forms of therapy than others.

As we will see in the following chapters of this book, some forms of therapeutic practice do seem to be particularly suited to some kinds of therapeutic clients. However, despite the promise of the aptitude-treatment paradigm, findings, to date, have been fairly disappointing (Clarkin and Levy, 2004; Dance and Neufeld, 1988; Wampold, 2001). In the largest ever randomised controlled trial of psychological therapies, for instance, the Project MATCH study (1997) – which examined the effectiveness of CBT, motivational enhancement therapy and twelve-step facilitation for alcohol problems – could find no particular matches between specific client characteristics and the successfulness of the different therapies. Indeed, even some of the most seemingly obvious aptitude-treatment interactions, such as clients with cognitive problems will do better in cognitive therapy (Spangler et al., 1997), were not borne out. Most disturbingly, from an aptitude-treatment perspective, there is research to suggest that clients sometimes do *worse* when therapists try to tailor the therapy to the individual client, as opposed to offering them a standardised therapeutic programme (e.g. Schulte et al., 1992). Nevertheless, given the fact that there are an endless number of therapy factors and client characteristics, it may be no wonder that aptitude-treatment interaction research is still in its infancy.

Conclusion

Debates between the differential effectiveness and dodo bird positions continue to rage, with major implications for the practice, funding and development of therapeutic services (see, for instance, the recent UK government initiative 'Improving Access to Psychological Therapies'). Empirically, there is evidence to support both sides of the controversy, with much of it coming down to how much one trusts randomised controlled trials and their underlying assumptions.

At the same time, however, a number of contemporary researchers are attempting to transcend the dodo bird/differential effectiveness dichotomy by examining the particular factors that are associated with positive change: both those related to specific orientations and those not. Almost fifty years ago, Gordon Paul asked '*What* treatment, by *whom*, is most effective for *this* individual with *that* specific problem, and under *which* set of circumstances?' (1967: 111), and today, more and more psychotherapy researchers seem to be moving towards this question. Castonguay and Beutler's (2006b) Task Force focuses on three particular groups of factors that are related to therapeutic outcomes: participant factors (client and therapist), relationship factors and technique factors; and this structure is adopted for the following chapters of the book, with the exceptions that client and therapist factors are examined separately (Chapters 4 and 5). Throughout these chapters, aptitude-treatment interaction findings are discussed as and where relevant.

Summary of Key Findings

- Cognitive-behavioural therapies have been shown to be efficacious for a wide range of psychological difficulties, in particular anxiety disorders, depression, bulimia nervosa, sexual dysfunctions, schizophrenia and health-related problems.
- Evidence for the efficacy of non-CBT therapies is limited, though there are some indications that psychodynamic therapies, experiential therapies, family therapies and interpersonal therapy are helpful for some problems.
- When bona fide therapies are compared with each other, they are usually found to be about equivalent in efficacy.
- There is some evidence to indicate that different clients do better in different kinds of therapy.

QUESTIONS FOR REFLECTION

1 How do you *feel* when you read about the relative efficacy of the different psychological therapies? Demoralised? Pleased? Incredulous? Angry? What might this say about your own assumptions and beliefs?
2 How do the findings presented in this chapter resonate with your own experiences of receiving or providing therapy?
3 To what extent do you trust the findings of randomised controlled trials and their underlying assumptions (e.g. that discrete forms of psychological distress exist)?
4 How do you think that the debate between the differential effectiveness position and the equivalent effectiveness (dodo bird) position can best be resolved? To what extent do you think that a focus on principles of change can take the field forward?
5 What common factors do you think are most likely to be predictive of positive therapeutic change? For instance, empathy? Firm boundaries? The therapist's use of self?
6 What aptitude-treatment interactions would you predict to exist? For instance, who do you think might do better with insight-orientated approaches to therapy as opposed to behaviourally orientated ones?

4

Client Factors: the Heart and Soul of Therapeutic Change

This chapter discusses:

- The extent to which client qualities and characteristics are related to the outcomes of therapy.
- The relationship between clients' attitudes towards therapy and therapeutic outcomes.
- The relationship between clients' levels of psychosocial functioning and therapeutic outcomes.
- The relationship between clients' demographic characteristics and therapeutic outcomes.

For many counsellors and psychotherapists, a basic assumption may be that it is what *they* do – or the conditions that they create – that is the principal factor in determining therapeutic change. However, the empirical research suggests something very different: that it is actually the other member of the therapeutic dyad, *the client*, who is primarily responsible for change in therapy (Bohart and Tallman, 1999). As Duncan and colleagues (2004: 12) put it, 'clients, not therapists, make therapy work'. We have already seen an indication of this in Lambert's pie (1992, see Figure 3.2), which estimates that around 40 per cent of therapeutic improvement is due to 'client variables and extra-therapeutic events'. However, if we add to this the fact that hope and expectancy is really a client factor, and that the therapeutic relationship is as much created by clients as it is by therapists, this suggests that 75 per cent or more of the change in psychotherapy may be directly attributable to client factors.

Bohart and Tallman (1999), in their classic work in this area, suggest a number of lines of evidence which support this emphasis on client factors. First, as we have seen in Chapter 3, clients tend to do about as well in different therapies (the 'dodo bird verdict'), and this suggests that the specific things that therapists do may not be that important to therapeutic outcomes. Rather, the dodo bird verdict is more consistent with the hypothesis that the primary determinant of therapeutic outcomes is the degree to which *clients* can make use of the therapeutic resources available to them. Such an argument is further supported by the fact that people often make substantial gains without any therapy at all or only a minimal degree of therapist input: for instance, through using self-help material (den Boer et al., 2004).

More direct evidence for the importance of client factors comes from studies which show a strong relationship between the amount of change brought about in therapy and specific client factors, with more client variables predictive of outcomes than any other kinds of variables (Crits-Christoph et al., 1991). For instance, in an analysis of the NIMH TDCRP data (which compared CBT and interpersonal therapy for depression, see Box 3.3, Ablon and Jones, 1999), virtually all of the aspects of therapy found to correlate significantly with outcomes in both CBT and interpersonal therapy were to do with clients' characteristics, experiences and qualities – for instance, 'patient conveys positive expectations about therapy', 'patient is clear and organised in self-expression' – rather than therapists' qualities or experiences. However, in examining such data, it is essential to bear in mind that evidence of an association between client factors and outcomes does not *prove* that the former causes the latter (see Box 4.1).

RECOMMENDED READING

Bohart, A.C. and Tallman, K. (1999) *How Clients Make Therapy Work: The Process of Active Self-Healing.* Washington: American Psychological Association. Possibly one of the finest contemporary contributions to the psychotherapy and counselling literature, drawing together empirical research, theory and clinical illustrations to argue that it is the client, and not the therapist, who is the key agent of therapeutic change.

Duncan, B.L., Miller, S.D. and Sparks, J.A. (2004) *The Heroic Client: A Revolutionary Way to Improve Effectiveness through Client-directed, Outcome-informed Therapy.* San Francisco: Jossey-Bass. Impassioned call for counsellors and psychotherapists to abandon therapist-centred, medically based models of practice; and to recast clients as 'the main characters, the heroes and heroines of the therapeutic stage' (p. 52).

> ### Box 4.1   Correlation does not imply causation
>
> The fact that client factors (or any other factors) are *associated* with therapeutic outcomes cannot be taken as proof that the former *cause* the latter. For a start, it may be that a third factor is responsible for changes in both these variables. For instance,
>
> *(Continued)*

> *(Continued)*
>
> higher levels of client motivation might be associated with better outcomes (see below) because clients who are highly motivated are also highly intelligent, and it is the higher levels of intelligence that cause these clients to get more out of therapy. Alternatively, the direction of causality might actually be in the other direction: that as client starts to feel better in therapy, so they become more motivated to engage with it. This means that we must always be careful not to infer cause-and-effect relationships from evidence that two variables are related – that may be the case, but we cannot know for certain.

For the purposes of this chapter, 'client factors' are defined as those that exist 'within' the person of the client (Beutler, Blatt et al., 2006). In other words, they are identifiable outside of what takes place in therapy (so not just the client's immediate feelings towards the therapist), and are relatively enduring and stable ways of being (for instance, the client's personality traits; Beutler, Blatt et al., 2006). These client factors can be further divided into those that are *inferred* (i.e. implicit qualities that can only be known through extrapolation, such as levels of motivation) and those that can be considered more *objective* (i.e. qualities that are generally observable and verifiable from an external standpoint, such as age).

Inferred Characteristics

Attitudes Towards Therapy

Motivation and Involvement

Across a range of client-, therapist- and relational-variables, studies have found that clients' levels of active participation in therapy is one of the strongest predictors of outcomes – and possibly 'the most important determinant' (Orlinsky et al., 1994: 361) – accounting for 20 per cent or more of the improvement alone (e.g. Bachelor, 1991). A good example of this comes from an early study by Heine and Trosman (1960), who found that 67 per cent of clients who saw themselves as having an active part to play in the therapeutic process continued with psychotherapy beyond six weeks, compared with just 28 per cent of clients who placed responsibility completely in the hands of their therapists. This relationship would seem to be as strong in the more directive therapies as it is in those therapies which place greater emphasis on client agency (e.g. Nelson and Borkovec, 1989). In behaviour therapy, for instance, Keijsers and colleagues (1994) found that obsessive–compulsive clients who were more motivated had greater reductions in levels of obsessive fear. Even for clients with some of the most hard-to-help psychological problems (for instance, 'personality disorders' – see below), significant correlations have been found between levels of motivation and therapeutic outcomes (McCallum and Piper, 1999). This link between motivation and outcomes also comes through in the effectiveness research, with 'active shoppers' (i.e. clients whose idea it was to seek therapy, who asked their therapists about the services they offered and who took a proactive role in the therapeutic tasks) doing better than 'passive recipients' (Seligman, 1995).

Closely related to, and sometimes overlapping with, this research is the finding that clients who are more willing to adopt the 'client role' and work collaboratively and cooperatively with their therapists – for instance, by keeping appointments, doing homework and persevering with the therapy – tend to do better in therapy (Orlinsky et al., 2004; Tryon and Winograd, 2002). The converse of this is that clients' levels of 'resistance' to the therapeutic processes are a strong predictor of poorer outcomes (Orlinsky et al., 2004). For instance, in a study of brief psychodynamic therapy, the item that most strongly correlated (in a negative direction) with outcomes across clients', therapists' and independent evaluators' ratings was 'patient resists examining thoughts, reactions, motives related to problems' (Jones et al., 1992: 27). Along somewhat similar lines, clients' 'openness' – as opposed to defensiveness – appears to be a particularly strong predictor of positive therapeutic outcomes (Orlinsky et al., 2004).

Resistance

Client behaviour that exhibits a reluctance to participate in the tasks of therapy.

While the above research indicates that clients do well in therapy when they are willing to engage in the client role, a more recent study suggests that a particularly strong predictor of outcomes may also be clients' level of intrinsic or 'autonomous' motivation for therapy. This is the extent to which they experience themselves as having freely chosen to enter therapy and the choice is felt to emanate from themselves (Zuroff et al., 2007). Zuroff and colleagues found that clients who scored high on autonomous motivation for therapy (whether CBT or interpersonal therapy) were almost twice as likely to respond well to therapy as those with average levels of autonomous motivation, and almost four times as likely to respond well as those with low levels of autonomous motivation.

Outcome Expectation

As most practitioners will have experienced, some clients come to therapy brimming with confidence that their lives are about to be transformed, while others seem to think that therapy is pointless before it has even started. Does this 'outcome expectancy' (Glass et al., 2001), 'faith' (Wampold, 2001) or 'hope' (Glass et al., 2001) in the therapeutic process relate to outcomes? The research suggests that it does (Snyder et al., 1999); indeed, as we saw in Chapter 3, Lambert (Asay and Lambert, 1999) estimates that a full

15 percent of the variance in therapeutic outcomes can be accounted for by clients' beliefs in its efficacy. In other words, just as social psychologists talk of a 'self-fulfilling prophecy', in which people's predictions of what will happen tends to come true (Aronson et al., 1999), so clients who have a lot of faith in the therapeutic process tend to do better than those who are sceptical about it (Beutler, Blatt et al., 2006; Glass et al., 2001). Research also indicates that the more credible clients believe a therapy to be, the more they tend to improve (Ilardi and Craighead, 1994).

This link between expectations and outcomes is supported by a range of further findings in the counselling and psychotherapy field (Snyder et al., 1999). For instance, as we saw in Chapter 2, clients tend to improve most in the first few weeks of therapy, and they can even show quite considerable improvement after their assessment session or even just by being offered therapy. Such improvements are hard to explain in terms of therapists' techniques or even the relationship that they create with their clients – particularly if the client has not even started therapy yet. Rather, what these findings suggest is that, for some clients, just knowing that they are going to be embarking on a therapeutic process is of considerable psychological benefit, and a likely explanation of this is because it engenders hope within the client, or what has also been termed 'remoralisation' (Frank and Frank, 1993). This fits in with the idea that, for some clients, a substantial part of their problem is that they feel hopeless about ever being able to extricate themselves from their psychological distress (Teasdale, 1985). Hence, the experiencing of hope can be an enormously important first step on the road to psychological recovery. Similarly, the finding that clients can experience considerable psychological improvements in placebo experimental conditions (see Chapter 2) suggests that a belief that one is being helped, in itself, can have a powerful ameliorative effect.

RECOMMENDED READING

Snyder, C.R., Michael, S.T. and Cheavens, J.S. (1999) 'Hope as a foundation of common factors, placebos, and expectancies', in M. Hubble, B.L. Duncan and S.D. Miller (eds), *The Heart and Soul of Change: What Works in Therapy*. Washington, DC: American Psychological Association, pp. 179–200. Introduces 'hope therapy'.

As emphasised above, however, it is essential to remember that correlation does not imply causation. It may be, for instance, that clients are just relatively good judges of how likely they are to change; or that a third factor, such as therapists' levels of empathy, bring about both hope and positive outcomes. Also, as research in the wider psychological field suggests (e.g. Baumeister, 1991), while realistic or slightly over-optimistic positive expectations tend to be associated with good psychological health, extremely high and unrealistic positive expectations also tend to be related to poorer outcomes (Piper et al., 1998; Sloane et al., 1977); and, as many therapists might have experienced, these may be just as common in therapy (Tinsley et al., 1993).

An emerging body of data also suggests that expectations may be more related to outcomes for some client groups than others. In particular, while clients with substance abuse and anxiety problems would seem to do best when they have high expectations, there is less evidence that this is also the case for clients with depression (Beutler, Castonguay et al., 2006).

IMPLICATIONS FOR PRACTICE

Based on the research, Glass and Arnkoff (2000: 1469) write that: 'Words of encouragement, hope and expecting and conveying to clients that they can recover and not be this way forever are essential.' Encouraging clients to see therapy as something which can be of benefit to them (when done in an honest and supportive way) would also seem to be of value. For instance:

- 'It's really good that you sought help for this.'
- 'What you're concerned about is exactly the kind of thing that therapy can help with' (Glass et al., 2001: 459).

However, clients who have excessively high hopes for therapy may need to be encouraged to develop more realistic expectations.

Process Expectations

As well as looking at the relationship between what clients expect to get from therapy and what they actually do, researchers have also looked at the relationship between what clients expect to *happen* in therapy and the eventual outcomes. Here, as with outcome expectations, the research indicates that clients who have a relatively realistic expectation about what will happen in therapy tend to get the most out of it. In particular, clients who 'do not anticipate pain or embarrassment' (Mohr, 1995: 13) tend to respond less positively to therapeutic interventions. Also, the research suggests that clients who have a relatively clear understanding of the process and goals of therapy and their role within it tend to get the most out of the therapeutic work, while those who have a more ambiguous understanding of role are less satisfied, less productive and more defensive (Bednar et al., 1974).

Much of the evidence for these findings comes from research into the effects of 'role induction interviews': pre-therapeutic procedures in which clients are educated about the goals and nature of therapy and encouraged to have realistic expectations about what will happen. In an early study by Hoehn-Saric and colleagues (1964), for instance, clients met with a psychiatrist prior to therapy and were given a general outline of psychotherapy; a description and explanation of the expected behaviour of therapists and clients; a preparation for certain phenomena that typically arose in therapy, such as resistance; and the induction of realistic expectations for improvement within four months of therapy. Hoehn-Saric and colleagues found that clients who had participated in these interviews, as opposed to control clients, were significantly more improved by the end of therapy and also attended significantly more therapy sessions. Subsequent studies have shown that similar induction procedures can also reduce drop-out rates and anxieties about therapy (Guajardo and Anderson, 2007; Van Audenhove and Vertommen, 2000).

IMPLICATIONS FOR PRACTICE

Helping clients to develop realistic and relatively clear expectations of what will happen in therapy may be an important element of initial and assessment sessions. It may even be something that could be offered to clients prior to therapy: for instance, through presenting a role play of a therapeutic session on a website. 'Role-induction' procedures may be particularly important when working with clients from different socio-cultural backgrounds, who may have very different expectations and understandings of the therapeutic process.

Predilections

One aspect of clients' expectations about the process of therapy is their expectations about how change will happen. Does a client, for instance, think that change will come about through psychological mechanisms (for instance, by having greater insight), or does he or she think that the cause of his or her problems is biological, and how does this relate to outcomes? Elkin and colleagues (1999) refer to this as clients' 'predilections' for therapy, and categorised the clients in the NIMH TDCRP study (see Box 3.3) according to whether they had a psychotherapy predilection (i.e. they tended to account for their depression in terms of psychological factors and thought that psychological treatment would be best), or a medication predilection (i.e. they tended to account for their depression in terms of poor physical health and biochemical problems and thought that medicine would be most helpful). The researchers then looked at whether clients who received a treatment that was 'congruent' with their predilections did better than those who received a non-congruent treatment. What they found was that drop-out rates were quite markedly reduced in those who received a congruent treatment, and that those groups also had a significantly better therapeutic alliance. In other words, clients who see the roots of their problems as psychological, and believe that psychological processes will be helpful for them, *do* seem to engage more fully at the early stages of psychological therapy.

Predilection

Clients' beliefs about the origins of their distress and what they expect will be helpful to them.

To some extent, these findings simply re-state what was established above: that clients who think that psychological therapy is going to help them have better outcomes. However, with the concept of predilection, we can also look at whether clients who attribute their problems to *particular* psychological causes, and think that *particular* psychological processes are going to help them, do better when they participate in a congruent psychological therapy. For instance, do clients who think that their difficulties are caused by being too self-critical and perfectionist do better in CBT than clients who construe their problems and solutions in interpersonal terms?

Evidence that such an aptitude-treatment interaction may, indeed, exist, comes from a study by Addis and Jacobson (1996). They showed that the more clients understood their depression in relatively abstract terms, the better they did in cognitive therapy (which gave them an opportunity to examine their personal meanings), but the worse they did in behavioural therapy (which focused on more discrete behavioural changes). Furthermore, Addis and Jacobson found that the more clients understood their problems in relationship terms, the less well they did in cognitive therapy (with its intra-personal orientation). Gaston and colleagues (1989) also found that, in cognitive therapy, clients who expected to be changed through cognitive and behavioural mechanisms (for instance, by becoming more flexible in thinking), did do better. However, the same was not true for clients in brief psycho-dynamic therapy: that is, clients who expected to be changed through such dynamic mechanisms as achieving insight and understanding did no better than those who were not expecting to be changed in those ways. While some findings, then, do suggest that clients do better in therapies that match their own predilections, the evidence is far from unequivocal. Also, there is some evidence to suggest that what may be important is that clients *perceive* their therapists as having similar predilections – and hence experience them as more credible and understanding – rather than similarities, *per se* (Atkinson et al., 1991).

IMPLICATIONS FOR PRACTICE

In initial and assessment sessions, it may be helpful to explore with clients what they see as the cause(s) of their problems, and how they think that they can best be helped. Duncan and colleagues (2004: 73), for instance, suggest asking such questions as:

- What ideas do you have about what needs to happen for improvement to occur?
- Many times people have a pretty good hunch not only about what is causing a problem but also what will resolve it. Do you have a theory of how change is going to happen here?

If clients' predilections are highly incongruent with your own – for instance, if they think they are going to be helped by being given advice and you want to practice in a non-directive way – it may be important to discuss this openly with the client and, if necessary, consider onward referral.

Preferences

People's expectations are what they think will happen; their preferences are what they would most like to happen, and there is research to indicate that clients are quite able to distinguish between their anticipations and their ideals (Tracey and Dundon, 1988). Do clients who express a preference for psychological therapy – as opposed to, say, medication – get more out of it? Interestingly, results here are actually quite mixed, and suggest that clients' preferences for psychological therapy over other forms of treatment may be less predictive of outcomes than their predilections. For instance, Iacoviello and colleagues (2007) found that clients who expressed a preference for psychotherapy, as compared with those who expressed a preference for drug treatments, experienced greater improvements in the psychotherapeutic alliance over time; but Bakker and colleagues (2000) found that panic-disordered clients who had expressed a strong preference for psychological treatment did not do any better in cognitive therapy than clients who were randomly allocated to it.

Results are equally mixed when clients' preferences for particular types of therapy are investigated as a potential aptitude-treatment interaction. On the one hand, there are some studies which show that clients who get the therapy they want have better outcomes. For instance, Devine and Fernald (1973) showed snake phobics videotapes of four different therapists describing, and then illustrating, their particular ways of working. Clients were then asked to rate each of the four therapies, and were assigned to a therapeutic condition that they had either rated as strongly disliking or strongly liking. The results showed that clients who had been allocated to their preferred form of treatment did significantly better than those allocated to their non-preferred form of treatment, and they also did significantly better than clients who had been randomly allocated to those therapies. However, in another study, no significant relationships were found between the successfulness of the counselling and the clients' ratings of how much their counsellors did what they wanted them to do (Pohlman, 1972). Moreover, a systematic review of thirty-two randomised controlled studies in which clients had the option of choosing a particular treatment found that those who received their preferred approach, in general, did not do any better than those who were randomly allocated to it, and were no less likely to drop out (King et al., 2005).

Psychosocial Functioning: the Rich Get Richer and the Poor ...

One of the most interesting paradoxes in the counselling and psychotherapy research is this: if you look at the relationship between levels of emotional distress and outcomes, what you tend to find is that clients with higher levels of *manifest*, overt distress have better clinical outcomes (e.g. Mohr and Beutler, 1990). This may be because such clients have more motivation to change (Mohr and Beutler, 1990), or because there is more 'room for improvement'. However, when one looks at more *latent*, underlying, characterological levels of psychological, social and interpersonal functioning, the reverse tends to be true: that is, individuals with higher levels of psychosocial dysfunction tend to get the *least* out of therapy (Castonguay and Beutler, 2006a; Clarkin and Levy, 2004) (see Box 4.2). The sections below look at six specific areas of psychosocial functioning in which this link between greater functionality and more improvements in therapy has been particularly well demonstrated.

Box 4.2   Compensation or capitalisation?

Does therapy help clients to compensate for areas of deficiency, or does it help them capitalise upon their strengths? In general, the research tends to support the latter, 'capitalisation' hypothesis (Rude and Rehm, 1991): clients who are already functioning well tend to improve more than those who have greater need for improvement. The evidence suggests, however, that the rich do not only get richer at a global level, but also with respect to more specific domains of functioning. For instance, in the NIMH TDCRP study, 'the least cognitively impaired patients responded more favourably to cognitive therapy, and the least socially impaired patients responded most favourably to interpersonal psychotherapy' (Sotsky et al., 1991: 1005–6). In this respect, it may be helpful to work with clients in ways that allow them to capitalise upon their strengths: for instance, more expressive ways of working with clients who are more emotionally open, and more cognitive ways of working with clients who take pride in their intellectual abilities.

Personality Disorders

'Personality disorders' can be defined as 'constellations of inflexible and maladaptive personality traits that result in significant functional impairment and subjective distress' (Ogrodniczuk and Piper, 2001: 105). Within the *DSM-IV*, ten different personality disorders have been defined (see Table 4.1).

Personality disorders

Constellations of relatively enduring, maladaptive traits that can result in significant subjective distress and functional impairment.

In approximately 50 per cent of cases (Hardy et al., 1995), individuals coming to therapy with an 'Axis I' disorder are also diagnosed as having one or more 'Axis II' personality disorders, and research suggests that such comorbid clients tend to benefit less from therapy (Castonguay and Beutler, 2006a). For example, after eight weeks of CBT for bulimia nervosa, clients who had also been diagnosed with a personality disorder made up 52 per cent of poor outcome cases and only 17 per cent of good outcome cases (Fahy and Russell, 1993). In specific treatments for personality disorders, greater severity of disorders has also been shown to relate to poorer outcomes (Ryle and Golynkina, 2000).

Table 4.1   DSM-IV personality disorders

	Characteristics
***Cluster A* (odd or eccentric disorders)**	
Paranoid PD	Distrust and suspiciousness of others; interpreting their motives as malevolent
Schizoid PD	Detachment from social relationships; restricted range of expression of emotions in interpersonal settings
Schizotypal PD	Need for social isolation; odd behaviour and thinking; unconventional beliefs, such as being convinced of having extra-sensory perception
***Cluster B* (dramatic, emotional or erratic disorders)**	
Antisocial PD	Disregard for, and violation of, the rights of others
Borderline PD	Emotional dysregulation; extreme 'black and white' thinking; chaotic relationships
Histrionic PD	Excessive emotionality and attention seeking
Narcissistic PD	Extreme focus on oneself
***Cluster C* (anxious or fearful disorders)**	
Avoidant PD	Social inhibition; feelings of inadequacy; hypersensitivity to negative evaluation
Dependent PD	Excessive need to be taken care of leading to submissive and clinging behaviour and fears of separation
Obsessive–compulsive PD	Psychological inflexibility; rigid conformity to rules and procedures; perfectionism; excessive orderliness

DSM-IV

One of the most widely used systems of diagnosis: *The Diagnostic and Statistical Manual of Mental Disorders* of the American Psychiatric Association. Now in its 4th edition, with a 5th edition expected in 2011 (see www.dsm5.org).

Axis I disorder

A clinical syndrome, such as social phobia or major depressive disorder – the first dimension in the *DSM-IV*.

Axis II disorder

A personality or developmental disorder, such as borderline personality disorder or autism – the second dimension in the *DSM-IV*.

More recent research, however, has suggested that it may not be the presence or absence of personality disorders, *per se*, that predicts outcome, but the number of personality disorders that an individual is diagnosed as having (Ogrodniczuk et al., 2001). Moreover, there are some indications that certain personality disorders are more predictive of poor outcomes than others: in particular, clients who are diagnosed with borderline and schizoptypal personality disorders seem to do particularly poorly across a range of clinical problems (Clarkin and Levy, 2004), while clients diagnosed with dependent personalities seem to experience some of the worst outcomes in treatments for depression (Beutler, Blatt et al., 2006).

RECOMMENDED READING

Benjamin, L.S. and Karpiak, C.P. (2002) 'Personality disorders', in J.C. Norcross (ed.), *Psychotherapy Relationships that Work: Therapist Contributions and Responsiveness to Patients*. New York: Oxford University Press, pp. 423–38.

Attachment and Interpersonal Style

Individuals' 'attachment styles' describe their 'comfort and confidence in close relationships, their fears of rejection and yearning for intimacy, and their preference for self-sufficiency or interpersonal distance' (Meyer and Pilkonis, 2002: 367). The concept emerged from the work of attachment theorists, in particular, John Bowlby (1979) and Mary Ainsworth (Ainsworth et al., 1978), who hypothesised that infants are inherently motivated to form close emotional bonds with their caregivers, and that the achievement, or disruption, of these bonds can have a profound psychological impact by determining the individual's mental models of self, other and relationship. Consistent with this hypothesis, empirical research shows that individuals' attachment styles show considerable stability across time (Meyer and Pilkonis, 2002).

Attachment style

Individuals' particular patterns of behaving, thinking and feeling in close relationships.

In terms of the particular attachment patterns that children and adults display, there is general agreement that three different styles can be reliably discriminated: 'secure', 'preoccupied' and 'dismissive' (Meyer and Pilkonis, 2002). The latter two of these styles are referred to as 'insecure' attachment patterns (see Table 4.2). In addition, if, as indicated in Table 4.2, styles of attachment can be understood in terms of two dimensions – positive/negative

Table 4.2 Principal attachment styles

	Secure/ insecure	Characteristics	Mental model of self and other
Secure, autonomous	Secure	Confidence and comfort in relating	Positive self Positive other
Preoccupied, anxious– ambivalent	Insecure	Fear of rejection and yearning for intimacy	Negative self Positive other
Dismissing, avoidant	Insecure	Discomfort with closeness and defensive self-sufficiency	Positive self Negative other

models of self, and positive/negative models of others – then a fourth insecure style of attachment emerges. This has been labelled a 'fearful', or 'fearful–avoidant' one, in which individuals hold negative models of both themselves and others. Closely related to this, a classification of 'unresolved' is sometimes used in the adult attachment literature (e.g. Fonagy et al., 1996) and is associated with experiences of abuse and trauma.

Given that individuals who are securely attached tend to have higher levels of psychological functioning than those with insecure attachment styles (Meyer and Pilkonis, 2002), it would be reasonable to predict that individuals with more secure attachment styles are likely to get more out of therapy. And, indeed, this is what the research tends to show (e.g. Meyer, Pilkonis et al., 2001). For instance, Saatsi and colleagues (2007) found that 93.3 per cent of securely attached individuals showed clinically significant and reliable change in cognitive therapy for depression, compared with 52.5 per cent of avoidant clients, and 38.5 per cent of ambivalent clients; and they also found that ambivalently attached clients were significantly less likely to complete therapy. More broadly, what a range of studies indicates is that clients with higher levels of interpersonal difficulties – in particular, higher levels of hostility, social avoidance and non-assertiveness (Paivio and Bahr, 1998) – tend to have poorer therapeutic outcomes (Clarkin and Levy, 2004; Newman, Crits-Christoph et al., 2006).

Studies have also shown that more securely attached clients and those with better interpersonal relationships form better alliances with their therapists (e.g. Eames and Roth, 2000) and, given that the quality of the therapeutic alliance is one of the best predictors of eventual therapeutic outcomes (see Chapter 6), this may explain why more securely attached individuals tend to do better in therapy. Indeed, the capacity to trust and engage with a therapist and form relatively stable alliances may be one of the main reasons why psychosocially well-functioning people, in general, tend to get more out of the therapeutic process.

There is one interesting exception to this, however: clients with dismissive attachment styles actually tend to do quite well in therapy (Fonagy et al., 1996), and also seem to form quite strong therapeutic alliances (Eames and Roth, 2000; Meyer and Pilkonis, 2002). It is not clear why this is the case, but it may be that individuals who have tended to deal with their relational insecurities by avoiding intimacy are more willing and able, after an initial wariness, to connect emotionally with their therapists. This is in comparison to preoccupied attached clients, who are likely to have had a long history of difficult and tumultuous relationships, and therefore may find it more difficult to 'unlearn' previous modes of relating.

RECOMMENDED READING

Meyer, B. and Pilkonis, P.A. (2002) 'Attachment style', in J.C. Norcross (ed.), *Psychotherapy Relationships that Work: Therapist Contributions and Responsiveness to Patients.* New York: Oxford University Press, pp. 367–82.

Perfectionism

One of the most interesting findings to come out of the NIMH TDCRP study was that, across all four treatment conditions, one of the most robust predictors of therapeutic outcomes was clients' levels of perfectionism (Blatt et al., 1995; Blatt et al., 1998). More specifically, clients with high levels of perfectionism (as assessed prior to therapy) showed less improvement on a range of indicators than those with lower levels of perfectionism. For instance, while the most perfectionist clients ended therapy with an average BDI score of 11.55, those with the lowest levels of perfectionism had scores of just 6.39 (remember, higher scores means more depressed, Blatt et al., 1995). Further analysis of the data revealed that this difference seemed to come about in the latter part of therapy. Up until about half-way through the sixteen weeks, clients who were high and low on perfectionism did about equally well; but in the second half of the therapy, clients low on perfectionism continued to improve, whereas those with moderate or high levels of perfectionism showed only very slight additional progress. Blatt and colleagues suggest: 'patients with elevated perfectionism may find their degree of therapeutic change in brief treatment to be insufficient and experience disillusionment with their therapist; the treatment process; and, most of all, their sense that they had failed to meet the high expectations they set for themselves' (1998: 427). Research also indicates that clients with higher levels of perfectionism may have poorer therapeutic alliances (Beutler, Blatt et al., 2006).

IMPLICATIONS FOR PRACTICE

When working with clients who seem strongly perfectionist, it may be particularly important to convey an accepting and non-judgmental attitude, and to encourage them to appreciate any therapeutic gains they make.

Psychological Mindedness

An emerging body of data suggests that an important predictor of a client's ability to benefit from therapy may be their 'psychological mindedness' (Piper et al., 1998; Piper et al., 2001). This can be defined as 'a person's ability to understand people and their problems in psychological [particularly psychodynamic] terms' (Piper et al., 1998: 559), and ranges from a simple awareness that others have internal experiences, to a complex awareness of the internal motivations, conflicts and defensive manoeuvres that others may have. In a study of time-limited group therapy for complicated grief, for instance, Piper and colleagues (2001) found that the more psychological minded clients were, the more favourable their outcome, and this was as true for clients in a supportive form of group therapy as it was for clients in a more interpretative context.

Psychological mindedness

A person's ability to understand people and their problems in psychological terms.

Stage of Change

One of the most popular and innovative developments in recent years in the psychotherapy and behavioural change field has been Prochaska and DiClemente's 'Stages of Change' model (see, for instance, Prochaska, 1999). The basic assumption behind this model is that behavioural changes, such as giving up smoking, are not instantaneous events but processes that unfold over time, and can be conceptualised in terms of a series of stages:

- *precontemplation*: no motivation or intention to change in the next six months or so
- *contemplation*: ambivalence, with an intention to change at some point in the future
- *preparation*: an intention to change in the next month or so
- *action*: overt behavioural change
- *maintenance*: a focus on preventing relapse
- *termination*: no further temptation and a sense of total self-control.

On the basis of such a model, it can be hypothesised that clients who come into therapy further along the stages of change continuum are more likely to achieve, and sustain, overt behavioural changes than those at earlier stages; and, indeed, this is what the research shows. Ockene and colleagues (1992), for instance, found that success rates for a smoking cessation programme approximately doubled across stages, with 22 per cent of precontemplators not smoking at six-months follow-up, 43 per cent of contemplators not smoking, and 76 per cent of individuals in the action stage giving up smoking. Research also suggests that clients in the precontemplation stage are most likely to drop out of therapy, with those in the action phase least likely to drop out (Brogan et al., 1999).

Such findings, however, do not suggest that clients in the earlier stages of change are unsuitable for therapy. Rather, as Prochaska and colleagues (1993; 2001) suggest, it may be that therapeutic interventions need to be tailored to the specific stages that clients are at, rather than assuming that all clients are ready to take action. Consistent with this analysis, Prochaska and colleagues (1993) have shown that behavioural change programmes are more successful when they are individualised to clients' particular stages of change, as opposed to being standardised across participants.

IMPLICATIONS FOR PRACTICE

Therapeutic interventions may be most effective if they are tailored to the particular stage of change that a client is at. A gambling addicted client who seems to be at the contemplation stage, for instance, may be more helped by an exploration of the pros and cons of gambling than by direct encouragement to change his or her behaviour. Setting realistic goals for change may also be important (see 'outcome expectations', above). Prochaska (1999) suggests that, within brief therapy, a progression of one or two stages is a fairly realistic goal; and this means that helping a client move from precontemplation to contemplation or preparation should be perceived as a successful outcome. As Lebow (2006: 59) writes, it is important for therapists and clients to 'honor every stage of change'.

Level of Social Support

Within the psychological literature, it is a well-established fact that levels of social support – in particular, the presence of close confiding relationships – are closely connected to psychological wellbeing (Segrin, 2001). Given, then, that 'the rich get richer', one would expect clients with higher levels of social support to do better in therapy and this is, again, what the research tends to show (Beutler, Castonguay et al., 2006; Newman, Crits-Christoph et al., 2006). In one qualitative study, for instance, peer support was described by consumers of mental health services as 'extremely beneficial' to their treatment (Glass and Arnkoff, 2000). And, in their analysis of the NIMH TDCRP data, Zlotnick and colleagues (1996) found that clients with more satisfying close friendships were less depressed at six months after therapy; and, at twelve and eighteen months after therapy, clients with higher levels of social support and more close friends were still less depressed than those without.

To some extent, this relationship may be independent of what takes place in therapy. A study by Vallejo and colleagues (1991), for instance, found that individuals with higher levels of social support also improved significantly more in *pharmacological* treatments, suggesting that social support brings about greater mental health improvements even in the absence of psychological treatment. At the same time, it is important to bear in mind that, for many clients, the ability to engage in close confiding relationships may be substantially augmented through therapy, such that the therapeutic process is by no means incidental to their improvement. Indeed, another in-depth study of clients' therapeutic experiences (Maluccio, 1979) suggests that counselling and psychotherapy may play a critical role in 'triggering' clients to establish new friendships, re-establish ties with old friends, or develop more satisfying relationships with family members, and through that process play a key role in helping to improve the quality of their lives.

IMPLICATIONS FOR PRACTICE

Working with clients to find ways of developing and extending their social support networks outside of the therapeutic relationship may be an important part of helping them to achieve greater psychological wellbeing. In particular, the more that clients can be helped to develop close, trustworthy, confiding relationships with others – for instance, through looking at ways of overcoming barriers to intimacy – the more that therapy may be of help.

Observed Characteristics

Gender

Who does better in therapy, male clients or female clients? In general, the research indicates that the outcomes for the two genders are pretty similar (Clarkin and Levy, 2004). However, in the few instances where significant differences have been found, they consistently favour female clients over males (Sue and Lam, 2002).

Sexual Orientation

As with gender, the research indicates that, overall, lesbian, gay and bisexual (LGB) clients do about as well as heterosexual clients in therapy and are equally satisfied with it (Beutler, Blatt et al., 2006). Indeed, the research indicates that lesbian, gay and bisexual clients are actually *more* likely to use psychotherapeutic services and to see therapists for a longer duration than heterosexual clients (King et al., 2007), with one study finding an average of eighty-two sessions per therapist for lesbian and gay clients, compared with twenty-nine sessions per therapist for heterosexual clients (Liddle, 1997). There is also some evidence to suggest that LGB clients' experiences of therapy are improving over time (Jones et al., 2003). Episodes of therapy that began prior to 1970, for instance, were given an average rating by LGB clients of 5.3 on a 10-point scale (1 = *very destructive*, 10 = *very beneficial*); while those that began after 1990 were given an average rating of 8.3. Jones and colleagues suggest that this may be because of the greater acceptance of LGB people in recent years – both by themselves and by mental health professionals – and it is interesting to note that, as recently as 1977, 69 per cent of members of the American Psychiatric Association still held the personal belief that homosexuality was a pathological adaptation (as opposed to a normal variation) (Rochlin, 1985). It may also be related to the reduced prevalence of 'conversion therapies' (therapies designed to 'cure' or extinguish homosexuality), which were given consistently low ratings by LGB clients (average of 2.2 on the 10-point scale). As a final point, it is worth noting that LGB clients, as well as transsexual clients (for whom very little data is available), come to therapy for a diversity of reasons, many of which are not directly to do with issues of sexual orientation: for instance, financial problems, work issues and relationship and family issues (King et al., 2007).

RECOMMENDED READING

King, M., Semylen, J., Killaspy, H., Nazareth, I. and Osborn, D. (2007) *A Systematic Review of Research on Counselling and Psychotherapy for Lesbian, Gay, Bisexual and Transgender People.* Rugby: BACP.

Age

Age also seems to bear little relationship to therapeutic outcomes, with both older and younger clients gaining substantially from therapy (Clarkin and Levy, 2004). The one exception to this seems to be in the treatment of depression, where there is some evidence that younger clients respond better to therapy than older ones (Beutler, Blatt et al., 2006).

Ethnicity

In general, clients of different ethnicities do about equally well in therapy (Clarkin and Levy, 2004). However, a few US studies have suggested that clients from African-American backgrounds may have slightly poorer outcomes on average (Beutler, Blatt et al., 2006), and Asian-American clients have also reported less satisfaction with their therapy and progress than Whites (Sue and Lam, 2002; Zane et al., 2004). There is also some evidence that clients from Black and minority ethnic (BME) backgrounds may attend for fewer sessions than White clients (Clarkin and Levy, 2004), be more likely to drop out (Zane et al., 2004) and utilise therapeutic services less than Whites (Zane et al., 2004). While it is not entirely clear why this should be the case, data from the Sainsbury Centre for Mental Health (2006: 6) in the UK indicates that 'Black people are less likely to be offered talking treatments, and more likely to be given medication and coercive treatments.'

RECOMMENDED READING

Sue, S. and Lam, A.G. (2002) 'Cultural and demographic diversity', in J.C. Norcross (ed.), Psychotherapy Relationship that work: Therapist Contributions and Responsiveness to Patients. New York: Oxford University Press, pp. 401–21

Zane, N., Hall, G.C.N., Sue, S., Young, K. and Nunez, J. (2004) 'Research on psychotherapy with culturally diverse populations', in M.J. Lambert (ed.), *Bergin and Garfield's Handbook of Psychotherapy and Behavior Change* (5th edn). Chicago: John Wiley & Sons, pp. 767–804.

Socio-Economic and Employment Status

In many respects, the relationship between class and therapeutic outcomes is similar to that of ethnicity and outcomes – a consequence, perhaps, of the substantial degree of overlap between these two groups. On the one hand, clients of different socio-economic backgrounds seem to do about as well as each other in therapy (Beutler, Blatt et al., 2006). However, low-income clients *do* seem more likely to drop out of treatment as compared with middle- and high-income clients (Clarkin and Levy, 2004).

Within the UK, a couple of recent studies have also indicated that poorer outcomes in therapy may be associated with employment status. In an evaluation of cognitive analytic therapy for individuals with borderline personality difficulties, for instance, Ryle and Golynika (2000) found that nine out of ten full-time employed clients could be classified as improved at six months, while only three out of twelve unemployed clients could be classified in the same way.

Summary of Key Findings

- Client factors are some of the strongest predictors of therapeutic outcomes.
- High levels of client motivation and involvement in therapy are closely associated with positive therapeutic outcomes.
- Clients tend to do best in therapy when they have a positive, but realistic, attitude towards the outcomes and process of therapy; in particular, when they are:
  - expecting that their therapy will be beneficial (within reason)
  - aware that therapy may sometimes be challenging and difficult
  - clear about what therapy is and why they are doing it.
- Clients with higher levels of psychological functioning tend to get more out of therapy than clients with lower levels. In particular, better therapeutic outcomes have been found with clients who:
  - are not diagnosed with personality disorders
  - have secure attachment styles and good interpersonal functioning

- do not have high levels of perfectionism
- are psychologically minded
- are ready to change
- have high levels of social support.

• Clients of different gender, age, sexuality, race and class seem to do about equally well in therapy. However, there is some evidence that clients from Black and minority ethnic backgrounds, as well as those of lower socio-economic status, are more likely to drop out of therapy and may use therapeutic services less.

RECOMMENDED READING

Clarkin, J.F. and Levy, K.N. (2004) 'The influence of client variables on psychotherapy', in M.J. Lambert (ed.), *Bergin and Garfield's Handbook of Psychotherapy and Behaviour Change*. Chicago: John Wiley & Sons, pp. 194–226.

QUESTIONS FOR REFLECTION

1 If you have been a client in counselling or psychotherapy:

   (a) How would you describe your attitude to therapy at that time (e.g. level of motivation, expectation of outcome, expectation of process, predilection and preference)?
   (b) How would you describe your level of psychosocial functioning?

2 Given your answers to (a) and (b), how much would the research predict that you would get out of therapy? *To what extent was this the case?*
3 If you are working with clients, how much do the findings presented in this chapter match your own experiences of the kinds of clients that seem to get the most and least out of therapy?
4 Based on your personal experiences as a therapist or client and/or your reading of the literature, what other client factors do you think might relate to outcomes?
5 Why do you think that therapy seems to help clients *capitalise* on their strengths, rather than *compensate* for their deficiencies?

5

Therapist Factors: Who Works for What?

This chapter discusses:

- The extent to which therapist qualities and characteristics are related to therapeutic outcomes, and the particular factors that seem to relate.
- The extent to which therapists vary in their effectiveness.
- The relationship between therapists' personality characteristics, levels of psychological wellbeing, beliefs and values, and clients' outcomes.
- The relationship between therapists' demographic characteristics and clients' outcomes, and the importance of therapist–client match.
- The relationship between therapists' professional characteristics and clients' outcomes.

What kinds of therapists are associated with the best client outcomes: males or females, extroverts or introverts, religious or non-religious therapists; or is it that therapists who are matched to their clients on these kinds of variables tend to be associated with the best results? Chapters 6 and 7 will look at the relationship between therapists' styles of relating and techniques on client outcomes; but this chapter focuses specifically on how 'therapist factors' – enduring and relatively stable traits of therapists that exist outside of the therapeutic relationship (Beutler, Blatt et al., 2006) – relate to clients' levels of improvement.

'Supershrinks' and 'Pseudoshrinks'

Before doing so, however, a more fundamental question needs to be addressed: are different therapists (aside from orientation factors) of differential effectiveness; or is it the case that, as with therapeutic orientations (see Chapter 3), different therapists are about equivalent in their outcomes? This is much more than an academic question, and not just because it might have implications for referral and employment policies or for therapists' feelings of self-worth. Its importance comes from the fact that, if there are wide variations in the effectiveness of individual therapists, then the orientations that they are aligned with are less likely to be of particular importance to outcomes (see Chapter 3): person-centred or psychodynamic, cognitive or transpersonal, what will be important is the particular therapist offering the therapy, and a therapeutic orientation will only be as good as the practitioners providing it (Luborsky et al., 1985). If, on the other hand, it does not really matter much who is providing the therapy, then the crucial factor is likely to be the kind of therapy that they are providing: the 'differential effectiveness' position outlined in Chapter 3.

So what does the research say? An early study by Ricks (1974) showed that two therapists, working with severely disturbed adolescent boys, could have strikingly different outcomes. In the case of 'Therapist A', for instance, whom one of the boys labelled 'supershrink', just 27 per cent of the clients went on to develop schizophrenia in adulthood. By contrast, in the case of 'Therapist B', who was subsequently labelled 'pseudoshrink' (Bergin, 1975, cited in Lambert, 1989), a full 84 per cent of the clients went on to develop schizophrenia.

More recent research, with larger samples of clients and therapists, has tended to confirm these findings, demonstrating significant differences in outcomes across more and less effective therapists. In a classic study, for instance, Luborsky and colleagues (1985) looked at the relative effectiveness of nine different therapists: three practising CBT, three practising supportive-expressive therapy (a form of psychodynamic therapy), and three practising drugs counselling, with over one hundred veterans struggling with drugs dependency. Overall, the researchers found that the supportive-expressive and cognitive-behavioural psychotherapists had somewhat better results than the drugs counsellors, but what was even more striking was the considerable variation in outcomes among therapists of the same orientation. For instance, while the ten clients of supportive-expressive psychotherapist 'A' demonstrated a large average improvement (effect size = 0.74), the eight clients of supportive-expressive psychotherapist 'C' demonstrated only a small average improvement (effect size = 0.19). In another study (Okiishi et al., 2003), clients of the most effective therapist had an average rate of change ten times greater than the mean of the sample, while clients of the least effective therapist actually showed a worsening of symptoms.

Combining such findings from fifteen studies, Crits-Christoph and colleagues (1991) calculated that around 9 per cent of the variance in psychotherapeutic outcomes is due to variations across individual therapists. This is similar to the 6 per cent calculated from the Project MATCH data (Project MATCH Research Group, 1998), the 8 per cent calculated from the NIMH TDCRP data (Kim et al., 2006), and the 8 per cent calculated from a multi-centre trial into CBT for panic disorder (Huppert et al., 2001) – all large-scale, carefully controlled studies in which therapists practised according to clearly-defined, manualised procedures. Wampold (2001) converts this 9 per cent into an effect size of around 0.6, which, although modest in effect size terms, is described by Wampold as 'impressively large' when compared with the effect size of differences across therapies (0.2 at most, see Chapter 3). In other words, the differences in effectiveness from one

CBT practitioner to another, or from one person-centred therapist to another, would seem to be considerably greater than the differences in effectiveness between *all* CBT practitioners and *all* person-centred therapists, or all therapists of any other orientation.

Needless to say, not everyone agrees with this analysis. In particular, in an alternative examination of the NIMH TDCRP data, Elkin and colleagues (2006) calculated that clinical outcomes did *not* differ significantly across therapists, and they highlight a number of problems with some of the data presented above. For instance, in the Project MATCH data, they point out that much of the variation across therapists was due to individual 'outliers': i.e. single therapists who had much poorer, or much better, outcomes than everyone else. They conclude that 'there is, as yet, very little evidence of statistically significant therapist effects' (Elkin et al., 2006: 154). Crits-Christoph and colleagues (1991) have also shown that therapist effects tend to be reduced among more experienced therapists, and therapists practising according to a manual.

Given that the differences between Elkin and colleagues' (2006) and Kim and colleagues' (2006) analyses of the same data-set seem to comes down to complex methodological differences regarding 'multi-level modelling' (Soldz, 2006), definitive answers to the question of therapist effects are likely to be some time. However, some tentative conclusions can be made. First, it seems that improvement and deterioration rates of different therapists can vary quite considerably, even when they are attempting to follow the same set of highly manualised procedures. Nonetheless, there are some indications that this variation may be primarily due to a few therapists performing very well and a few very badly (Elkin et al., 2006), with the majority of therapists performing at a relatively middling range. What is almost certainly also the case is that some therapists perform better with some groups of clients while other therapists perform better with others. In the remainder of this chapter, we will explore this possibility, as well as the kinds of therapist factors that, in general, are related to positive client outcomes.

RECOMMENDED READING

Luborsky, L., McLellan, A.T., Woody, G.E., O'Brien, C.P. and Auerbach, A. (1985) 'Therapist success and its determinants', *Archives of General Psychiatry*, 42 (6): 602–11.

Inferred Characteristics

Psychological Functioning

In Chapter 4, we saw that clients with high levels of psychosocial functioning tended to do better in therapy, but is the same also true for therapists? In general, the research seems to indicate that it is – though not to the extent that one might imagine. A recent meta-analysis of nine studies, for instance, found a significant positive relationship between therapists' wellbeing and clients' outcomes, albeit a relatively small one (equivalent to an effect size of about 0.24, Beutler et al., 2004). For example, in the Luborsky et al. (1985) study of differential therapist effectiveness (see above), therapists who were judged by their peers as psychologically healthy and well-adjusted (as well as capable, skilful and non-authoritarian) tended to have better client outcomes on such indices as drug use, employment, and psychological functioning, with correlations in the moderate to high range. In another study (Henry et al., 1990), therapists who were more hostile towards themselves were found to be more hostile towards their clients. There is also some evidence to suggest that therapists with more secure attachment styles (see Table 4.2) have better client outcomes (e.g. Tyrrell et al., 1999), while those with more preoccupied styles tend to respond less empathically, particularly to clients who have secure or dismissive attachment styles (Beutler, Blatt et al., 2006).

Box 5.1   Should therapists have their own therapy?

Around four out of five psychotherapists have had, or are having, their own psychotherapy (Rønnestad and Ladany, 2006). Given that therapists who are more psychologically healthy tend to have better outcomes, and that therapy has been shown to improve levels of psychological health (see Chapter 2), shouldn't all therapists be required to have their own personal therapy? One problem with this argument is that the research has yet to demonstrate a direct relationship between client outcomes and therapists' engagement with their own personal therapy (Beutler et al., 2004; Rønnestad and Ladany, 2006). Indeed, a recent study of long-term psychotherapy in Sweden found that psychoanalysts with the longest periods of training analysis had some of the poorest client outcomes (Sandell et al., 2006). On the other hand, a small number of correlational studies *have* suggested that experiences of personal therapy are positively related to therapists' levels of warmth, empathy, genuineness, as well as their awareness of countertransference (Macran and Shapiro, 1998). Psychotherapists also tend to identify personal therapy as one of their most important developmental experiences, with around 90 per cent rating it as helpful (Norcross, 2005). This is for a range of reasons, some of the most frequent being:

- taking care of self
- knowing how it feels to have therapy
- experiencing a role model
- learning to separate own feelings and client's feelings
- learning to hold back from jumping in to help
- knowing what *not* to do.
  (Macran et al., 1999)

Norcross (2005: 847), in his comprehensive review of the research, concludes that the evidence is probably not sufficient to compel personal therapy for all healthcare psychologists, but he does endorse the view that practitioners should engage in 'a variety of individually tailored personal development exercises and other life-enhancing activities, prominently including personal therapy'.

Personality

Research indicates that clients consider their therapists' 'personalities' one of the most important factors in therapy: 72 per cent of clients in behaviour therapy, for instance, rated it as 'extremely' or 'very' important' (Sloane et al., 1977), but there is little strong evidence to link specific personality traits to outcomes. An early study by Antonuccio and colleagues (1982), for instance, failed to find any significant correlations between client outcomes and a wide range of therapist characteristics. There is also no clear evidence on whether therapists whose personalities match their clients have better outcomes than therapists whose personalities are opposite to their clients (Beutler et al., 2004).

There are, however, one or two exceptions to this equivocal state of affairs. In particular, there is some evidence to suggest that therapists who have more dogmatic and controlling 'introjects' (i.e. unconscious attitudes or ideas) tend to have poorer client outcomes (Henry et al., 1990). Such characteristics, however, overlap considerably with therapists' relational styles, and in Chapter 6 we will look much more extensively at how therapists' interpersonal qualities, such as their levels of warmth and understanding, relate to clients' outcomes.

Beliefs and Values

As with personality characteristics, there is little empirical evidence to indicate that particular therapists' beliefs or 'values' – i.e. enduring beliefs 'that a specific mode of conduct or end state of existence is personally or socially preferable' (Kelly and Strupp, 1992: 34) – are directly related to client outcomes (Beutler et al., 2004) (although, interestingly, the research does show that the more clients' values converge on those of their therapists, the more therapists (but not clients) rate their clients as improved – e.g. Martinez, 1991). A study by Lafferty and colleagues (1989: 78), for instance, found that more effective and less effective trainee therapists differed on only three out of forty values: 'More effective therapists placed significantly less importance on having a comfortable (i.e. a prosperous) and exciting (i.e. a stimulating and active) life and placed significantly more importance on being intellectual (i.e. intelligent and reflective) than did less effective therapists.' These findings, however, have yet to be replicated. Nevertheless, there is some evidence to suggest that therapists who hold prejudicial attitudes towards particular disadvantaged groups – such as homosexual clients, women and BME (black and minority ethnic) clients – are less able to engage with these clients and form effective working alliances (Beutler et al., 2004); and, given that these factors are closely related to client outcomes (see Chapter 6), it seems reasonable to conclude that the clients of such therapists may achieve less positive outcomes.

What about matching on beliefs and values: would a client who holds conservative values, for instance, do better with a therapist of a similar outlook, or would they do just as well with a therapist with a liberal worldview? Research on this question, as one might expect, is relatively sparse, but one aspect of it that has been researched in some depth is that of the effect of a convergence of religious and spiritual values in therapy and counselling.

Here, findings are relatively complex. On the one hand, the research suggests that, in themselves, therapist and client similarities on levels of religious commitment do not predict better outcomes (see Worthington and Sandage, 2002). Indeed, one study found that initial *dissimilarity* of religious values correlated significantly with clients' self-ratings of improvement (Martinez, 1991). On the other hand, if one looks solely at highly religious clients, there is some evidence that they do have a preference for therapists with more religious *values* (though not necessarily more religious *beliefs)* (McCullough and Worthington, 1995), and may assume that such therapists will be more effective (Ripley et al., 2001).

Why might this be the case? Studies suggest that religious people may anticipate negative experiences with secular or non-religious therapists (Keating and Fretz, 1990; Worthington and Sandage, 2002), fearing that their values may be undermined, or that they would be misunderstood or misdiagnosed in some way (Worthington et al., 1996). For instance, Wikler (1989) found that, based on past and present experiences of therapy, 45 per cent of Orthodox Jewish respondents would prefer to see an Orthodox Jewish therapist, and much of this was to do with fears that non-Orthodox therapists would react negatively to them. One respondent said, for instance, 'Someone not *frum* [Orthodox] would try to channel me in non-*frum* directions' (Wikler, 1989: 137). Interestingly, however, those respondents who expressed a preference *not* to see an Orthodox Jewish therapist (20 per cent of respondents) did so for similar reasons: i.e. they feared that an Orthodox Jewish therapist would judge or criticise them: for instance, 'I really chose someone ... who was really "off-the-wall" in Judaism, because I kind of felt I could say some of the things I wanted to without any fear of ... "How can you even *think* of such things?!"' (Wikler, 1989: 139). This indicates that the key factor in determining clients' preferences for particular kinds of therapists may not be similarity in values, *per se*, but whether or not clients believe that they will be accepted and understood by their therapists. Such an interpretation is supported by the finding that, when religious people are actually exposed to counselling, religious or non-religious therapists who behave in similar ways are seen as being equally attractive (Worthington et al., 1996).

Observed Characteristics

Gender

A review of ten recent studies that compared drop-out and improvement rates for male and female therapists found no significant difference between the sexes, with a mean effect size of just 0.01 (Beutler et al., 2004). In those few studies where differences did exist, however, female therapists outperformed males (Beutler, Blatt et al., 2006). A study of gender effects in brief psychodynamic psychotherapy, for instance, found that clients of female therapists were, on average, more satisfied with their therapy than clients of male therapists; and, in a subsequent study, were rated by judges as experiencing less negative affect, appearing more trusting and secure, and being less worried about the kinds of impressions they were making on their therapists (Jones et al., 1987). In addition, Jones and colleagues found that male therapists were rated as experiencing more countertransferential difficulties than female therapists (see Chapter 6); while female therapists were characterised as more assured and more direct in their communications, and more accurate in their perceptions. Similarly, there is research to indicate that female therapists generally hold more positive attitudes towards their clients than male therapists (Bowers and Bieschke, 2005); and are more empathic, relational, and less likely to disempower female clients, though not all studies find significant differences on such variables (e.g. Zlotnick et al., 1998).

Current research also indicates that therapists who are matched with their clients by gender (i.e. male therapists with male clients or female therapists with female clients) do not tend to do any better or any worse than therapists who are of a different gender from their clients (Beutler, Blatt et al., 2006). However, some studies have found that men and women express a preference for a therapist of the same gender (Zlotnick et al., 1998); and a handful of studies have suggested that clients matched on gender with their therapists may be somewhat more satisfied with therapy and may stay in therapy for longer (Sue and Lam, 2002).

Sexual Orientation

While no evidence exists on the comparative effectiveness of lesbian, gay, bisexual, transgendered (LGBT) and heterosexual therapists, in general, the question of whether LGBT therapists are more helpful than non-LGBT therapists to LGBT clients has been the subject of considerable recent research. With respect to outcomes, some studies have found that LGB clients (there is no evidence regarding transgendered clients) report greater benefits when working with therapists of a similar orientation (King et al., 2007; Sue and Lam, 2002); although two recent studies have suggested that it may primarily be *male* heterosexual therapists that LGB clients find less helpful (Jones et al., 2003; Liddle, 1996). This may be because, in general, male therapists have less positive attitudes towards lesbian and gay clients than female therapists (Bowers and Bieschke, 2005). Research also shows that LGB clients tend to prefer working with therapists of a similar sexual orientation, and this seems particularly true for lesbians (Burckell and Goldfried, 2006; King et al., 2007). However, the importance of having a LGB therapist may depend on the kinds of issues that LGB clients want to talk about in therapy. For instance, Burckell and Goldfried found that this preference was stronger when the issue was related to sexual orientation. Also, it would be wrong to assume that *all* LGB individuals prefer working with LGB therapists, or that the preferences of lesbian, gay and bisexual people are identical. Liddle (1997), for instance, found that lesbian clients were most likely to select a lesbian therapist to work with, and least likely to select a heterosexual male; by contrast, gay male clients were most likely to select a gay male therapist, and least likely to select a lesbian. It is also important to note that some gay and lesbian clients have concerns about, or are actively opposed to, working with therapists of a similar sexual orientation (King et al., 2007). For instance, one gay man felt that working with a gay therapist 'would not allow him the freedom to explore views which might not be considered "politically correct"' (Mair, 2003: 36).

Such responses suggest that, as with the research into matching on values, the key issue may not be therapists' sexual orientation, *per se*, but their perceived ability to accept and understand the client. This was the finding of a recent systematic review of research on counselling and psychotherapy with LGBT people by King and colleagues (2007: 3). They write: 'Our principal findings were that therapists' attitude, knowledge and practice are more important than their sexual orientation.' A good illustration of this comes from the recent study by Burckell and Goldfried (2006), which asked LGB individuals to describe the kinds of characteristics they would look for in a therapist. Here, while it was seen as 'beneficial' for therapists to be LGB, behaving in LGB-affirming ways and having LGB-specific knowledge were considered 'essential'. Such findings are supported by research which shows that, once behaviours and attitudes are controlled for, sexual orientation makes little difference to clients' preferences (e.g. Liddle, 1996). King and colleagues (2007: 9) write: 'Therapy that affirms and normalises a client's homosexual or bisexual orientation and/or their transgendered identity, regardless of the therapist's sexual orientation, appears to be particularly helpful in making clients feel safe and secure in therapy.'

In terms of specific ways of working with an LGBT population, Table 5.1 presents four practices rated as particularly exemplary, and four rated as particularly inappropriate, by LGB clients (Liddle, 1996). Note, in this, as in similar research (Burckell and Goldfried, 2006), LGB clients particularly emphasised the importance of being seen as a 'whole person' by the therapist, and not solely in terms of their sexual orientation.

Age and Experience

Like gender, the research tends to indicate that therapists' age, in itself, does not have much relationship to the outcomes of counselling and psychotherapy (Beutler et al., 2004). In other words, there is no evidence that the clients of older therapists do any better, or any worse, than the clients of younger therapists. Similarly, there does not seem to be any strong relationship between the matching of therapists and clients on age and the outcomes of therapy (Beutler et al., 2004). However, a couple of studies have suggested that therapists who are ten or more years younger than their clients may have lower positive outcomes overall than those who are within ten years of their clients' age (Beutler, Blatt et al., 2006). In addition, there is very preliminary evidence to suggest that therapist–client age similarity is particularly important to clients under 30 (Lasky and Salomone, 1977), and that these clients may do better with a therapist within ten years of their age (Dembo et al., 1983).

Table 5.1 LGB clients' ratings of inappropriate and exemplary practices (Liddle, 1996: 397)

	per cent of therapists exhibiting this practice who were rated as 'not at all helpful' or 'destructive'
Inappropriate practices	
1 Your therapist suddenly refused to see you any more after you disclosed your sexual orientation.	100
2 Your therapist discounted, argued against, or pushed you to renounce your self-identification as a lesbian or gay man.	80
3 Your therapist indicated that he or she believed that a gay or lesbian identity is bad, sick or inferior.	78
4 Your therapist blamed your problems on sexual orientation or insisted on focusing on sexual orientation without evidence that your sexual orientation was relevant to your problem.	76
Exemplary practices	
1 Your therapist helped you feel good about yourself as a gay man or lesbian.	4
2 Your therapist was quite knowledgeable about the lesbian and gay communities and other resources.	7
3 Your therapist was not afraid to deal with your sexual orientation when it was relevant.	8
4 Your therapist never made an issue of your sexual orientation when it was not relevant.	9

With respect to these findings, however, it might be hypothesised that the key factor related to outcomes is not therapists' age, *per se*, but their *life experience*: the amount that they have struggled with life's challenges and found their way through them. Unsurprisingly, perhaps, psychotherapy researchers have yet to find a way of measuring such experience; hence, its correlation with client outcomes is yet to be established. However, what some researchers have looked at is whether therapists who have been through similar issues and difficulties to their clients have better outcomes than those who have not, and the general finding here is that matched therapist–client life experiences does not make much difference to outcomes (Beutler, Castonguay et al., 2006). For instance, the Project MATCH (1998: 470) study of therapy for alcohol problems found that 'Client outcomes were unrelated to therapists' self-reports of being "alcoholic", having had alcohol problems, or being "in recovery"'. They go on to state: 'This is consistent with a large literature showing that a therapist's personal history of alcoholism and recovery neither benefits nor hinders his or her effectiveness in the treatment of substance abuse.'

Ethnicity

Overall, there is no evidence to indicate that therapists of any particular ethnic origin have outcomes that are any better, or any worse, than therapists of any other ethnic origin (Beutler et al., 2004). As with sexuality, however, therapist–client matching on ethnicity does seem to make some difference to improvements in therapy (e.g. Farsimadan et al., 2007), as well as to lower drop-out rates (Beutler et al., 2004). One study, for instance, found that African-American clients averaged 17 sessions with White therapists, compared with 25 sessions with African-American therapists (Rosenheck et al., 1995). Evidence is strongest indicating that ethnic matching is of importance for clients experiencing depression (Castonguay and Beutler, 2006a). There is also some evidence to suggest that BME (Black and minority ethnic) clients prefer therapists from similar ethnic backgrounds, are more satisfied with them and experience greater feelings of rapport; and that therapists who are from a similar ethnic background to that of their clients feel that they have more understanding of their clients' problems (Murphy et al., 2004; Zane et al., 2004). However, other studies have found that ethnically matched and non-ethnically matched clients are just as satisfied with their therapy (Murphy et al., 2004); and where differences do exist on indicators of therapeutic success they tend to be quite small. For instance, in the Beutler (2004) meta-analysis discussed above, the average difference in outcome and drop-out rates between ethnically matched and non-ethnically matched pairs was equivalent to an effect size of only about 0.04 (i.e. very, very small). Moreover, it is not clear how consistent this effect is across ethnic groups. For instance, there is some evidence to indicate that matching may be most important to Asian-American and Latino groups, and less so to African-American clients (Beutler et al., 2004). As a final point, while there are some indications that White therapists are less successful with BME clients than ethnically matched therapists, 'cultural sensitivity training programs' – which help therapists deepen their understanding of cultural differences – have been shown to have a positive impact on how BME clients experience their therapists (Zane et al., 2004).

RECOMMENDED READING

Sue, S. and Lam, A.G. (2002) 'Cultural and demographic diversity', in J.C. Norcross (ed.), *Psychotherapy Relationships that Work: Therapist Contributions and Responsiveness to Patients*. New York: Oxford University Press, pp. 401–21.

Zane, N., Hall, G.C.N., Sue, S., Young, K. and Nunez, J. (2004) 'Research on psychotherapy with culturally diverse populations', in M.J. Lambert (ed.), *Bergin and Garfield's Handbook of Psychotherapy and Behavior Change* (5th edn). Chicago: John Wiley & Sons, pp. 767–804.

Socio-Economic Status

Whether or not therapists of different socio-economic statuses have different client outcomes is a research question that has yet to be explored. There is also an almost complete dearth of literature on the question of whether therapist–client matching on socio-economic variables relates to the successfulness of therapy (Sue and Lam, 2002). However, a recent qualitative study by Balmforth (2006) (see Box 5.2) throws some interesting light on what it might be like for working-class clients to participate in therapy with middle- and upper-middle-class therapists.

Box 5.2   The process of therapy: working with therapists from a higher social class

As a research project for a Masters in Counselling, Jane Balmforth (2006) interviewed six working-class clients about their experiences of being in therapy with middle- or upper-class therapists. Many of the participants talked about feeling inferior, uncomfortable and silenced by their therapists; criticised and misunderstood; and unable to form good therapeutic alliances because of the inequality of power. For instance, one interviewee said, 'there was a barrier up which was tangible and palpable in the room and which we never acknowledged' (p. 220). Another client said, 'she struggled with my values, um, she found that quite novel … she'd say things like "Oh, how interesting!" and I'd be thinking "What do you mean 'interesting'?!"' Given the small-scale nature of this study and the fact that the respondents were self-selected, these experiences cannot be taken as representative of *all* working-class clients' experiences. However, they do highlight some of the potential difficulties that clients may experience when working with therapists of a higher social class.

IMPLICATIONS FOR PRACTICE

When working with clients from marginalised social groups (e.g. LGBT clients, BME clients, working-class clients), it would seem to be very important that therapists can relate in non-pathologising, affirming ways, helping clients to feel good about who they are in both their personal and social identities. It may be useful, therefore, for therapists to take some time to reflect on their own possible stereotypes and prejudices (whether in training, in supervision or otherwise), and to try to ensure that these do not impede their therapeutic work. The evidence also indicates that therapists should try to develop an understanding of the particular issues and difficulties that clients from marginalised groups may face (for instance, the stress that can be experienced by LGBT people when 'coming out') and the culturally specific resources that may exist within the client's community. It is also important that therapists should not expect, or rely on, clients to provide them with this knowledge.

Professional Characteristics

Training

Does training make therapists more effective? Certainly, research suggests that training increases the development of therapeutic skills (Lambert and Ogles, 1997); and, in the most comprehensive meta-analysis to date, Stein and Lambert (1995) found that clients of therapists with more training experience did achieve better overall outcomes. Such clients also had lower drop-out rates, tended to stay in therapy for longer and were more satisfied with their therapy. However, effect sizes across all indicators were relatively small (less than 0.30, Stein and Lambert, 1995). It is also important to bear in mind that, with many of these data-sets, the degree of training is confounded with such variables as levels of experience and age, such that it is difficult to be certain that training, *per se*, is the key factor associated with more positive outcomes.

In terms of what kinds of training are most effective, Beutler and colleagues (2004: 239) suggest that 'training that is directed by specific, manualised concepts and tasks tends to produce enhanced results over non-specific and general training'. However, while some research does suggest that skill-specific training improves and increases therapists' utilisation of those particular practices (e.g. Hilsenroth et al., 2006; Stein and Lambert, 1995), there is other research which suggests that training on specific competences only marginally increases therapists' abilities to practice in those ways (e.g. Crits-Christoph et al., 2006). Moreover, one well-known study found that training therapists in manualised, systematic procedures led them to behave in colder, less friendly ways to their clients, with a greater expression of negative attitudes (Henry et al., 1993). What is clear from the research, however, is that therapists' skilfulness, as well as their credibility – whether rated by clients, therapists, or external judges – is generally associated with more positive outcomes (Orlinsky et al., 2004).

Professional Status

The assumption that a direct relationship exists between therapists' levels of training and clients' outcomes is further questioned by research which compares the outcomes of clients of professionally trained therapists with those of 'paraprofessional' therapists (i.e. those who have had no formal mental health training, such as nurses, clergy and minimally trained volunteers). Somewhat worryingly for the counselling and psychotherapy professions, early studies suggested that clients who sought help from paraprofessionals were actually *more likely* to achieve resolution of their problems than those who consulted professionals (Durlak, 1979; Hattie et al., 1984). Such findings are supported by research which shows that clients who participate in paraprofessional-led therapy groups, such as Alcoholics Anonymous, can experience just as much therapeutic improvement as those who participate in therapy with fully trained mental health professionals (e.g. Project MATCH Research Group, 1997). A more rigorous meta-analysis by Berman and Norton

(1985) challenged the finding that paraprofessionals had better outcomes than professionals, but did not provide much further comfort for the psychological professions, calculating that the overall difference in effect size between the two groups was 'strikingly close to zero' (Berman and Norton, 1985: 403). A very recent meta-analysis also found no differences between professionals and paraprofessionals in the treatment of anxiety and depression (den Boer et al., 2005), with a non-significant, very small effect size of 0.09 favouring the paraprofessionals. What Berman and Norton did find, however, was that professionals were somewhat more effective in short-term work, while paraprofessionals had better outcomes in the long term. Also, professionals seemed to achieve better outcomes with older clients, while paraprofessionals were superior with a younger age group. In support of this latter finding, a meta-analysis of the efficacy of play therapy with children found a mean effect size of 1.15 when the therapy was conducted by a parent (i.e. a paraprofessional), compared to just 0.72 when it was conducted by a mental health professional (Bratton et al., 2005).

Paraprofessional

A mental health care worker, paid or voluntary, who is not formally qualified in the psychological treatment of mental distress.

Alongside these findings, however, there is quite good evidence to suggest that clients who are seen by a professional specifically trained in mental health work (for instance, a psychologist or psychiatrist), do better than those clients who are seen by a more generally trained *medical* professional, such as a GP (Balestrieri et al., 1988), or someone who has a biological orientation to treatment (Blatt et al., 1996). In the US-based *Consumer Studies* report (see Chapter 2), for instance, 62 per cent of clients were 'highly satisfied' with their treatment when it was provided by a mental health professional, while only around 50 per cent were 'highly satisfied' when it was provided by a family doctor (Consumer Reports, 1995). Similarly, while the improvement scores of mental health professionals and family doctors were similar in the short term, the mental health practitioners had significantly better improvements in the long term (Seligman, 1995). And while the Consumer Reports study did not find significant differences in the outcomes of psychologically and psychiatrically treated clients, the results of a meta-analysis by Smith, Glass and Miller (1980, cited in Beutler et al., 2004) slightly favoured psychologists over psychiatrists. Psychologically trained therapists also rated themselves as experiencing higher levels of engagement and skilfulness in their work than medically trained therapists (Orlinsky and Rønnestad, 2005) – what Orlinksy and colleagues refer to as 'healing involvement' (see below). Finally, a couple of studies have indicated that the professional group with the best therapeutic outcomes may be social workers, who undertake much of the therapeutic work in the US (Consumer Reports, 1995; Jones et al., 2003).

> **Healing involement**
>
> A broad, underlying dimension of counsellors' and psychotherapists' experience of therapeutic practice (Orlinsky and Rønnestad, 2005), characterised by a sense of positive involvement, effectiveness, skilfulness, flow and affirming interaction. The two other principal dimensions identified by Orlinsky and colleagues were 'stressful involvement' and 'controlling involvement'.

Supervision

Within the UK, organisations such as the BACP oblige counsellors and psychotherapists to receive supervision or consultative support (British Association for Counselling and Psychotherapy, 2007), but is there any evidence that this improves clinical outcomes? Research on this question is scarce (Wheeler and Richards, 2007), with mixed results from a couple of early studies (Holloway and Gonzáles-Doupé, 2002). However, one recent study from Australia suggests that clinical supervision of qualified CBT therapists does lead to better client outcomes, with 67 per cent of clients in supervised therapy conditions (both process-focused supervision and skills-focused supervision) achieving clinical remission from depression, compared with 47 per cent of those in an unsupervised therapy condition (Bambling et al., 2006). In this study, clients of therapists who were supervised were also significantly more likely to complete therapy than clients of non-supervised therapists. In addition, a range of studies has indicated that supervision can enhance therapists' self-awareness, help them apply skills and knowledge in a more consistent way, and help them experience greater self-efficacy (Wheeler and Richards, 2007); and total years of formal supervision correlates quite strongly with experiencing healing involvement with clients (Orlinsky and Rønnestad, 2005). A recent qualitative study also found that therapists experienced supervision as having a direct impact on their client work, leading to increased confidence, congruence, focus, freedom and safety; though several respondents also noted that their supervisor's attitudes, values or beliefs could sometimes get in the way and be counter-productive (Vallance, 2005). In addition, around half of trainees report that they have experienced at least one ineffective supervisory relationship (Worthen and McNeill, 1996).

In terms of what kind of supervision is experienced by counsellors and psychotherapists as most helpful, qualitative studies indicate that supervisees place particular value on:

- *Safety and acceptance*: a feeling of not being threatened and judged; feeling affirmed in one's work and orientation; trust; empathy; a sense of being able to disclose all aspects of one's practice.
- *Equality*: a sense of collaboration, collegiality and mutuality, which may be enhanced through the supervisor's self-disclosure.
- *Challenge*: the development of new insights.
  (Weaks, 2002; Worthen and McNeill, 1996)

There is also some evidence to indicate that supervisees prefer supervisors to observe them directly, either live or through video tapes; and that beginning therapists particularly value structure, teaching and encouragement as a means of helping them to gain competence (Neufeldt et al., 1997).

Box 5.3   The process of therapy: what supervisees don't say

A study by Ladany and colleagues (1996) found that over 97 per cent of trainee psychotherapists had failed to disclose at least one thought, feeling or reaction to their supervisors to date, with an average of approximately eight non-disclosures per psychotherapist. The two most common categories of non-disclosure were:

- *Negative reactions to supervisor* (at least one instance given by 90 per cent of all participants): for example, 'I thought he was an arrogant asshole who had a big blind spot on how to help me in supervision.'
- *Personal issues* (60 per cent): for example, 'I have not told my supervisor that I am pregnant.'

Other categories of non-disclosure included:

- *Clinical mistakes* (44 per cent): for example, 'I think I sometimes confuse my clients with interventions that are not at the level of the client's understanding.'
- *Negative reactions to clients* (36 per cent): for example, 'that sometimes I'm bored'.
- *Client–counsellor attraction issues* (25 per cent): for example, 'found a male client attractive, reminded me of the type of guys I used to like'.
- *Supervisor appearance* (9 per cent): for example, 'He wears clothes out of the seventies.'

The principal reasons that *supervisees* gave for not disclosing was that the material was unimportant (particularly for attraction issues); that it was too personal (particularly for personal issues); or that it evoked too many negative feelings, such as shame. In 66 per cent of instances, however, non-disclosures were discussed with someone other than the supervisor, primarily a peer-friend in the field. In most instances, supervisees non-disclosed by simply not bringing up the issue, rather than actively refusing to discuss it or by diverting the dialogue away.

Interestingly, when *supervisors* were asked what they do not disclose to their *supervisees*, negative reactions – to both supervisees' therapeutic work (given by 74 per cent of supervisors) and their performances in supervision (56 per cent) – were again amongst the most frequent non-disclosures (Ladany and Melincoff, 1999). Other things that supervisors did not disclose were their own personal issues (67 per cent), feelings of attraction to the supervisee (10 per cent), and reactions to the supervisee's appearance (18 per cent): for example, 'Trainee constantly blows nose and leaves tissues on table – it repulses me.'

RECOMMENDED READING

Wheeler, S. and Richards, K. (2007). *The Impact of Clinical Supervision on Counsellors and Therapists, their Practice and their Clients: A Systematic Review of the Literature. Rugby:* BACP.

Professional Experience

While practitioners tend to assume that therapist experience is a strong predictor of outcome (Boisvert and Faust, 2006), early reviews did not find any significant relationship between therapists' years of professional experience and clients' improvements (e.g. Christensen and Jacobson, 1994; Shapiro and Shapiro, 1982). A study by Hill and colleagues (1992) also found that more experienced therapists were no more able to 'read' clients' reactions. However, more recent studies, which have disentangled professional experience from related variables, such as years of training, have suggested that more experienced therapists do *have* better outcomes (Beutler et al., 2004). Propst and colleagues (1994), for instance, found that experienced therapists were more associated with positive outcomes than inexperienced ones, though the effect sizes were consistently small (less than 0.1). Other studies, however, have found larger effects. In a study of CBT for clients with panic disorder, for instance, Huppert and colleagues (2001) found a large average effect size (equivalent to a Cohen's *d* of about 0.87) between therapists' years of experience and clients' post-therapy levels of anxiety and distress. Interestingly, however, clinical outcomes only seemed to correlate with years of experience, *per se*, and not with years of experience in practising CBT. Beutler et al. (2004: 240) conclude: 'Such findings suggest that what is relevant about experience may be general clinical contact rather than the development of specific proficiencies.' Recent research by Orlinksy and colleagues (2005) also suggests that therapists who have been practising for longer, and who have a greater depth and breadth of experience, experience more healing involvement with their clients.

Conclusion

At first glance, there may appear to be something of a contradiction in the findings presented in this chapter. On the one hand, the evidence seems to indicate that therapists vary quite considerably in their levels of effectiveness; but when one looks at particular therapist characteristics and their relationship to client outcomes, there is rarely more than a small association between the two.

One possible explanation for this is that we have yet to find the key therapist characteristic, or characteristics, that relate to client outcome. For instance, it may be that some of the more obvious therapist characteristics, like gender and age, are really only 'proxies' (i.e. stand-ins) for the more meaningful variables, such as levels of masculinity and femininity or levels of maturity (Shoham-Salomon and Hannah, 1991).

Another possibility, however, is that the key therapist factors are not so much to do with *who* therapists are, but *how* they relate to their clients. Much of the evidence presented in this chapter points in this direction. For instance, in Wikler's (1989) study of Orthodox Jews' preferences for therapists, the key issue was not whether the therapists were Orthodox or non-Orthodox Jews, but who the clients thought would be most likely to understand and accept them. Similarly, Balmforth's (2006) study of working-class clients with middle-class therapists showed that clients reacted against, not the class status of their therapists, *per se*, but the fact that they were experienced as un-empathic and judgemental.

RECOMMENDED READING

Beutler, L.E., Malik, M., Alimohamed, S., Harwood, M.T., Talebi, H., Noble, S. et al. (2004) 'Therapist variables', in M.J. Lambert (ed.), *Bergin and Garfield's Handbook of Psychotherapy and Behavior Change* (5th edn). Chicago: John Wiley & Sons, pp. 227–306.

Summary of Key Findings

- Client outcomes vary quite considerably across counsellors and psychotherapists.
- Therapists with higher levels of psychological wellbeing tend to have some-what better client outcomes.
- Although clients rate their therapists' personalities as important, there are no clear indicators of personality characteristics associated with greater or lesser degrees of client improvement.
- Clients who hold strong or extreme values express a preference for thera-pists with similar values, possibly because they feel that such therapists are more likely to understand and accept them.
- Female therapists have outcomes that are as good as, and possibly slightly better than, male therapists, particularly with female clients.
- Clients from marginalised social groups show some preference for work-ing with therapists from similar groupings, and there is evidence that such matching may be associated with more positive outcomes but, in many instances, the therapists' attitudes and values may be of greater importance.
- Therapists' age and personal experiences do not seem to relate to clients' outcomes.
- Professional development through training, supervision and experience have some relationship to therapeutic outcomes, although the size of the effect tends to be small, and paraprofessionals seem to have as good outcomes as professionals.
- In general, therapists' traits (their enduring and relatively stable characteris-tics) seem to be a less important predictor of therapy outcomes than the way in which they relate to their clients.

QUESTIONS FOR REFLECTION

1 Do you agree or disagree with the general conclusion of this chapter that it is not *who* you are, as a therapist, that counts, but *how* you relate to your clients? What arguments are there to support, and challenge, this hypothesis?
2 If you have been a client in counselling or psychotherapy, were there any personal traits of the therapist (i.e. qualities that could be assumed to exist outside of the therapeutic relationship) that made the therapy more or less effective? If so, is this consistent or contradictory with the empirical research findings?
3 Without thinking about it too much, conjure up in your mind an image of the ideal therapist. Now write down five traits that you would imagine them to have. Are these the traits identified in the empirical research in this chapter?
4 If you are practising, or training to practice, as a therapist, which of your personal qualities (i.e. those that exist outside of the therapetutic relationship) do you think will be most important to your clients? Is this supported by the empirical evidence?

6

Relational Factors: it's the Relationship that Heals … or is it?

This chapter discusses:

- The extent to which relational factors are linked to therapeutic outcomes.
- The extent to which *qualities* of the therapeutic relationship are linked to outcomes:

  – therapeutic alliance
  – goal consensus and collaboration.

- The extent to which therapists' '*generic*' *relational skills* are linked to outcomes:

  – empathy
  – positive regard
  – congruence.

- The extent to which therapists' *specific relational skills* are linked to outcomes:

  – management of countertransference
  – self-disclosure
  – feedback
  – repairing alliance ruptures
  – relational interpretations.

In Chapters 4 and 5 we looked at the relationship between client outcomes and factors that were 'internal' to the client and therapist. In this chapter, we turn our attention to the way in which client outcomes are related to relational factors: 'the feelings and attitudes that therapist and client have toward one another, and the manner in which these are expressed' (Gelso and Carter, 1985: 159).

Within the psychotherapy research field, there has been considerable discussion and disagreement over the importance of relational factors for client outcomes. To a great extent, again, this is because of its implications for the 'Does orientation matter?' debate (Chapter 3). For a start, if relational factors turn out to be a key determinant of therapeutic success, then this is severely undermining for those who argue that different therapies are of differential effectiveness, because it suggests that it does not really matter what you 'do' with your clients, it is how you relate to them that counts. Also, however, if relational factors are the key determinants of therapeutic success, then this provides strong support for the relational forms of therapy (such as person-centred counselling and contemporary psychodynamic therapy), as compared with the more technique-oriented approaches, such as CBT.

As we saw at the end of Chapter 3, Lambert (Asay and Lambert, 1999), a leading figure in the counselling and psychotherapy research field, estimates that relational factors account for around 30 per cent of the variance in outcomes. This is twice the amount of variance that he attributes to therapists' techniques. A classic illustration of this relative efficacy comes from an analysis of the NIMH TDCRP data (Box 3.3; Krupnick et al., 1996). As we saw in Chapter 3, CBT and interpersonal therapy were found to be about equivalent, overall, in their effectiveness (Elkin et al., 1989); but what did correlate strongly with therapeutic improvements, in both CBT and interpersonal therapy, was the degree of 'therapeutic alliance' (see below) between therapist and client. Indeed, Krupnick and colleagues calculated that the therapeutic alliance, alone, contributed about 20 per cent of the variance in therapeutic outcomes.

Studies which ask clients to describe what they found most helpful in therapy also show that relational factors are considered among the most important aspects of the therapeutic process. Bohart and Tallman (1999: 51) write: 'From a client perspective, the most important aspects of therapy typically are the "nontechnological" factors: having a time and place to talk; having someone care, listen and understand; having someone provide encouragement and reassurance; and having someone offer an external perspective and advice.' Research also indicates that therapists can underestimate the importance of these relational dimensions, conceiving their aid as 'issuing strongly from their professional mastery' (Feifel and Eells, 1963: 317) when, to a large extent, it may come from helping to create an atmosphere of interest, warmth and tolerance.

What the research also suggests, as evident in the NIMH TDCRP findings, is that relational qualities are as important in non-relationally oriented therapies (e.g. CBT) as they are in relationally oriented ones. An extensive review of the impact of relational variables on outcome in CBT, for instance, summarised that there was 'conclusive empirical evidence' that relational factors, such as empathy and positive regard, *did* have a consistent impact across a variety of client groups (Keijsers et al., 2000). In fact, in a review of five retrospective studies in which clients were asked what had been the most helpful aspect of their CBT, it was consistently found that clients rated their relationship with their therapist as more helpful than the cognitive-behavioural techniques employed. In one of these studies, for instance, Ryan and Gizynski (1971: 8) found no correlation between the implementation of behaviour modification techniques and outcomes; rather, what they found was that, for the clients, 'the most universally helpful elements of their experiences were the therapist's calm, sympathetic listening, support and approval, advice, and "faith"'.

Such research suggests that the relative efficacy of relational factors – against technique factors, in particular – may be considerable; and although allegiance effects may play some part here, even advocates of cognitive-behavioural and empirically supported therapies tend to accept that relational factors do influence the outcomes of therapy (Chambless and Ollendick, 2001; Emmelkemp, 2004) (although, contrary to a common misconception, very few CBT therapists have ever claimed otherwise – see, for instance, Chapter 3 on 'The therapeutic relationship', in Beck et al., 1979). However, what some researchers in these, and related, fields *have* questioned is the extent to which relational factors determine the efficacy and effectiveness of therapy. In their extensive review, for instance, Beutler and colleagues (2004) estimate that relational factors contribute between 7 per cent and 17 per cent of the variance in outcomes, while Chambless and Ollendick give the figure of 9 per cent. Writing in 2004, Beutler et al. (2004: 282) state that 'The collection of meta-analytic findings over the past 10 years indicates that relationship quality accounts for a far more modest proportion of the variance in outcome than the 30 per cent suggested by Lambert.' More recent studies have also challenged the assertion that clients in cognitive and behavioural therapies rate relational factors as *the* most important elements of therapy. In a qualitative analysis of CBT clients' 'end of therapy' evaluations, for instance, Clarke and colleagues (2004) found that clients cited both relational and technique factors as helpful, with no clear evidence that the former were more important than the latter. Also, as emphasised in Box 4.1, *correlation cannot be taken to imply causation*: good therapeutic relationships do seem to correspond with positive therapeutic outcomes, but this cannot be taken to mean that the former causes the latter. Some studies of cognitive therapy with depressed clients, for instance, have suggested that it is the symptom change that is responsible for bringing about the improvements in the alliance, rather than *vice versa* (DeRubeis and Feeley, 1990; Feeley et al., 1999).

What also provides a very strong challenge to the assumption that the relationship is *the* key agent in therapeutic change is the fact that entirely, or predominantly, 'non-relational' therapies – such as self-help manuals and web-based therapeutic programmes – can be highly efficacious, with effect sizes that are often close to those in face-to-face therapies (Barak et al., in press; Gould and Clum, 1993). Given that many of these studies are conducted with relatively specific behavioural problems (such as smoking cessation, Gould and Clum, 1993) and that some interpersonal contact *does* seem to boost the efficacy of these self-help therapies (e.g. van Boeijen et al., 2005), it cannot be concluded from this that the therapeutic relationship is entirely redundant. Nevertheless, contrary to Rogers' (1959) hypotheses regarding the necessary and sufficient conditions for constructive personality change, it would seem quite possible for clients to experience positive therapeutic development without any kind of 'real' interpersonal encounter.

In discussing this link between relational factors and outcomes, it is also important to bear in mind that many of these factors – such as the degree of goal agreement – may be as much to do with how the client relates to his or her therapist as with how the therapist relates to his or her client. Indeed, in support of this hypothesis, there is actually more evidence that the client's contribution to the therapeutic relationship is linked to outcomes than there is for the therapist's contribution (Bachelor, 1991; Orlinsky et al., 2004). For instance, Orlinsky and colleagues report that, while 56 per cent of studies show a positive relationship between therapists' affirmation of their clients and outcomes, *69 per cent* show a positive relationship between *clients' affirmation of their therapists* and outcomes. Furthermore, clients' (and observers') ratings of the therapeutic alliance, as with all relational variables, tend to be more predictive of outcomes than therapists' ratings (Horvath and Bedi, 2002). At the same time, a very recent study has suggested that it *is* the therapist's capacity to relate to his or her clients, and not *vice versa*, that is the principal determinant of outcomes (Baldwin et al., 2007). In this study, they found that outcomes were dependent on a therapist's general ability to form positive alliances, and that, beyond this, it did not matter how well or poorly individual clients got on with individual therapists.

A final point: one of the biggest challenges in researching the therapeutic relationship is attempting to identify discrete, distinguishable relational factors. '[T]he therapy relationship is like a diamond, a diamond composed of multiple, interconnected facets … a complex, reciprocal and multidimensional entity' (Norcross, 2002a: 8). How do you distinguish, for instance, between 'congruence,' 'feedback' and 'self-disclosure'? Certainly, the research indicates that many of the relational factors are highly correlated (e.g. Salvio et al., 1992), with some studies indicating that, from the clients' perspective, there is really just one main relational variable: an experiencing of the therapist as *caring/involved* (e.g. Williams and Chambless, 1990). These high levels of inter-correlation were acknowledged by the Steering Committee of the American Psychological Association's Division of Psychotherapy (Division 29) Task Force on Empirically Supported Therapy Relationships, which conducted the largest ever review of empirical evidence in this area (Norcross, 2002b). Nevertheless, the Task Force distinguished between eleven general elements of the therapeutic relationship, as well as ten 'moderating' and 'mediating' variables; and these will serve as the basis for the present chapter.

Mediating variable

A factor that accounts for the relationship between two variables: for instance, greater levels of empathy might lead to better outcomes because of the feelings of being valued it engenders.

Moderating variable

Factors that affect the relationship between two variables: for instance, levels of empathy might lead to better outcomes in males but not females – hence, gender would be a moderating variable.

For the purposes of this chapter, one other useful distinction is between *qualities* of the therapeutic interaction (such as the degree of goal agreement between therapist and client) and the extent to which therapists exhibit certain relational *skills* (such as the amount of positive regard that they extend to their clients) (Castonguay et al., 2006). (Some readers may object to the use of the term 'skills' to include less 'doing'-orientated 'ways of being'; but the term is used here in the broadest sense, as an 'ability' or 'proficiency' at something.) 'Skills' can be further broken down into more *generic* interpersonal competencies (such as being empathic and positively regarding), and those that are more *specifically* orientation-based (such as making relational interpretations). (Again, some readers may object to competences generally associated with person-centred therapy being termed 'generic', but there are few therapeutic orientations that would not subscribe to the importance of these modes of relating.) Hence, in the following sections, we will look at the evidence that links therapeutic outcomes to three types of relational factors: qualities of the therapeutic interaction, interpersonal skills and clinical relational skills. We will also use the framework adopted by the Division 29 Task Force to distinguish between those relational factors which, on the strength of the research evidence, can be considered 'demonstrably effective', and those that can be considered 'promising and probably effective' (Norcross, 2002a).

Quality of the Therapeutic Interaction

Therapeutic Alliance

What is it?

Within the world of counselling and psychotherapy training and practice, the concept of the 'therapeutic alliance' (also called the 'working alliance', 'therapeutic bond', 'helping alliance' or simply the 'alliance') tends to be less familiar than other relational factors, such as 'empathy'. In the world of counselling and psychotherapy research, however, it reigns supreme, with over 4,000 papers and dissertations written on it in the last thirty years and more than 24 different scales developed to measure it (Horvath and Bedi, 2002; Martin et al., 2000). The 'therapeutic alliance' emerged from the field of psychoanalytic and psychodynamic psychotherapy, where it was conceptualised as the conscious, adult-to-adult working bond between therapist and client, as opposed to the unconscious, transferential and countertransferential dynamic. Today, however, it is generally considered a pan-orientation concept (i.e. shared by many different therapeutic approaches), with humanistic, cognitive-behavioural and many other researchers interested in its links to clinical outcomes (see, for instance, Watson and Geller, 2005).

The therapeutic alliance has been defined in many ways, but perhaps the simplest definition is that it is the 'quality and the strength of the collaborative relationship between client and therapist' (Horvath and Bedi, 2002: 41). Bordin (1979) conceptualised this collaborative relationship as having three main components:

1 The therapist's and client's agreement on the *goals* of therapy: i.e. the targeted outcomes of their work.
2 Therapist and client consensus on the *tasks* of therapy: i.e. the in-therapy behaviours and processes that form the substance of their work.
3 The existence of a positive affective *bond* between therapist and client: i.e. the positive personal attachments between therapist and client, including levels of mutual trust, acceptance and confidence.

The therapeutic alliance

The quality and the strength of the collaborative relationship between therapist and client.

This three-way conceptualisation has been widely accepted in the psychotherapy research field, and is the basis for the most commonly used alliance measure (Martin et al., 2000), the 'Working Alliance Inventory' (Horvath and Greenberg, 1989). However, it should be noted that considerable overlap exists between the three sub-scales of the measure (goal agreement, task agreement and bond), as well as with other relational variables, such as empathy (Horvath and Greenberg, 1989).

How Does it Relate to Outcomes?

A recent meta-analysis of the data suggests that the correlation between alliance and outcomes is in the range of 0.21 to 0.25 (Horvath and Bedi, 2002; Martin et al., 2000). This is equivalent to a Cohen's *d* of about 0.45 (i.e. a moderate effect), and suggests that about 5 per cent of the variance in overall therapeutic outcomes can be related to the quality of the therapeutic alliance. On the basis of the strength of this evidence – both in terms of the magnitude of the relationship and the amount and consistency of the data – the Division 29 Task Force concluded that the therapeutic alliance was one of four 'demonstrably effective' elements of the therapeutic relationship (Steering Committee, 2002) (another demonstrably effective factor being 'cohesion' in group psychotherapy (Burlingame et al., 2002), a variable closely related to alliance but within a group context). Qualitative studies of the factors that clients perceive as helpful in therapy also indicate the value of a collaborative relationship 'that deemphasises the power imbalance and in which both therapist and client are working together' (Glass and Arnkoff, 2000: 1469). In addition, the more positive the therapeutic alliance, the less likely clients are to drop out of therapy (e.g. Piper et al., 1999).

Moderators and Mediators

As indicated in the introduction to this chapter, this relationship between alliance and outcomes seems to be independent of the type of therapy being practised (Horvath and Bedi, 2002), with large correlations (equivalent to a Cohen's d of about 1.12 and more) for some of the less relationally oriented therapies, such as CBT (Castonguay et al., 1996; Safran and Wallner, 1991). In other words, agreement on the goals and methods of therapy and having a good sense of working together would seem to be of no less importance in the cognitive and behavioural therapies than in the more relational ones; and the evidence also indicates that therapists working in such orientations have just as strong an alliance as in more relationally oriented therapies (e.g. Marmar et al., 1989). There is some evidence, however, that measures of the alliance in the early stages of therapy (i.e. the third to the fifth sessions) are especially strong predictors of positive therapeutic outcomes (Bachelor and Hovarth, 1999; Horvath and Bedi, 2002); and this suggests that therapists should be particularly mindful of establishing a strong collaborative relationship in the first few sessions of therapy. Indeed, based on the empirical data, Hovarth and Bedi (2002: 60) state that therapists should make the development of the alliance 'the highest priority in the early phases of therapy'. There is also some evidence to suggest that a 'high–low–high' pattern of alliance development (i.e. where the alliance starts off well, dips, and then improves again towards the end of therapy) is particularly predictive of positive outcomes (Kivlighan and Shaughnessy, 2000); indicating that a therapeutic relationship in which alliance 'ruptures' are experienced, and repaired, may be of particular value to clients (see below).

IMPLICATIONS FOR PRACTICE

In the first few sessions of therapy, one of the main priorities should be to establish a strong therapeutic alliance with the client: a positive affective bond, a sense of working together towards the same goals, and some agreement about how therapy should proceed. Until such an alliance has been fostered, therapists should be cautious about using more challenging interventions.

Goal Consensus and Collaboration

What Are They?

Goal consensus can be defined as 'therapist–client agreement on therapy goals and expectations' (see Box 6.1) while collaborative involvement can be defined as 'mutual involvement of patient and therapist in a helping relationship' (Tryon and Winograd, 2002: 109). Both are very closely related to the concept of therapeutic alliance, particularly as defined in Bordin's tripartite formulation (see above), but their relationship to outcomes is also analysed independently by the APA Division 29 Task Force.

Box 6.1   The process of therapy: clients' goals

What do clients want from therapy? Research indicates that clients often have a range of diverse goals, with an average of 3.25 per client (Holtforth and Grawe, 2002). A study of Swiss psychotherapy outpatients found that the following types of goals were most common (in descending order):

- *Interpersonal goals* (74.5 per cent of all clients had one or more of these goals): for instance, increased assertiveness and developing greater intimacy.
- *Coping with specific problems/symptoms* (60.3 per cent): for instance, overcoming depressive symptoms or coping with trauma) (note: fewer than one in ten clients gave symptom-relief goals alone, though these goals were more prevalent in a sample of psychiatric inpatients, Holtforth et al., 2004).
- *Personal growth* (45.9 per cent): for instance, enhanced attitude towards self.
- *Wellbeing/functioning* (13.4 per cent): for instance, becoming more relaxed.
- *Existential issues* (11.1 per cent): for instance, reflecting on self and future.

These goals correspond relatively well to what counsellors and psychotherapists believe is most important for clients to realise in therapy (in descending order):

- To have a strong sense of self-worth and identity.
- To improve the quality of their relationships.
- To understand their feelings, motives and/or behaviours.
- To integrate excluded or segregated aspects of experience.
- To experience a decrease in their symptoms.

(Orlinsky and Rønnestad, 2005: 227)

How Do They Relate to Outcome?

As one component of the therapeutic alliance, we have already seen that agreement on the goals of therapy tends to be related to outcomes. However, Tryon and Winograd (2002) found that, reviewed in isolation, evidence for a relationship between goal agreement and therapeutic outcomes was 'mixed'. On the one hand, some studies have shown that these two variables are related (Dormaar et al., 1989); and low levels of client–therapist goal consensus have also been related to difficulties in therapy. Also, in an in-depth qualitative study of clients' experiences of therapy, Maluccio (1979) found that client dissatisfaction was often related to a failure to discuss, or agree, concrete and specific goals between therapist and client. In one 'failure' case, for example, a therapist attempted to help a couple work through their desire to control their son's life, while the parents wanted the therapist to induce their son to return to school. On the other hand, a number of studies have failed to find a relationship – or shown only a weak, non-significant relationship – between goal agreement and outcomes (Tryon and Winograd, 2002). Overall, Tryon and Winograd found that goal consensus and outcomes were significantly, positively related on at least one measure in around 65 per cent of studies, though this was higher when just clients' ratings of agreement were focused on.

With respect to the relationship between client–therapist collaborative involvement and outcomes, the evidence here is stronger (Tryon and Winograd, 2002). As we have already seen, clients' motivation and involvement in therapy are among the strongest predictors of therapeutic outcomes (see Chapter 4), and around 90 per cent of studies find that collaborative involvement and outcome are significantly related on at least one measure (Tryon and Winograd, 2002). Overall, the Division 29 Task Force concluded that goal consensus and collaboration was one of the four 'demonstrably effective' elements of the therapeutic relationship (Steering Committee, 2002).

Therapist Interpersonal Skills

Empathy

What is it?

Empathy is most closely associated with the person-centred tradition, being one of the six conditions that Carl Rogers (1957) hypothesised to be necessary and sufficient for constructive personality change to occur. It also assumed central importance in the Self-psychology of psychoanalyst Heinz Kohut and, today, is generally considered by psychotherapy researchers as a pan-orientation concept, as Rogers (1957) originally intended it to be. Rogers (1980a: 142) defined empathy as the therapist's ability to enter the private perceptual world of the client – 'being sensitive, moment by moment, to the changing felt meanings which flow in this other person' – and this is the definition used by Bohart and colleagues (2002) in their Division 29 Task Force review of the research. It is important to note, however, that considerable debates and controversies have existed regarding the nature of empathy (see, for instance, Bohart and Greenberg, 1997; Gladstein and Associates, 1987), and it is probably best understood as a multi-dimensional construct, with cognitive, affective (emotional) and somatic (bodily) elements all intertwined (Cooper, 2001).

Empathy

Entering the private perceptual world of another and having an accurate, felt understanding of their experiencing.

Within the psychotherapy research literature, empathy has most frequently been measured through the Barrett-Lennard Relationship Inventory (BLRI), a measure developed by the person-centred scholar Godfrey Barrett-Lennard in the late 1950s (Barrett-Lennard, 1986). The BLRI asks clients, therapists or observers to rate the therapist on a series of items from +3 (*Yes(!), I strongly feel that is true*) to –3 (*No(!), I strongly feel that it is not true*). Examples of the empathy items from this measure are:

- '[Name of therapist] nearly always knows exactly what I mean.'
- '[Name of therapist] understands me.'

Measured in this way, empathy has been shown to correlate strongly with the other Rogerian (1957) conditions of positive regard and congruence (Gurman, 1977). As discussed above, it has also been found to correlate strongly with measures of the therapeutic alliance, to the extent that some studies have suggested that the BLRI and the Working Alliance Inventory are really only measuring one, underlying factor (Salvio et al., 1992): a good/bad relationship dimension. However, in one of the most extensive reviews of this research to date, Gurman (1977: 511) concludes that empathy and the other BLRI scales, 'while overlapping to some extent, are consistently measuring different dimensions of the patient's perception of the therapeutic relationship'.

How Does it Relate to Outcome?

Based on the findings of forty-seven studies, Bohart and colleagues (2002) calculated that the correlation between levels of empathy and outcomes is around 0.32, equivalent to a Cohen's *d* of about 0.68. This is a medium to large effect size, and suggests that therapists' levels of empathy may make considerably more contribution to the outcomes of therapy than the specific techniques used, and may even be more significant than the therapeutic alliance, *per se*. This relative importance for clients of being understood by their therapists is particularly evident in studies which ask clients to rate the factors that they found most helpful in therapy (e.g. Lorr, 1965). Paulson and Worth (2002), for instance, found that clients with a history of suicidal behaviour rated 'feeling the counselor understood me' as one of the four most important aspects of their therapy (out of 65 items), with a mean score of 4.44 on a 1 (*not important*) to 5 (*extremely important*) scale. Conversely, one of the characteristics most consistently associated with negative outcomes is therapists' lack of understanding (e.g. Mohr, 1995). On the basis of such evidence, the Division 29 Task Force concluded that empathy is a 'demonstrably effective' element of the therapeutic relationship (Steering Committee, 2002).

Moderators and Mediators

Not only is there evidence that empathy is related to outcomes in the less relationally orientated therapies (e.g. CBT, Miller et al., 1980), but the review by Bohart and colleagues (2002) actually found a stronger relationship between empathy and outcomes in the cognitive-behavioural therapies (equivalent to an effect size of about 1.12) than in the experiential/humanistic therapies (equivalent to an effect size of about 0.52). Why this is the case is not clear, but it may be that empathic understanding is particularly important to provide the ground for more technical interventions. Bohart and colleagues (2002) also found that empathy was more predictive of outcomes for inexperienced, as compared with more experienced, therapists, perhaps because the former group tended to vary more in empathy overall. However, some reviews of the evidence suggest that not all clients respond favourably to explicit empathic expressions. In particular, Beutler and colleagues (cited in Bohart et al., 2002: 100) suggest that clients 'who are highly sensitive, suspicious, poorly motivated, and reactive against authority perform relatively poorly with therapists who are particularly empathic'. Also, what is experienced as empathic may be different for different clients. While some clients, for instance, have been found to experience cognitive-type responses as most helpful (for instance, 'The therapist really seemed to *understand* what I was saying'), others have been found to experience affective-style responses as most meaningful (for instance, 'I really think he *felt* my despair') (Bachelor, 1988).

Positive Regard

What is it?

Positive regard is known by a number of names in the literature, including 'unconditional positive regard', 'non-possessive warmth', 'therapist affirmation', 'acceptance', 'prizing', 'caring', 'unconditionality' and 'warmth' (Farber and Lane, 2002). Rogers (1957: 98), from whose work the concept is derived, defines unconditional positive regard as the extent to which 'the therapist finds himself experiencing a warm acceptance of the client's experience as being a part of that client'. However, Barrett-Lennard (1986; 2003), whose Relationship Inventory has been one of the principal means of measuring positive regard, distinguishes between 'level of regard' (the extent to which the therapist experiences positive feelings towards the client, such as respect, caring and appreciation) and 'unconditionality' (the extent to which the therapist's attitudes or feelings towards the client 'hold steady' regardless of what the clients shows of his or her inner experiencing). Analyses of Barrett-Lennard Relationship Inventory (BLRI) scores indicate that this is a valid distinction (Gurman, 1977). Indeed, while considerable overlap seems to exist between level of regard, empathy and congruence, unconditionality is only moderately correlated with the other variables (Gurman, 1977).

Positive regard

A warm acceptance of the other and their experiences without conditions.

How Does it Relate to Outcome?

Reviews of the research indicate that positive regard – as measured by ratings on such items as 'Shows a real liking and affection for me' (Lorr, 1965) – is generally, but not always, associated with positive outcomes. Farber and Lane (2002), for instance, found significant positive relationship in about half of the studies; while Orlinsky and colleagues (2004), as discussed above, found them in about 56 per cent. These percentages increase substantially, however, when only clients' ratings of therapists' positive regard are taken into account. Indeed, many studies of the factors that clients find helpful in therapy indicate that the experiencing of a warm and positively regarding relationship with a likeable therapist are amongst the most valued aspects of therapy (e.g. Conte et al., 1995) (see Box 6.2), right from the very initial contact (Bedi et al., 2005). Conversely, unhelpful and hindering therapeutic experiences have been associated with therapists who have a 'bored, rote, cold, or impersonal manner of relating, a sense of arrogant superiority …; lack of compassion, warmth and understanding; lack of respect' (Glass and Arnkoff, 2000: 1470). Therapists' feelings of irritation, anger and boredom have also been rated as non-helpful by clients (Feifel and Eells, 1963). Given the number of non-significant findings, however, and also the relatively modest effect sizes that tend to exist between positive regard and outcomes, the Division 29 Task Force (Steering Committee, 2002) concluded that it was a 'promising and probably effective' element of the therapeutic relationship.

Box 6.2   Going 'the extra mile': genuine care in counselling and psychotherapy

In a recent presentation entitled 'Relational depth from the point of view of the client', John McLeod (2006) argued that clients may particularly value a sense that their therapists *genuinely care* about them. This is something more than experiencing positive regard in the therapeutic hour; it is a feeling of really mattering to their therapists: that they are genuinely interested in their wellbeing and have been willing to 'go the extra mile' for them (see McMillan and McLeod, 2006). Such a hypothesis is borne out in much of the research (e.g. Jones et al., 2003). In their study of 'critical incidents' that led to the formation or strengthening of a positive therapeutic alliance, for instance, Bedi and colleagues (2005: 318) found that 'service beyond normal expectation' was mentioned by about 40 per cent of clients. One client, for instance, recalled 'The therapist said, "Call anytime, or just come in anytime, and there will be someone here, even if I'm not here."' Does this mean that therapists should abandon their boundaries? Given the need for therapists to behave in ethical ways, and to 'look after themselves', obviously not. But letting clients know how much they are cared for, and being willing to be flexible around boundaries, may sometimes be important contributors to positive therapeutic outcomes.

Moderating and Mediating Variables

Like other relational factors, there are some indications that positive regard is associated with outcomes irrespective of therapeutic orientation. In one particularly interesting study, Najavitis and Strupp (1994) looked at the qualities associated with more effective and less effective psychodynamic therapists – a way of working which is generally associated with a more neutral style of relating. The researchers found that more effective therapists, in contrast to the less effective therapists, scored significantly higher on such variables as warmth, friendliness and affirmation; and significantly lower on such variables as attacking, blaming, rejecting, belittling, ignoring and neglecting.

Congruence

What is it?

Also termed 'genuineness', 'authenticity', 'openness', or 'realness', congruence is the third of Rogers' (1957) necessary and sufficient conditions for constructive personality change. For Rogers (1957: 96), congruence means that 'within the relationship, [the therapist] is freely and deeply himself, with his actual experience accurately represented by his awareness of himself. It is the opposite of presenting a façade, either knowingly or unknowingly.' More recently, Lietaer (1993) has distinguished between two sides of congruence: an inner one and an outer one. The inner side, which Lietaer (1993: 18) labels 'congruence,' 'refers to the degree to which the therapist has conscious access to, or is receptive to *all* aspects of his flow of experiencing'. By contrast, the outer side, which Lietaer labels 'transparency', refers 'to the explicit communication by the therapist of his conscious perceptions, attitudes and feelings'. Like the other Rogerian conditions, a principal way in which congruence has been measured has been through the Barrett-Lennard Relationship Inventory (BLRI). Examples of congruence items are:

- 'I feel that [name of therapist] is genuine with me.
- '[Name of therapist] is willing to say whatever is on his/her mind with me, including feelings about either of us or how we are getting along.'

Congruence

Being freely and deeply oneself in a relationship, with one's experiences accurately represented in awareness.

How Does it Relate to Outcome?

In his later works (e.g. Rogers, 1980b), Rogers came to believe that congruence was the most important of the three therapist-provided 'conditions'. However, the research is generally more ambivalent. In the most extensive review of the literature to date, Klein and colleagues (2002) found that, in around two-thirds of the seventy-seven results reviewed, no significant relationship existed between levels of congruence and outcomes, with only one-third of studies showing positive results. Similarly, Orlinsky and colleagues (2004), in their classic review of the research, found only around 38 per cent of results showing a significant positive relationship between congruence and outcomes, although this was somewhat higher when only clients' and therapists' ratings (and not observers') were taken into account. Studies which ask clients to describe the most important aspects of their therapy also tend not to indicate strong links between congruence and outcomes, with therapists' 'realness', 'genuineness' or 'openness' rarely cited as key elements of the therapeutic work (e.g. Burckell and Goldfried, 2006; Feifel and Eells, 1963). However, it is interesting to note that, in some studies, therapists' 'trustworthiness' has emerged as one of their most important characteristics (Burckell and Goldfried, 2006; Conte et al., 1995), suggesting that this may be a more important factor than congruence, *per se*. In part, the low correlation between congruence and outcomes may also come about because genuineness is a relatively 'high-frequency' event in therapy. That is, therapists are experienced as relatively genuine most of the time, such that the likelihood of a significant co-variation between experiencing the therapist as congruent and positive experiences is likely to be small. It may also be, however, that some clients do not like a congruent, 'natural' therapist style. One client in the Maluccio (1979) study, for instance, equated professional competence with formality and structure. Hence, she experienced the 'informal and spontaneous' style of her therapist as 'overly casual' and, lacking confidence in his ability to help her, withdrew from therapy after a few sessions. Overall, however, the Division 29 Task Force (Steering Committee, 2002) concluded that congruence was a 'promising and probably effective' element of the therapeutic relationship.

Therapists' Clinical Skills

Management of Countertransference

What is it?

'Countertransference' was first remarked on by Freud in 1910, and over the last century has been defined in the psychodynamic field to varying degrees of breadth, from 'the therapist's unconscious, conflict-based reactions to the patient's transference', to the much more general and contemporary '*all* of the therapist's emotional reactions to the patient' (Gelso and Hayes, 2002: 267). Hayes and Gelso (2001: 1042), two of the leading researchers in the countertransference field, attempt a mid-point between these poles, defining it as 'therapists' reactions to clients that are based on therapists' unresolved conflicts'. Countertransferential reactions can be thought of as either *acute* (i.e. irregular and uncharacteristic reactions to specific clients) or *chronic* (i.e. habitual needs and behavioural patterns of the therapist); and they can also be thought of as existing as either an *internal* state or as an *external* expression (Gelso and Hayes, 2002). *Positive* countertransferential behaviours (for instance, being overly friendly to a client to meet one's own needs for affection) can also be distinguished from *negative* countertransferential behaviours (for instance, excessively criticising a client because they resemble one's mother). See Box 6.3 for research findings on countertransference and transference in therapy, outside of its immediate relationship to outcomes.

Countertransference

Therapists' reactions to clients that are based on therapists' unresolved conflicts.

Transference

The process of transferring to and repeating early patterns of behaviour with present-day partners.

Box 6.3   The process of counselling and psychotherapy: transference and countertransference

Transference can be defined as the process of transferring to and repeating early patterns of behaviour with present-day partners (Cutler, 1958: 349). Consistent with the psychodynamic assumption that this is a principal element of the therapeutic encounter, research indicates that parallels *do* exist between how clients relate to their therapists and their patterns of relating to significant others in their lives (Luborsky et al., 1990).

A qualitative study of psychodynamic therapists' recollections of transference in cases of successful long-term therapy (Gelso et al., 1999) found that mothers were cited as the source of transference in all cases, with fathers also cited as sources in the majority of cases. In terms of transferential themes, fear or mistrust of the therapist was evident in all cases, with wishes for a 'good parent' or dependency wishes evident in most. Development of transference issues was typically stimulated by both changes in the structure of therapy, such as an increase in therapy fees, and by events in the clients' lives outside of therapy, such as the death of a parent. In terms of how transference issues were dealt with, therapists used a range of classic psychoanalytic strategies, such as offering interpretations and focusing on the relationship, but also seemed to use less traditional methods, such as teaching clients about transference and self-disclosing. As with other research (Luborsky et al., 1990), resolution tended to be characterised by greater insight and mastery over the transference rather than the transference patterns actually going away.

With respect to countertransference, a qualitative study of seasoned therapists found that this phenomenon was identified in about 80 per cent of sessions (Hayes et al., 1998). Most commonly, its origins were attributed to family issues; with the therapists' needs and values, such as a need to be needed or narcissistic tendencies, also identified as common sources. In terms of what triggered the countertransferential reaction, the most common response was to do with perceptions of the client (for instance, that he was becoming dependent). Other triggers included the content of the clients' material, comparisons between the client and others, the clients' progress (or lack of) in therapy, emotional arousal, and changes in the therapy structures or procedures (for instance, missed sessions).

As indicated above, countertransference was described as taking both 'positive' and 'negative' forms, with therapists describing it in terms of both greater nurturing and identification with their clients, and also greater desires for distance and negative feelings. Research has also shown that male therapists may be more likely to distance themselves when countertransference is aroused, while female therapists are more likely to become over-involved (Hayes and Gelso, 2001). Therapists who have more 'integrated' personalities tend to have less countertransferential reactions (Hayes and Gelso, 2001), and the same has been shown for therapists who have greater awareness of their feelings (Robbins and Jolkovski, 1987). Interestingly, however, greater awareness of *theory* only seems to lead to reduced countertransference when therapists also have high awareness of their feelings (Latts and Gelso, 1995; Robbins and Jolkovski, 1987). By contrast, therapists who have high theoretical awareness but low awareness of feelings actually show *more* countertransferential responses than therapists who were low on both dimensions, suggesting that intellectual insight without emotional awareness may be more hindering than helpful.

Because of its 'unconscious' nature, countertransference tends not to be empirically assessed through therapists' or clients' ratings, but through the ratings of experienced external judges. The Inventory of Countertransference Behaviours (Friedman and Gelso, 2000), for instance, asks therapists' supervisors or observers to rate practitioners from 1 (*to no extent*) to 5 (*to a great extent*) on a range of items – for instance, 'The therapist rejected the client in the session' and 'The therapist talked too much during the session' – with higher overall scores taken as an indication of higher levels of countertransference.

In terms of its relationship to other relational factors, Ligiéro and Gelso (2002) found that negative countertransference was associated with lower scores on all three dimensions of the Working Alliance Inventory, with some indications that positive countertransference was also associated with a weaker client–therapist bond.

How Does it Relate to Outcome?

According to analytical thinking, the more therapists can manage their countertransferential reactions – i.e. the more they can reduce the probability of countertransference reactions occurring, or, if countertransference reactions do occur, the more they can reduce the likelihood of it adversely affecting the therapy (Goldfried et al., 1997) – the better the therapeutic outcomes should be. Unfortunately, very few studies have empirically examined this hypothesis. In probably the most relevant to date, Gelso and colleagues (2002) found a positive relationship between supervisors' ratings of therapists' abilities to manage countertransference and ratings of clients' outcomes. More specifically, clients' outcomes were related to the therapists' abilities to manage their own anxiety, levels of self-integration, and to the therapists' abilities to conceptualise client dynamics in terms of the therapeutic relationship and clients' pasts. In a similar study, Hayes and colleagues (2001) found that therapists who were judged by their supervisors to be more 'self-integrated' behaved in less avoidant ways with their clients. That is, they were less likely to inhibit, discourage or divert their clients from exploration or expression of a theme. Hayes and Gelso (1997) also found that greater levels of countertransference behaviour were associated with lower levels of client satisfaction and self-reported gain. However, this only seemed to be the case in the least successful therapy cases. In other words, when therapy was going well, countertransference did not seem to be a particular issue, but when therapy was otherwise going badly, high levels of countertransference seemed to be highly predictive of even poorer outcomes. Findings such as these suggest that therapists who are more able to manage their countertransference reactions may have better client outcomes, and the Division 29 Task Force (Steering Committee, 2002) concluded that management of countertransference was a 'promising and probably effective' element of the therapeutic relationship.

Self-Disclosure

What is it?

The practice of self-disclosure is 'one of most controversial therapist interventions' (Hill and Knox, 2002: 255). In particular, while humanistic and existentially orientated therapists have emphasised the need for practitioners to be transparent, real and open with their clients (e.g. Rogers, 1957; Yalom, 2001), more psychodynamically orientated therapists have cautioned against too much personal openness, fearing that it will impede clients' capacities to develop transference to their therapists (Hill and Knox, 2002). Consistent with this, research indicates that humanistic and behavioural therapists are most likely to self-disclose, and analytical therapists least (Edwards and Murdock, 1994). Given this polarisation, considerable research has been undertaken into the effects of self-disclosures on both the process and outcomes of a therapeutic encounter, though much of it has been of an 'analogous' nature (i.e. based on 'artificial' therapist–client dyads, or raters' perceptions of therapists, rather than bona fide therapeutic relationships).

Self-disclosures can be defined as 'therapist statements that reveal something personal about the therapist' (Hill and Knox, 2002: 255). In this respect, they overlap considerably with the external aspect of congruence ('transparency', see above). However, in contrast to transparency, self-disclosures are an *event* rather than a *quality*; and, by definition, are verbal, whereas transparency may include many non-verbal elements.

Self-disclosure

Therapist statements that reveal something personal about the therapist.

Self-involving statements

A form of self-disclosure, in which the therapist expresses a personal response to the client in the here-and-now.

Within the literature, a distinction is frequently made between 'self-involving' statements (or 'immediacy'), and 'self-disclosures' (or 'self-revelations') (e.g. Hanson, 2005). Self-involving statements are expressions of the therapist's personal response to the client in the here-and-now: for instance, 'Every time you raise your voice I start to feel anxious.' Self-disclosures, on the other hand, are statements of factual information on the part of the therapist that are about his or her existence outside of the therapeutic relationship: for instance, 'When I left University I also had no idea what I was going to do.' Within the literature, *positive* self-disclosures (for instance, 'I feel very warm to you when you share that') have also been distinguished from *negative* self-disclosures (for instance, 'I feel really critical of you when you describe how you are with your son') (Andersen and Anderson, 1985; Hill and Knox, 2002). Because of their event-like nature, self-disclosures tend to be identified and assessed in the research by external observers, rather than by therapists or clients.

How Does it Relate to Outcome?

In probably the most relevant and carefully conducted study to date, Barrett and Berman (2001) compared the outcomes of two conditions: one in which therapists (mainly of a CBT and supportive psychotherapy orientation) were instructed to increase their self-disclosures in response to similar client self-disclosures, and one in which they were told to restrict their disclosure of personal information. By the end of therapy, the researchers found that clients in the increased disclosure condition reported significantly less symptom distress. These clients also liked their therapists more, and several other analogous studies have shown that the more therapists self-disclose, the more they tended to be rated as likeable, warm and attractive by observers (Dowd and Boroto, 1982; Nilsson et al., 1979; VandeCreek and Angstadt, 1985). Given that clients' feelings of affirmation towards their therapists are predictive of positive outcomes (Orlinsky et al., 2004), this could be taken as further evidence of the therapeutic value of self-disclosures.

Studies which ask clients to rate different therapist responses also provide some further evidence that self-disclosures can be of value. Hill and colleagues (1988), for instance, found that self-disclosures were rated by clients as *the* most helpful therapist response mode, with ratings that were superior to such other responses as interpretation, paraphrasing and open questioning. (Interestingly, therapists in this study gave self-disclosures the *lowest* rating on helpfulness.) Of all the response modes, self-disclosures were also most strongly related to clients' levels of experiencing which, as we will see in Chapter 7, is also linked to outcomes. In another study, Bedi and colleagues (2005) found that around 30 per cent of clients, when asked to describe incidents that were critical to the formation or strengthening of the therapeutic alliance, gave instances of self-disclosure: for example, 'The therapist said, "You know what? I can really understand that. I've gone through that experience too."' In a third study of this type, Hanson (2005) found that self-disclosures were more than twice as likely to be rated as helpful than unhelpful by clients, while non-disclosures (i.e. times when therapists did not reveal personal information about themselves when it might have been appropriate) were twice as likely to be rated as unhelpful than helpful. Consistent with the findings of the Bedi et al. study, Hansen found that self-disclosures were experienced as particularly helpful – and non-disclosures particularly unhelpful – because of their effect on the therapeutic alliance.

It would be wrong to assume, however, that the above studies indicate that the more therapists self-disclose, the better the outcomes are likely to be. In the Barrett and Berman (2001) comparative study above, for instance, the frequency of self-disclosures in the 'increased' condition was still fairly limited, with an average of fewer than five self-disclosures per session, and an average time of less than fifteen seconds per disclosure. Also, studies which directly correlate the amount of self-disclosure with outcomes generally fail to find a positive relationship (Orlinsky et al., 2004), although Hill and Knox (2002) suggest that the definition and ways of assessing self-disclosures in these studies tend to be vague and inconsistent. Even so, such findings are not particularly surprising: in contrast to generic interpersonal skills such as empathy or positive regard, no one has ever suggested that therapists should simply self-disclose as much as possible. Rather, what has been suggested is that a judicious and moderate use of self-disclosure can be of value to clients (e.g. Yalom, 2001), and this is what analogous studies indicate, with therapists who disclose at moderate being often levels viewed most favourably by observers (Watkins, 1990). Based on such research, the Division 29 Task Force (Steering Committee, 2002) concludes that self-disclosure is a 'promising and probably effective' element of the therapeutic relationship.

Mediators and Moderators

With respect to whether self-involving or self-disclosing statements are more helpful, results here are mixed. On the one hand, there is research to indicate that clients rate self-involving therapists as significantly more expert and trustworthy than self-disclosing therapists, and that such immediate disclosures stimulate more client self-reflection (McCarthy and Betz, 1978). Other studies, however, have not confirmed these findings (e.g. Dowd and Boroto, 1982); and a study by Knox and colleagues (1997) found that clients, when asked to give an example of a therapist self-disclosure that had been helpful to them, consistently described non-immediate self-disclosures, such as revelations about the therapist's past history of drug use. What is clear, however, is that positive self-involving statements tend to be rated more positively than negative self-involving statements (e.g. Andersen and Anderson, 1985). The evidence would seem to suggest, then, that positive self-involving statements are regarded most favourably by clients, certainly more than negative self-involving statements, and probably more than both positive and negative self-disclosing statements (Watkins, 1990). Finally, there is some evidence to indicate that disclosures of relatively non-intimate material by therapists (such as professional issues and demographic details) are viewed more positively than disclosures of more intimate material, such as personal feelings and sexual issues (Edwards and Murdock, 1994; Watkins, 1990).

IMPLICATIONS FOR PRACTICE

Based on their review of the empirical literature, Hill and Knox (2002: 262) make the following suggestions regarding self-disclosing in therapy:

- Disclose infrequently.
- It is usually more appropriate to disclose less intimate material, such as professional background, than intimate material, such as religious beliefs.
- Use disclosures to validate the client's reality, normalise, strengthen the alliance, or to offer alternative ways to think or act.
- Avoid disclosures that are for your own needs, remove the focus from the client, interfere with the flow of the session, burden or confuse the client, are intrusive, or blur the client–therapist boundaries.
- Self-disclosures may be particularly appropriate as a response to similar client disclosures, normalising and reassuring clients.
- Carefully observe how clients respond to disclosures and ask about their reactions, using this information to judge the appropriateness of further disclosures – be responsive to the needs of individual clients.

In addition, the research indicates that positive self-involving statements may be of particular value to clients: for instance, 'I get such a sense of excitement and energy when you talk about your future.'

Feedback

What is it?

Feedback can be defined as information provided to a person, from an external source, about the person's behaviour or the effects of that behaviour (Claiborn et al., 2002). Conceptually, feedback overlaps quite considerably with self-involving forms of self-disclosures (see above), but the term tends to be used to refer to less personal disclosures of information, and more 'objective' appraisals of another's behaviour. In contrast to self-disclosure and the other relational factors discussed in this chapter, it is also a relatively new concept in the counselling and psychotherapy field, coming from such areas as electrical engineering and performance appraisal (Claiborn et al., 2002).

Feedback

Information provided to a person, from an external source, about the person's behaviour or the effects of that behaviour.

Claiborn (2002) outlines four types of feedback that may take place in therapy:

- *Observation* or *description* of clients' behaviours: for instance, 'I can really see you shaking when you come into the room.'
- *Emotional reactions* to clients' behaviour (this is closest to self-involving statements): for instance, 'I find myself getting frustrated every time you arrive at sessions 30 minutes late.'
- *Inferences* about something not directly observable: for instance, 'I get a sense that you really don't like visiting your parents.'
- *'Mirroring'* – i.e. presenting clients with a sample of their behaviour: for instance, by inviting them to watch a recording of their interactions in a group.

Like self-involving statements, feedback can also be a 'positive' (e.g. affirming or supportive), or have a more negative tone (e.g. critical, Claiborn et al., 2002).

How Does it Relate to Outcome?

Studies which look at the relationship between feedback and outcomes in individual therapy have primarily focused on the impact of descriptive behavioural feedback and mirroring within cognitive and behavioural practice. Leitenberg and colleagues (1975), for instance, examined the effects of providing phobic clients with feedback on how long they had managed to endure anxiety-evoking situations. The researchers found that precise feedback on performance led to dramatic increases in rates of improvement. In another study, Rapee and Hayman (1996) found that socially anxious clients could make more realistic (i.e. more positive) assessments of their performances after viewing themselves on video. Research from the US also indicates that clients who are given feedback on psychological test scores, and who are invited to participate actively in assessment procedures, experience greater gains than those in control conditions (Finn and Tonsager, 1997; Goodyear, 1990). Based on such findings, Claiborn and colleagues (2002) conclude that feedback can be a powerful intervention, and the APA Division 29 Task Force (Steering Committee, 2002) conclude that it is a 'promising and probably effective' element of the therapeutic relationship.

Mediators and Moderators

As with self-disclosures, research indicates that positive feedback is experienced as more acceptable and helpful to receivers than negative feedback (Goodyear, 1990); indeed, there is evidence that negative feedback delivered in high proportions can reduce clients' sensitivity to an entire session (Kivlighan, 1985). However, based on the research, Claiborn and colleagues (2002: 226) write that: 'As the working alliance becomes established and the goals of the client (and thus the criteria for judging the effectiveness of the client's behavior) are clear, negative feedback is likely to be accepted as accurate and useful, as well.' Similarly, negative feedback also seems to be more acceptable when it is preceded by positive feedback (Claiborn et al., 2002; Kivlighan, 1985) or sandwiched between it (Morran et al., 1998); and there is evidence that, in groups, those who do the best are those who receive high levels of both positive and negative feedback (Kivlighan, 1985). A study by Thelen and Lasoski (1980) also suggests that mirroring feedback is most helpful when therapists provide 'focusing comments': i.e. when the therapist actively attempts to direct the person's attention to the crucial aspect of their behaviour. Different individuals also seem to process feedback in different ways. In particular, clients with low self-esteem and who are more depressed tend to 'hear' feedback more negatively; and there is also evidence that clients may vary in their desire for feedback, with different implications for how they hear positive and negative information.

IMPLICATIONS FOR PRACTICE

When giving challenging feedback to clients, it may help:

- to give positive feedback first
- to ensure that a safe and trusting therapeutic relationship has been established
- to make the aims and function of giving the feedback clear to the client
- to share the feedback in a collaborative, rather than didactic manner, and to be open to the possibility that the feedback may be wrong or unhelpful
- to bear in mind that clients with low self-esteem or who are in a depressed mood may hear feedback more negatively than it is intended.

Repairing Alliance Ruptures

What is it?

The concept of 'alliance ruptures' may be unfamiliar to many counsellors and psychotherapists, but within the psychotherapy research field it is one of the most innovative and exciting areas of development, principally through the work of Jeremy Safran and colleagues in New York (see Safran and Muran, 2000a). Informed by psychodynamic, cognitive, humanistic and relational thinking, the work on alliance ruptures starts from the premise that a strong therapeutic alliance, as suggested above, is a key ingredient of effective therapy. Hence, 'a tension or breakdown in the collaborative relationship between patient and therapist', as Safran and colleagues (2002: 236) define alliance ruptures, has the potential to detrimentally affect the therapeutic work. Such a rupture could involve disagreements over the goals or tasks of the therapeutic work, or a breakdown in the therapeutic bond. For instance, a client might become frustrated and angry with a therapist who offers her non-directive reflections when she wants guidance and advice (task); or a therapist may notice herself becoming more and more distant from a client because she experiences the client as critical and patronising (bond). Safran and Muran (2000b: 240) identify two main sub-types of ruptures: confrontation and withdrawal. 'In confrontation ruptures, the client directly expresses anger, resentment, or dissatisfaction with the therapist or some aspect of the therapy. In withdrawal ruptures, the client withdraws or partially disengages from the therapist, his or her own emotions, or some aspect of the therapeutic process.' Safran and colleagues (2002) report that alliance ruptures are a fairly common occurrence in therapy, with one study identifying their presence in 11–38 per cent of sessions.

Alliance rupture

A tension or breakdown in the collaborative relationship between client and therapist.

How Does it Relate to Outcome?

Safran and colleagues (2002) suggest that repairing alliance ruptures is not only important to allow the therapeutic work to continue, but because learning to overcome breakdowns and tensions in relationships is a critical developmental task. At the present time, however, little direct evidence supports the contention that improvements in therapy are related to the capacity to repair alliance ruptures. Nevertheless, a substantial body of indirect evidence exists. First, as we have seen above, there is good evidence that outcomes in therapy are related to a strong therapeutic alliance. Second, as also discussed above, the fact that a high–low–high pattern of alliance development seems particularly predictive of good outcomes suggests that experiencing ruptures in the alliance, and then overcoming them, may be a particularly helpful aspect of therapy. Third, a brief relational therapy, developed by Safran and colleagues (2002) with a particular emphasis on repairing alliance ruptures, has been shown to have significantly lower drop-out rates (20 per cent) than either CBT (37 per cent) or psychodynamic therapy (46 per cent). Fourth, there is some evidence to suggest that, when therapists act to address alliance difficulties and misunderstandings rather than avoiding them, clients have better outcomes, are less likely to drop-out of therapy, have better alliances, and experience more of a feeling of resolution (Foreman and Marmar, 1985; Rhodes et al., 1994). As suggested by Safran and colleagues (1990), greater resolution of rupture events also seems to come about when therapists respond to their clients in an accommodating way (for instance, by apologising or by changing their behaviour). On the basis of such findings, the APA Division 29 Task Force (Steering Committee, 2002) concluded that repairing alliance ruptures is a 'promising and probably effective' element of the therapeutic relationship.

IMPLICATIONS FOR PRACTICE

Safran and colleagues (1990: 159) offer the following general principles for therapists for resolving alliance ruptures.
- Attend to the rupture. Indicators of a rupture may include the following client behaviours:
  - overt expression of negative sentiments
  - indirect communication of negative sentiments or hostility
  - disagreement about the goals or tasks of therapy
  - compliance
  - 'avoidance manoeuvres', such as skipping particular topics
  - self-esteem enhancing operations, such as self-justification
  - non-responsiveness to interventions.
- Develop an awareness of how you feel in relation to the rupture.
- Take responsibility for your part in it and talk about that with your client – avoid using transference interpretations to put all of the responsibility on to the client.
- Try to empathically understand the client's experience.
- Maintain the stance of a participant/observer rather than getting hooked in to a dysfunctional cycle.

Where ruptures emerge over the goals and tasks of therapy, it may also be useful to review and discuss with clients what it is that they are trying to achieve in therapy, and how that might most effectively be achieved (Safran et al., 2002). If necessary and appropriate, revise the goals and tasks of therapy accordingly.

Transference Interpretations

What Are They?

Transference interpretations are rooted in the psychodynamic and psychoanalytic tradition, and can be considered a sub-set of interpretations: 'going beyond what the client has overtly recognised, including establishing connections between statements or events, pointing out themes, patterns, or causal relationships in the patient's behaviour or personality, or giving alternative meanings for old behaviours or issues' (Hill, 1978, in Crits-Christoph and Gibbons, 2002: 287). Transference interpretations can be understood as those interpretations 'that help the patient to understand the link between their interactions with the therapist and the interactions they experience with others' (Connolly et al., 1999: 487). Crits-Christoph and Gibbons (2002), in their APA Task Force Review of the literature, focus more broadly on 'relational interpretations', which include both transference interpretations and interpretations of other relational experiences (for instance, parallels between how a client relates to his or her spouse and his or her father). For the purposes of this book, however, this section will focus primarily on transference interpretations, with relational interpretations covered more extensively in Chapter 7.

Interpretations

Therapist statements which go beyond what the client has overtly recognised, to suggest new understandings of experiences.

Transference interpretations

Interpretations that try to help the client understand the link between their interactions with the therapist and the interactions they experience with others.

How Do they Relate to Outcome?

Research that looks at the relationship between interpretations and outcomes has focused on two main variables: *frequency* of interpretations ('concentration') and *quality* of interpretations ('correspondence' or 'correctness') (Piper et al., 1993). With respect to the first of these variables, research over the last twenty years (primarily conducted by psychodynamically orientated researchers) has indicated that higher frequencies of transference interpretations are actually associated with *poorer* outcomes in therapy, particularly for certain groups of clients (see below) (e.g. Høglend, 1993). In the most extensive study of this type, for instance, Piper and colleagues (1991) found a correlation of 0.37 between proportion of transference interpretations and general symptoms and distress at outcome (equivalent to a Cohen's *d* of about 0.80 – a large effect) and a similarly negative relationship with quality of the therapeutic alliance. There is also evidence that greater focus on transference is associated with higher rates of drop-out, with clients who drop out more likely to be exploring transference issues in their final sessions than completers (Piper et al., 1999; see Box 6.4). Crits-Cristoph and Gibbons (2002: 298) conclude their review of this research by stating that 'High levels of transference interpretations should be avoided'; while Orlinksy and colleagues (2004: 342), drawing on a similar body of evidence, write that the use of transference interpretations in brief psychotherapies 'probably should be abandoned'. Interestingly, too, while Orlinsky and colleagues' (1994) extensive review of the research found that a focus on life problems and on core personal relationships tended to be associated with positive outcomes, a focus on here-and-now involvements in therapeutic interactions was not.

Box 6.4   The process of therapy: transference and drop-out

For clients who dropped out of psychodynamic therapy where there was a high transference focus, Piper and colleagues (1999) identified a consistent pattern of interactions in the pre-termination sessions:

---

1 The patient made his or her thoughts about dropping out clear, usually early in the session.

2 The patient expressed frustration about the therapy sessions. This often involved expectations that were not met and the therapist's repeated focus on painful feelings.

3 The therapist quickly addressed the difficulty by focusing on the patient–therapist relationship and the transference. Links were made to other relationships.

4 The patient resisted the focus on transference and engaged in little dynamic exploration (work). Resistance was often active, for example, verbal disagreement, and sometimes passive, for example, silence.

5 The therapist persisted with transference interpretations.

6 The patient and therapist argued with each other. They seemed to be engaged in a power struggle. At times the therapist was drawn into being sharp, blunt, sarcastic, insistent, impatient, or condescending.

7 Although most of the interpretations were plausible, the patient responded to the persistence of the therapist with continued resistance.

8 The session ended with encouragement by the therapist to continue with therapy and a seemingly forced agreement by the patient to do so.

9 The patient never returned.

As with the research into alliance ruptures (see above), Piper and colleagues (1999) conclude that persistent use of transference interpretations does not resolve impasses; and that, faced with the threat of premature termination, therapists may be better advised to allow clients to save face and conclude the therapy more amicably.

As with the research on self-disclosures (see above), however, it is questionable how informative or surprising this correlation between frequency of transference interpretations and outcomes is. After all, has any psychodynamic theorist ever suggested that therapists should simply make as many transference interpretations as possible? A better indicator of the value of such interpretations, then, might be the relationship between accuracy of interpretations and outcomes. Here, accuracy of interpretations tends to be assessed by rating the extent to which therapists' interpretations correspond to expert clinicians' ratings of the client's central relationship patterns, as judged from session transcripts. What such research shows is that more accurate relational interpretations (both transference and otherwise) *do* tend to be related to better therapeutic outcomes (Crits-Christoph et al., 1988) as well as to a stronger therapeutic alliance (Crits-Christoph et al., 1993). This seems to be particularly the case when therapists accurately interpret what clients seem to want from others, and how they perceived others as reacting (Crits-Christoph et al., 1988). In summary, then, the research suggests that a low frequency of accurate relational interpretations can be helpful (Piper et al., 1993), and the APA Division 29 Task Force (Steering Committee, 2002) concluded that relational interpretations are a 'promising and probably effective' element of the therapeutic relationship.

Mediators and Moderators

One key issue in the research on transference interpretations is their efficacy in relation to clients' 'quality of object relations'. This is defined as a client's 'enduring tendency to establish certain types of relationships, ranging from primitive to mature' (Piper et al., 1993: 588). Here, 'primitive' means that the person reacts to perceived separation or rejection with intense anxiety and affect (similar to insecure attachment), while 'mature' means that the person can enjoy equitable relationships characterised by love and tenderness (similar to secure attachment, Piper et al., 2001). Overall, what the research seems to indicate is that clients with more primitive styles of relating tend to do poorly at high and moderate levels of transference interpretation but can handle very low levels; while clients who have relatively mature styles of relating can benefit from low and moderate levels of transference interpretations, and only have difficulties at high levels (Connolly et al., 1999). In other words, high rates of transference interpretations may be particularly counterproductive for clients who have poor relational abilities (Crits-Christoph and Gibbons, 2002) and also possibly depressed clients (Castonguay et al., 2006); although a more recent study has directly challenged this conclusion (Høglend et al., 2007).

What also seems clear from the research is that transference interpretations are most effective when embedded in the context of a strong therapeutic alliance and supportive interventions, and may be dangerous when the therapeutic alliance is not sufficiently formed, serving to further weaken an already tenuous bond (Bond et al., 1998). Given that clients with more severe forms of psychological distress, such as those diagnosed with borderline personality disorder, may find it particularly difficult to establish strong therapeutic alliances (see Chapter 4), particular caution with such clients would seem warranted. Indeed, Bond and colleagues (1998: 302) write that, with clients diagnosed with more severe personality disorders, 'transference interpretations are very high-risk interventions', and suggest the use of more supportive techniques, 'especially during the early phases of therapy until a firm alliance has been established'.

Finally, there is the question of whether transference interpretations are more effective than non-transference relational interpretations. Some interesting light is thrown on this in the study by Høglend and colleagues (2007) which compared the effectiveness of two forms of psychodynamic therapy: one in which the therapists were instructed to address transactions in the therapist–client relationship and to make transference interpretations, and one in which such techniques were proscribed and therapists could only refer to relational patterns outside of therapy. Overall, the researchers found that both forms of therapy were about equally effective, though those with more severe forms of pathology did better in the transference condition than in the non-transference condition, while the reverse was true for those with less severe forms of pathology (see above). This means that, overall, interpretations focused on the immediate therapeutic relationship may be no more helpful than those that are not, but different clients may respond to these different kinds of interventions in different ways.

Table 6.1 Summary of conclusions of Division 29 Task Force by category and in descending order of magnitude of relationship (Norcross, 2002b)

	Magnitude of the relationship	Evidence of causality	Number of studies
Demonstrably effective			
Goal consensus and collaboration	3.7	2.0	3.7
Therapeutic alliance	3.0	1.7	5.0
Empathy	3.0	2.0	4.0
Promising and probably effective			
Management of countertransference	3.3	2.7	2.0
Feedback	2.7	1.5	2.7
Positive regard	2.3	2.0	4.0
Congruence	2.3	1.3	3.0
Self-disclosure	2.3	1.0	2.0
Relational interpretations	2.3	1.3	2.0
Repair of alliance ruptures	2.0	1.3	2.0

Note: Ratings of all factors are on a 1 *(low)* to 5 *(high)* scale. 'Number of studies' indicates relative size, rather than the actual number of studies.

Conclusion

Table 6.1 presents a summary of the conclusions reached by the Division 29 Task Force on the effectiveness of the relational factors reviewed in this chapter. Also included in this table are informal ratings by members of the Task Force on the apparent magnitude of the relationship between the factors and therapeutic outcomes, the evidence that this relational factor would actually seem to be responsible for bringing about these outcomes, and the number of studies conducted – a rough indicator of the reliability of the evidence.

Summary of Key Findings

- The quality of the therapeutic relationship is closely associated with therapeutic outcomes, across both relationally orientated and non-relationally orientated therapies.
- The strength of the therapeutic alliance – in particular, the extent to which clients and therapists agree and collaborate on the goals and tasks of therapy – has consistently been shown to relate to therapeutic outcomes, and seems important to establish prior to more challenging interventions.
- Therapists' levels of empathy are closely associated with the outcomes of therapy.
- Therapists' levels of positive regard are modestly related to the outcomes of therapy.
- In some instances, therapists' levels of congruence have been found to relate to the outcomes of therapy.

- There are indications that therapists' abilities to manage countertransferential reactions are related to therapeutic outcomes.
- Moderate amounts of self-disclosure, particularly as positive self-involving statements, may be more helpful to clients than systematic non-disclosure.
- Feedback, particularly positive feedback, can be useful to clients.
- Indirect evidence indicates that the capacity to repair alliance ruptures is associated with positive therapeutic outcomes.
- High frequencies of transference interpretations should be avoided, particularly as a means of dealing with alliance ruptures or with highly dysfunctional clients; but low concentrations of accurate interpretations may be helpful.

RECOMMENDED READING

Norcross, J.C. (ed.) (2002) *Psychotherapy Relationships that Work: Therapists' Contributions and Responsiveness to Patients*. New York: Oxford University Press. Essential reading for therapists of all orientations, with chapters that clearly and comprehensively summarise the empirical data for each of the relational factors discussed in this chapter.

QUESTIONS FOR REFLECTION

1 If you have been a client in counselling or psychotherapy:

- What aspects of the relationship with your therapist, if any, were helpful for you?
- What aspects of the relationship with your therapist, if any, were unhelpful for you?
- Is this consistent with the empirical research findings?
- What other aspects of the relationship, based on your experience, might be considered helpful or unhelpful?

2 Based on your experience as a counsellor or psychotherapist (if you have any), how do you think your clients would answer these questions?

3 To what extent do you think that relational variables can be distinguished? Would you agree that, ultimately, clients experience their therapists along just one caring/involved relational dimension?

4 Based on the empirical evidence and/or your own experiences as a therapist, how important do you think it is that therapists are willing to 'go the extra mile' for their clients? How can this be reconciled with the need to maintain appropriate boundaries?

5 In 1957, Rogers concluded that the three 'core' conditions of empathy, congruence and unconditional positive regard were necessary for therapeutic personality development. What do you think Rogers would say today?

7

Techique and Practice Factors: is it What You Do or the Way that You Do It?

This chapter discusses:

- The extent to which therapists' techniques, in general, determine outcomes.
- The efficacy and effectiveness of different therapeutic techniques:
  - cognitive-behavioural
  - psychodynamic
  - humanistic.
- The relationship between outcomes and generic therapeutic techniques and practices.

A counselling or psychotherapy technique can be defined as a well-defined therapeutic procedure implemented to accomplish a particular task or goal. It is somewhat distinct from a skill (see Chapter 6), which can be defined as the ability or competency to do something. Therapists *have* skills, but techniques are something that therapists *do*: intentionally applied procedures designed to bring about particular responses or outcomes. This chapter reviews the evidence for things that therapists do: both those that clearly come under the definition of technique and those that can only loosely be described as intentionally applied procedures, such as listening and paraphrasing. For the purposes of this chapter, these latter activities are described as 'practices'.

Therapeutic technique

A well-defined procedure implemented to accomplish a particular task or goal.

Like the other factors discussed in this book, the extent to which technique factors relate to outcomes has important implications for the 'Does orientation matter?' debate. Unlike the 'common factors' discussed in Chapters 4 to 6, however, evidence in support of specific techniques tends to support the differential effectiveness position rather than the dodo bird one. This is because, in many instances, specific techniques are associated – or even synonymous – with specific orientations: for instance, hypnosis and hypnotherapy, coping skills training and coping skills therapy. Indeed, Lambert (1986) defines therapeutic techniques as 'factors unique to specific therapies'.

So what does the research say about the importance of techniques? On the one hand, thousands of studies indicate that therapeutic practices based around specific techniques (in particular, cognitive and behavioural ones) bring about substantial amounts of psychological improvement, above and beyond that achieved in control or placebo conditions (see Chapter 3). There are also studies which indicate that, at least in cognitive therapy, greater adherence to the concrete, technical aspects of the approach is associated with greater subsequent change (e.g. DeRubeis and Feeley, 1990). Studies which ask clients what they found helpful in therapy also demonstrate that, for some clients, specific technical interventions can be experienced as very valuable (e.g. Carey et al., 2007). In Clarke et al.'s (2004) study of cognitive therapy for clients with depression, for instance, one respondent described an exercise that involved listing key life events and core beliefs as, 'amazing, really useful'; and another spoke of the value of keeping a diary of his thoughts. Most interestingly, perhaps, technical interventions were cited by clients as *the* most common type of events that led to the formation and strengthening of the therapeutic alliance (Bedi et al., 2005) – cited far more frequently than such relational events as the therapist's candour or his or her use of humour. This suggests that the relationship between technical and relational factors is complex, and that techniques may be valuable to therapy by strengthening the therapeutic alliance (see Chapter 6), as well as through their direct impact.

At the same time, psychotherapy researchers such as Lambert have estimated that technique and orientation factors may contribute only 15 per cent or so towards the overall outcomes of therapy (Asay and Lambert, 1999); with Wampold (2001) calculating a much lower figure of just 1 per cent (this is based on the finding that the average difference in outcomes between therapeutic orientations is an effect size of just 0.2; see Chapter 3). Furthermore, as also discussed in Chapter 3, many studies which compare technique-orientated therapies (i.e. CBT) against bona fide non-technique-orientated therapies (i.e. non-directive counselling) have equivocal results (e.g. King et al., 2000). Also, as we saw in Chapter 6, when clients are asked to describe what they found most helpful in therapy, 'nontechnological' factors (Bohart and Tallman, 1999) *do* seem to be most strongly endorsed, and this is true even in the more technique-orientated approaches (Keijsers et al., 2000). Third, and perhaps most problematic for advocates of technique-orientated approaches, 'component studies' – i.e. studies which look at the effects of either adding particular techniques to a form of therapy ('additive designs') or taking them away ('dismantling designs') – rarely find that the presence or absence of specific techniques makes much difference to the overall outcomes (Ahn and Wampold, 2001). Finally, studies which directly compare the efficacy of one set of bona fide techniques against another tend to find few significant differences (e.g. Tarrier et al., 1999), again raising questions about the importance of technique-specific factors.

Component study

A study which looks at the efficacy of particular aspects of therapeutic practice: 'additive' designs look at the effect of adding a particular practice, while 'dismantling' designs look at the effect of taking away a particular practice.

In terms of the overall efficacy of techniques, it is also important to consider the possibility that they may be more effective with some clients than with others (i.e. an aptitude by treatment interaction). A qualitative study of clients' feelings about behaviour therapy (Ryan and Gizynski, 1971: 6), for instance, found that, while '[s]ome of the patients in this sample clearly liked the therapeutic methods, finding them efficient, precise, or "scientific"; an equal number … found them annoying, "silly," "phoney," or "pointless."' More specifically, there is a fairly consistent body of evidence to suggest that clients who have a predominantly 'externalising' coping style (i.e. who deal with new or problematic situations by behaving impulsively, actively and excessively), tend to do better with technique-oriented therapies than clients with an 'internalising' coping style (i.e. who deal with new or problematic situations by turning in on themselves and becoming self-critical or depressed) (Beutler et al., 1993; Beutler, Mohr et al., 1991). This is consistent with the capitalisation hypothesis discussed in Chapter 4: that clients do better with therapies that are aligned with their pre-existing ways of functioning.

A final point about the techniques and practices discussed in this chapter: although what is primarily reviewed here are the things that therapists *do*, it should be re-emphasised that there are no clear dividing lines between these factors and other aspects of the therapeutic process, such as relational and therapist factors. For instance, is self-disclosure an intentionally applied technique or a relational skill? Also, given the overlap between specific techniques and specific therapeutic orientation, there is a somewhat grey dividing line between what is reviewed here and what is reviewed in the Appendix on specific therapies. In general, however, this chapter focuses on particular techniques and practices that any therapist might, conceivably, incorporate into their one-to-one therapeutic work (with the appropriate training); while the Appendix reviews the evidence for practices at the more global, orientation level.

Cognitive-Behavioural Techniques

At their most basic, cognitive, behavioural and cognitive-behavioural techniques try to produce change by directly influencing thinking, behaviour or both (Hollon and Beck, 2004) (see Box 7.1). Numerous different cognitive and behavioural techniques have been developed, with over 150 in the behavioural field alone (Antony and Roemer, 2003). This section will focus on some of the most common and rigorously evaluated ones.

Exposure

Exposure is used primarily in the treatment of anxiety disorders – in particular, specific phobias and social phobia – where it has been shown to be highly effective with many individuals (see Chapter 3). Exposure can be defined as 'Purposefully invoking anxiety by direct confrontation with the situations that produce fear in the patient' (Abramowitz, 1996: 584), and is often undertaken in a hierarchically structured way, with clients moving from mildly to highly anxiety-inducing situations. An individual with a fear of needles, for instance, might be encouraged to touch, and then use, a needle. The basic principle behind exposure techniques is that, if individuals are directly confronted with and face their fear, they can learn that they are able to cope with it and the associated anxiety (Newman, Stiles et al., 2006).

Exposure

Purposefully invoking anxiety by direct confrontation with the situations that produce fear in the client. Exposure may be:

- *in vivo*: ('in life') actual exposure to the feared situation
- *imaginal*: actively visualising the feared situation
- *virtual reality*: simulated exposure, for instance through a flight simulator
- *interoceptive*: generation of bodily symptoms (e.g. feelings of choking, dizziness) that accompany the feared situation
- *exposure and response prevention:* in addition to exposure, encouraging clients to desist from engaging in ritual or compulsive behaviours (such as checking and re-checking that they have locked their front door)
- *cue exposure*: exposure to stimuli associated with substance-use behaviours (for instance, presenting a problem drinker with a whisky bottle), while addressing and attempting to reduce the desire to use
- *systematic desensitisation*: gradual exposure to a feared stimulus, generally in imagination, while in a state of deep muscle relaxation.

Research indicates that exposure procedures are most successful when carried out during a long uninterrupted period of time, as opposed to several shorter periods spaced over time (Emmelkemp, 2004).

In Vivo Exposure

In vivo exposure is one of the most intensively researched psychological techniques, and there is clear evidence of its efficacy with specific and social phobias, with gains either maintained or improved at around one-year follow-up (Choy et al., 2007; Emmelkemp, 2004).

Emmelkemp argues that *in vivo* exposure is *the* most effective form of exposure treatment; and studies which compare it with other cognitive and behavioural practices nearly always find it of equivalent or superior efficacy (e.g. Scholing and Emmelkemp, 1993; Wlazlo et al., 1990). Indeed, as introduced in Chapter 3, a classic study by Schulte and colleagues (1992) found that the consistent application of *in vivo* exposure techniques was more effective for phobic clients than individually tailored therapeutic programmes, with the extent of improvement directly related to whether or not the therapists used exposure techniques.

Imaginal Exposure

Although considered somewhat less effective than *in vivo* exposure (Emmelkemp, 2004), in situations where it is not possible or desirable to actually encounter the feared stimulus – for instance, with clients who have been traumatised by war – imaginal exposure has been shown to be efficacious and superior to a no-treatment control (Emmelkemp, 2004).

Virtual Reality Exposure

For individuals with flying and height phobias, computer-simulated exposure has been shown to be as effective as *in vivo* exposure – with as many as 90 per cent of aerophobics flying post-study (Wiederhold et al., 2002, in Choy et al., 2007) – and superior to control conditions and systematic desensitisation (Choy et al., 2007; Emmelkemp, 2004).

Interoceptive Exposure

Introceptive exposure has been shown to be of greater efficacy with panic disorder than some other cognitive and behavioural techniques, such as breathing retraining (Craske et al., 1997). There is also some evidence that it is effective in the treatment of claustrophobia, though to a lesser extent than an *in vivo* or cognitive intervention (Booth and Rachman, 1992).

Exposure and Response Prevention

Exposure and response-prevention procedures have been shown to be particularly efficacious in the treatment of obsessive–compulsive problems, with a pre-test to follow-up effect size on anxiety symptoms in excess of 2.0 (Abramowitz, 1996). For this client group, response prevention seems to be an essential component of the exposure treatment (Emmelkemp, 2004), with evidence that complete abstention from rituals brings about greater improvement than partial abstention (Abramowitz, 1996). Gradual exposure *in vivo*, however, appears to be as effective as *in vivo* 'flooding' (prolonged exposure to a fear-arousing stimuli of relatively high intensity).

Cue Exposure

Cue-exposure techniques have been shown to be effective in the treatment of alcohol abuse (Monti and Rohsenow, 1999) at a level similar to other CBT interventions (Dawe et al., 2002), with levels of efficacy generally equivalent – or superior to – other cognitive and behavioural practices. However, they were not found to be significantly more effective than a control condition in the treatment of opiate addiction (Dawe et al., 1993).

Systematic Desensitisation

Gradated imaginal exposure techniques, combined with muscular relaxation, have tended to receive more mixed empirical support than other exposure procedures, with evidence that they can improve subjective levels of anxiety, but do not necessarily reduce levels of fear-avoidant behaviours (Emmelkemp, 2004).

IMPLICATIONS FOR PRACTICE

Given the weight of evidence in support of exposure techniques, if clients come to therapy specifically wanting to overcome specific or social phobias, it may be important for counsellors or psychotherapists not trained in these practices to discuss with them the potential value of referral to an appropriately trained practitioner.

Paradoxical Intervention

Although advocated by therapists of widely divergent orientations (including the renowned existential therapist, Viktor Frankl, 1986), paradoxical interventions are generally classed as a behavioural technique. They can be defined as 'Any approach where the therapist seems to take an "antitherapeutic" stance vis-à-vis the client's problems' (Hill, 1987: 266) or, more simply, as 'prescribing the symptom' (Williams, 2002: 246). A client with insomnia, for instance, might be encouraged to try as hard as possible to stay awake each night. The basic rationale behind such interventions is that, in some instances, the more people try to achieve something the more difficult it becomes for them to do so, such that trying to do the opposite may sometimes have a beneficial effect.

Despite their somewhat counter-intuitive nature, paradoxical interventions have been shown to be highly effective therapeutic interventions. Indeed, in an extensive review of the research on a wide range of therapist interventions, paradoxical interventions were most consistently associated with positive therapeutic outcomes (Orlinsky et al., 2004). A meta-analysis of the use of paradoxical interventions with such problems as depression, insomnia, agoraphobia and procrastination found a large mean effect size, against controls, of 0.99, with 'no indication that paradoxical therapy is any more hazardous than other forms of treatment' (Hill, 1987: 269). Some research indicates that paradoxical interventions work best when they are unexpected (Williams, 2002); and they also seem to be most effective when they help clients to positively reframe their experiences rather than pointing out the negative consequences of change (Swoboda et al., 1990). Research also indicates that paradoxical interventions may be particularly effective with more reactant clients (i.e. those who have a greater tendency to perceive and react to situations as threats to their freedom), whereas clients with lower levels of reactance may do better with non-paradoxical interventions (Horvath and Goheen, 1990).

IMPLICATIONS FOR PRACTICE

If you are working with a client who seems to find something more and more difficult the more they try to do it, it might be helpful to explore with them whether they would find it useful to have a go at trying to do the opposite. For instance, if you are working with a client who seems to get more and more anxious at social functions the more they try to socialise, you could explore with them what it might be like to go to a party with the deliberate intention of not talking to anyone. Bear in mind, however, that the use of paradoxical interventions raises a number of ethical issues (see Foreman, 1990), and should not be practised without their full consideration.

Activity Scheduling

Activity scheduling is a technique used in cognitive and behavioural therapies in which clients are encouraged to plan and monitor their daily activities – for instance, through completing an hour-by-hour timetable – so that they can come to see how their moods are linked to what they do, increase the number of pleasant activities engaged in ('behavioural activation'), and challenge dysfunctional cognitions, such as a belief that they 'do nothing all day'. For clients with depression, activity scheduling has been shown to have a large effect size against controls ($d = 0.87$); indeed, in itself, a programme based on activity scheduling has been found to be as effective as full cognitive therapy (Jacobson et al., 1996).

RECOMMENDED READING

Emmelkemp, P.M.G. (2004) 'Behavior therapy with adults', in M.J. Lambert (ed.), *Bergin and Garfield's Handbook of Psychotherapy and Behavior Change*. Chicago: John Wiley & Sons, pp. 393–446. An excellent summary of the research on the effectiveness of behavioural practices with different psychological problems.

Cognitive Techniques

In contrast to the behavioural techniques reviewed above, there has tended to be less analysis of the efficacy of specific cognitive techniques. However, the principal practice within cognitive therapy – that of identifying and challenging dysfunctional beliefs through disputation and collection of evidence – has consistently been shown to lead to positive outcomes against control conditions (e.g. Dickerson, 2000), and is identified as a key principle in the effective treatment of depression (Follette and Greenberg, 2006) and other psychological problems (Castonguay and Beutler, 2006a). Other cognitive techniques, such as keeping a diary of thoughts and 'normalising' (i.e. helping clients to understand their experiences in non-stigmatising ways), have also been related to positive therapeutic outcomes (e.g. Clarke et al., 2004). In support of the efficacy of cognitive strategies, DeRubeis and Feeley (1990) showed a significant positive correlation between the use of concrete cognitive techniques early on in therapy – for instance, examining evidence concerning clients' beliefs, asking clients to record thoughts, and labelling cognitive errors – and subsequent improvements on the Beck's Depression Inventory.

However, other studies have found that improvements in CBT are unrelated to the extent to which CBT techniques are applied (e.g. Jones and Pulos, 1993). Indeed, in one study, improvements in CBT were only associated with the extent to which the therapist practised in ways that would be typically associated with *psychodynamic* therapy, such as interpreting unconscious wishes and emphasising the client's feelings (Jones and Pulos, 1993). Furthermore, in one of the most rigorous component studies yet conducted, Jacobson and colleagues (1996) found that the addition of cognitive techniques to a basic behavioural programme made no difference to its effectiveness: raising questions about the 'added value' of cognitive techniques. Studies and meta-analyses which compare cognitively orientated practices against behaviourally orientated ones also tend to find few differences in effectiveness (Lambert and Ogles, 2004). In a study of treatments for chronic post-traumatic stress disorder, for instance, Tarrier and colleagues (1999) found no significant differences between imaginal exposure, in which clients were instructed to 'describe the event as it was happening in the present tense while visualizing it' (1999: 15); and cognitive therapy, in which dysfunctional cognitions associated with the trauma were identified and modified (for instance, 'It was my fault it happened'). There is also the finding that much of the improvement in CBT happens in the first few weeks of therapy, and it has been argued that this is before the specific techniques designed to facilitate a reduction of dysfunctional thoughts are brought into play (Ilardi and Craighead, 1994). While cognitive techniques, then, do seem to lead to more positive change than an absence of intervention, there is little evidence to suggest that they are more (or less) effective than other bona fide therapeutic practices. Moreover, the lack of clear evidence to show that cognitive techniques work in the way that they are hypothesised to (see Box 7.1) raises further questions about their comparative efficacy.

Box 7.1   The process of therapy: does cognitive therapy work by changing dysfunctional cognitions?

Cognitive therapy is based on the assumption that psychological problems are a consequence of maladaptive thinking. Hence 'Correction of these faulty dysfunctional constructs can lead to clinical improvement' (Beck et al., 1979: 8). This is known as the 'cognitive mediation hypothesis', and is the basis of most cognitive techniques. However, although the efficacy of cognitive techniques is well established, it is by no means evident that it does so in this way (Hayes et al., 2006).

For a start, while research into 'sudden gains' in CBT (see Box 2.5) shows that dramatic improvements are preceded by large in-session cognitive changes (Tang and DeRubeis, 1999), there are also studies which indicate that clients can improve in cognitive therapy without significant reductions in levels of dysfunctional thinking (e.g. Serfaty et al., 1999). And while many cognitive therapy clients *do* experience a reduction in dysfunctional thinking, so do many clients in other therapies, and to a similar extent (Oei and Free, 1995). This suggests that a reduction in dysfunctional thinking may be a *consequence*, rather than a cause, of improvements in mood.

In one of the most sophisticated analyses to date, Burns and Spangler (2001) came to the conclusion that reduction of dysfunctional thinking did not cause improvements in mood in CBT but, equally, improvements in mood did not cause reduction of dysfunctional thinking. Rather, some third, 'unknown variable' – such as reduced feelings of hopelessness – was responsible for both of these changes.

However, such an analysis is based on the assumption that all clients in cognitive therapy change in the same way, and the qualitative interview study by Clarke and colleagues (2004) suggests that, for some clients at least, the correction of dysfunctional thoughts *is* a key part of the cognitive therapeutic process. 'Barbara', for instance, states: 'Once I started looking at my beliefs about myself I could see a lot of it was nonsense' (Clarke et al., 2004: 87); and for 'Carmen': 'It's helped me to have a more logical approach to my emotions, so that when horrible things happen I use the methods taught to sort of balance that out' (Clarke et al., 2004: 85).

Finally, Teasdale and colleagues (2001), in another sophisticated analysis, suggest that the key mediating factor may not be the *content* of someone's cognitions (for instance, 'I am to blame for getting depressed'), but rather their *form*: in particular, an absolutist, black-and-white style of thinking.

Psychodynamic Techniques

Interpretation

Interpretations, defined as therapist statements that go beyond what the client has overtly recognised (see Chapter 6), are one of the few psychodynamic or psychoanalytic techniques to be subjected to intensive empirical evaluation. Chapter 6 reviewed the research on transference interpretations but, as noted in that chapter, this is just one type of interpretation that psychodynamic therapists may offer. For instance, psychody-namic therapists may also point out links between clients' current experiences or rela-tionships (outside of therapy) and past experiences or relationships; they may suggest patterns of thoughts, feelings and behaviours in their clients' lives; they may posit thoughts, feelings or behaviours that their clients do not seem to be fully aware of; or they may suggest to clients particular links between their thoughts, feelings and behaviours (Andrusyna et al., 2006).

Used in this broader sense, 'There appears to be compelling evidence for the effective-ness of interpretations' (Williams, 2002: 237). In their review of the relevant studies, for instance, Orlinksy and colleagues (2004) found 24 results in which interpretations showed a positive relationship with outcomes, compared with 11 in which no relationship was found, and 3 in which a negative relationship emerged. Interpretations are also consis-tently rated by therapists and clients – as well as observers – as one of the most helpful therapist responses (e.g. Elliott et al., 1982; Hill et al., 1988). Elliott and colleagues, for instance, found that they were given a mean rating of 4.2 on a 6-point scale of helpfulness (1 = *not at all helpful* to 6 = *extremely helpful*), compared with 4.0 for reflections and 3.8 for self-disclosure. Interpretations in the form of diagrams – as used, for instance, in cog-nitive analytic therapy (CAT) – are also rated by a high proportion of clients as helpful (Bende and Crossley, 2000). Closely related to these findings, when clients are asked about the most helpful aspects of the therapeutic process, developing 'awareness', 'insight', or 'self-understanding' – for instance, 'Understanding how I react to my husband like I do to my dad' – is one of the most commonly given responses (Timulak, 2007). There is also evidence to suggest that interpretations can make an important contribution to the ther-apeutic alliance, with one study indicating that it had a larger effect than therapists' empathic or exploratory responses (Allen et al., 1996).

IMPLICATIONS FOR PRACTICE

Based on reviews of the evidence, Williams (2002: 237) suggests that interpretations may be most effective when they are:

- worded in a tentative, rather than absolute, manner
- just beyond the limits of the client's awareness
- mixed with other response modes, such as questions and direct guidance
- repeated several times
- later on in the therapeutic process
- tailored to the individual client.

As with transference interpretations (see Chapter 6), they would also seem to be most effective when they are:

- accurate
- embedded within a strong therapeutic alliance.

Humanistic and Experiential Techniques and Practices

Non-Directivity

A non-directive stance – defined as one in which the therapist tries to refrain from directing the client or the therapeutic process – is, in many respects, the antithesis of a therapeutic technique. Nevertheless, given that it is closely connected to so much of what humanistic, and particularly classical client-centred (e.g. Merry, 2004), therapists 'do', it is relevant to address in this chapter.

Non-directivity

A therapeutic stance in which the practitioner tries to refrain from directing his or her client in any particular way.

How does a non-directive stance relate to therapeutic outcomes? In fact, there is virtually no research on this question, because non-directivity, as defined above, is an attitude or an ethic (see, for instance, Grant, 2002) and, as such, has yet to be subjected to direct empirical evaluation. Nevertheless, a substantial body of evidence does exist on the relative efficacy of directive and non-directive *practices* (i.e. what a therapist does, as opposed to the values that they hold), and such research sheds some interesting light on the 'non-directivity versus directivity' debate.

On the one hand, as we saw in Chapter 3, the vast majority of therapies that have been shown to be effective for particular forms of psychological distress are of a relatively directive, structured nature. Indeed, in many instances (e.g. Blowers et al., 1987; Craske et al., 1995), the support for these therapies comes from the fact that they bring about significantly more improvement than a 'non-directive' control. As we also saw in Chapter 3, however, allegiance effects make such findings difficult to interpret, and the few studies which have compared directive therapies against bona fide non-directive therapies tend to find few differences in their effectiveness (Beutler et al., 2004; Elliott, Greenberg et al., 2004).

Research which focuses more specifically on the impact of directive therapist statements – for instance, guidance, advice and confrontation (Williams, 2002) – produces an equally mixed picture (Williams, 2002). On one hand, a number of studies have shown that more directive therapist behaviours lead to greater client resistance (e.g. Bischoff and Tracey, 1995) – a client characteristic that has been associated with poorer outcomes (see Chapter 4). Patterson and Forgatch (1985), for instance, found that clients became more non-compliant when therapists acted in didactic and confrontational ways, while supportive and facilitative therapist behaviours were associated with reduced non-compliance. Research into client deference (see Box 7.2) also shows just how vulnerable clients can be to following their therapists' leads. On the other hand, there is clear evidence that many directive therapist interventions, such as paradoxical interventions (see above) can be associated with positive therapeutic outcomes. Moreover, as will be discussed below, there is research to suggest that clients may *need* therapists to direct them towards deeper, and more productive, levels of processing; and that, without such directions, clients may stay at relatively superficial levels of therapeutic work (Sachse, 2004).

Box 7.2   The process of therapy: client deference

Many therapists, particularly those of a humanistic orientation, would like to believe that clients feel free to say and do whatever they want in therapy. Research into clients' experiences of therapy – humanistic or otherwise – suggests, however, that clients will frequently 'defer' to their therapists. This might take such forms as:

- withholding critical or challenging comments from their therapists
- concealing negative reactions and feelings (and, indeed, research shows that clients are much more likely to conceal negative reactions to their therapists than positive ones, e.g. Regan and Hill, 1992)
- overlooking, or making allowances for, therapists' mistakes and misunderstandings
- not asking questions about things that are not understood
- expressing agreement with therapists when they actually disagree with them
- trying to see things from the therapist's perspective.
  (Bury et al., 2007; Hill et al., 1992; Rennie, 1994; Rennie, 2004)

David Rennie (1994), who has led the work in this field, gives the example of a client who felt annoyed when her therapist answered the phone during sessions but said nothing.

In terms of why clients defer, research suggests that it can be for a number of reasons:

- because clients want to be seen as 'good clients'
- out of a fear that therapists will retaliate if they are challenged and the therapeutic relationship will be jeopardised
- because therapists are perceived as experts in the field
- because clients feel powerless
- to save the therapist's face.
  (Bury et al., 2007; Rennie, 1994; Rennie, 1998)

In support of the hypothesis that deference is prevalent in therapy, Hill and colleagues (1993) found that around 65 per cent of clients leave at least one thing unsaid during sessions; and 46 per cent of clients kept one or more secrets from their therapists, around half of these being of a sexual nature (for instance, 'I am more sexually attracted to my therapist than I have let on').

What are the implications of this research for practice? Given that therapists are only minimally aware of what clients are not saying in therapy (Hill et al., 1993; Regan and Hill, 1992) – particularly where it is a negative reaction (Thompson and Hill, 1991) – it might be argued that therapists should strive to be more aware of their clients' covert, negative responses; or to bring these more fully into the therapeutic dialogue. However, there is also research to suggest that therapists are actually *less* helpful when they are aware of these negative responses (Thompson and Hill, 1991) – perhaps because it undermines their self-confidence or draws attention away from clients' issues. In other words, therapists actually seem to operate more effectively 'under a slight delusion that clients are reacting positively to them' (Regan and Hill, 1992: 173). Rennie (1994: 435) concludes that 'Being deferential to the therapist is the client's way of protecting and fostering the alliance', and he suggests that whether or not it is helpful to invite clients to express their inner discontent depends on how disruptive that deference is to their productive use of therapy.

Recommended reading

Rennie, D. L. (1994) 'Clients' deference in psychotherapy', *Journal of Counseling Psychology*, 41(4): 427–37.

Hill, C. E., Thompson, B. J., Cogar, M. C. and Denman, D. W. (1993) 'Beneath the surface of long-term therapy: therapist and client report of their own and each other's covert processes', *Journal of Counseling Psychology*, 40 (3): 278–87.

Studies which ask clients what they found helpful and unhelpful in therapy are equally equivocal. On the one hand, a significant proportion of clients would seem to experience an absence of directivity as unhelpful and hindering (e.g. Conte et al., 1995). In their in-depth study of young people's experiences of psychoanalytic psychotherapy (a relatively non-directive practice), for instance, Lilliengren and Werbart (2005: 332) report that a number of clients felt that the therapist was too passive, and wanted more feedback, guidance and advice. One young person said: 'The therapist should have been more effective so that one didn't talk so much nonsense but concentrated on something important'. Along similar lines, Maluccio (1979) reports that some of his interviewees experienced therapist non-directivity as a lack of interest or rejection. One client said, 'He just sat there while I was trying to save my marriage … I didn't know if he really cared', and another, 'She could at least say what she thought … Sometimes I felt like I was just another case as far as she was concerned.' At the same time, a study by Paulson and colleagues (2001) found that clients could experience *both* a lack of counsellor directiveness and an excess of it as unhelpful. For instance, while 'My counsellor not telling me what to do' was given a mean rating of 2.05 on a 5-point scale of unhelpfulness (1 = *not at all hindering*, 5 = *extremely hindering*), 'The counsellor trying to tell me what to do' was given a mean rating of 3.25, and 'My counsellor being too directive' a mean rating of 2.80.

Such findings suggest that both high levels of directivity and high levels of non-directivity may be experienced by a significant proportion of clients as unhelpful. This is consistent with research from studies of both group and individual psychotherapy (e.g. Glass and Arnkoff, 2000), which suggest that highly authoritarian/directive stances, as well as highly laissez-faire/permissive ones, are associated with poorer outcomes as compared with more collaborative stances. The key question, then, may not be so much whether directivity or non-directivity is better, but about finding a way of working that avoids either extreme, and which has the potential to incorporate both directive and non-directive elements in a way that is responsive to individual clients. This is consistent with the principles of therapeutic change arrived at by Castonguay and Beutler (2006a: 361) in their extensive review of the research. They write: 'Positive change is likely if the therapist provides a structured treatment and remains focused in the application of his/her interventions,' but add, 'Therapists should be able to skillfully use "non-directive" interventions.'

A final point is that the relative efficacy of directive and non-directive ways of working may also be dependent on a particular client's characteristics. Indeed, one of the best established aptitude-treatment interactions in the psychotherapy field is that clients with high levels of resistance or reactance (i.e. who have a tendency to behave in oppositional ways) tend to benefit more from non-directive practices, whereas those who are judged to be non-defensive benefit more from directive therapeutic procedures (Beutler, Blatt et al., 2006; Beutler, Engle et al., 1991). Furthermore, there are some indications that clients who are particularly mistrustful and suspicious may become more so when faced with a therapist who actively tries to structure a session (Kolb et al., 1985). At the same time, data from a range of sources suggest that directive practices may be particularly useful for clients who are experiencing anxiety disorders (Woody and Ollendick, 2006).

Deepening Levels of Experiencing

In contrast to the non-directive emphasis of classical person-centred practice, other humanistic therapies – in particular, process-experiential therapy and gestalt therapy – use a range of techniques and practices (such as empathic probes or two-chair dialogue, see below) to help clients deepen (i.e. intensify) their level of 'experiencing'. Here, experiencing refers to the extent to which inner feelings and sensations are the foci of attention, and the extent to which attempts are made to focus on, expand and probe this data (Klein et al., 1986). In the psychotherapy research field, the concept of experiencing has primarily been assessed through the Experiencing Scale (Klein et al., 1986), in which client involvement in therapy can be rated from 'Stage 1' (impersonal, external focus, no personal content) down to 'Stage 7' (a steady and growing awareness of present feelings and internal processes).

Experiencing

The extent to which inner felt senses and processes are the foci of attention.

Research has shown that clients' levels of experiencing tend to be related to the outcomes of therapy, with the exploration of deeper, more internally felt material generally associated with better outcomes in both humanistic and non-humanistic practices (Hendricks, 2002; Orlinsky et al., 2004). On the basis of such findings, Klein and colleagues (1986) suggest that depth of experiencing can be taken as an indicator of a client's productive involvement in the therapeutic process: a factor which, as we saw in Chapter 4, is closely connected to levels of improvement.

Of crucial importance to the practice of the more 'process-guiding' (i.e. directive) humanistic therapies, however, is the question of whether such techniques actually serve to deepen clients' levels of experiencing; or whether it is simply the case that some clients are more in touch with their inner experiences, and therefore make more use of therapy, than others. Here, research suggests that some clients do seem to enter therapy with a greater capacity to experience at depth (Goldman et al., 2005); but, at the same time, participation in process-guiding interventions would seem to help people deepen their work. A range of studies, for instance, has indicated that levels of experiencing can be deepened in response to the presentation of focusing instructions or interventions (Hendricks, 2002, see below); and there is also evidence that two-chair dialogue can deepen levels of experiencing significantly more than non-directive reflections (see below).

Further support for the practice of process-guiding humanistic interventions comes from a series of 'microanalysis' studies by Rainer Sachse (see Sachse, 1990; Sachse and Elliott, 2002) who examined the effects of therapists' statements on clients' 'levels of processing'. This is a phenomenon similar to experiencing, assessed on an 8-point scale from 'No processing of relevant contents discernible' (Level 1) to 'Integration' (Level 8). Contrary to the views of many person-centred therapists (e.g. Bohart and Tallman, 1999), Sachse concluded that clients are not particularly good, by themselves, at deepening their levels of processing (and thereby making their therapeutic work more productive). Rather, he suggests that they are strongly influenced by their therapists' statements, such that 'deepening' therapist interventions (i.e. therapist statements at a deeper processing level than the preceding client statement) tend to bring about deeper client processing; while 'flattening' therapist statements (i.e. therapist statements at a shallower processing level than the preceding client statement) tend to bring about more superficial client processing. Based on his research, Sachse also claims that 'level-maintaining' therapist interventions (i.e. therapist statements at the same level as the preceding client statement) keep most clients at a similar level of processing. On the basis of such findings, Sachse (2004) concludes that therapists need to go beyond offering clients reflections or summaries that are at the same level of processing as the client's statements, and instead actively invite the client towards deeper levels of processing. However, it is worth noting that Sachse's research focuses only on the client's immediate response to the therapist's statements, such that the sustained impact of the therapist's level of processing on the client's experiencing level is not clear.

Deepening Levels of Emotional Processing

Closely related to levels of experiencing, there is also research to indicate that, across a range of different therapies, greater emotional arousal and expression – as facilitated by a range of humanistic techniques and practices (e.g. Pos et al., 2003) – tend to be related to positive therapeutic outcomes (Greenberg et al., 2002; Orlinsky et al., 2004). However, emotional catharsis, in itself, appears to be inadequate for producing positive change, with research indicating that it needs to be combined with some cognitive processing of the emotion (Bohart, 1980). Consistent with such a hypothesis, Mergenthaler (1996) has demonstrated that therapy is most effective when there are both high levels of emotion *and* high levels of cognitive abstraction in a session. Further support for the therapeutic value of emotion-processing comes from research in the field of acceptance and commitment therapy, which indicates that the acceptance of emotions is more effective in reducing psychological distress than its suppression. In one study, for instance, individuals with panic disorder were exposed to CO_2-enriched air (which can induce symptoms of panic in this client group), and told either to try to suppress any anxious thoughts or feelings, or to accept whatever feelings came up (Levitt et al., 2004). The researchers found that clients in the latter, 'acceptance' condition experienced significantly lower levels of anxiety than those in the former, suppression condition; and were also more willing to go through the task again. However, it should also be noted that emotion-intensifying therapies have been associated with higher rates of deterioration in therapy, with Mohr (1990: 17) suggesting that they may 'have a negative impact when applied to severely disturbed patients over a short period of time'.

Two-Chair and Empty-Chair Dialogues

'Two-chair dialogue' is a specific technique used in gestalt, process-experiential (emotion-focused) and various other humanistic and integrative therapies to deepen levels of experiencing and emotion processing through working with intra-personal 'splits'. These splits can be defined as 'in-therapy statements of conflict with recognizable distinctive features' (Greenberg, 1980: 143): for instance, 'I hate myself for being so lazy.' In two-chair dialogue, clients are invited to put different 'parts' of themselves in different chairs (for instance, the 'self-hating part' and the 'lazy part'), and to speak to and from these different sides, such that intra-personal conflicts can be addressed and resolved.

In general, research suggests that 'experiential confrontation,' in such forms as two-chair dialogue, is a 'potent form of intervention' (Orlinsky et al., 2004: 323), though it is important to bear in mind that virtually all of the relevant studies have been carried out by researchers (and often therapists) with an allegiance to these practices. In comparison with empathic reflections, for instance, two-chair dialogue has been shown to lead to significantly greater awareness and depth of experiencing, as well as greater behavioural change and self-reported progress on issues (Greenberg and Dompierre, 1981; Greenberg and Rice, 1981). Qualitatively, clients in process-experiential therapy have also made clear reference to the value of two-chair dialogue in helping them to change. Greenberg and Watson (1998: 221), for instance, report that a number of clients 'referred specifically to the identification of a harsh inner critic, early in therapy, as helping them to see how they were involved in generating their own depression'.

In contrast to two-chair dialogue, in 'empty-chair dialogue' clients have an opportunity to engage in an imaginary dialogue with a significant other as a means of resolving 'unfinished' emotional issues (Paivio and Greenberg, 1995). Such an intervention, embedded within a twelve-week course of process-experiential therapy, has been shown to be more effective than a psycho-educational group in resolving emotional issues with a significant other, with 81 per cent of clients resolved in the former condition at end of therapy compared with 29 per cent of individuals in the latter. This approach has also been shown to be effective for adult survivors of childhood sexual abuse (Paivio and Nieuwenhuis, 2001), with evidence that a reduction in traumatic symptoms is directly related to the amount of imaginal confrontation work undertaken (Paivio et al., 2001). However, Paivio and Bahr (1998: 403) report that 'clients with extreme problems in the area of nonassertiveness, emotional constriction, and social and performance anxiety found enactment and confronting an imagined other extremely anxiety provoking'; and, indeed, in the study of adults abused as children, 56 per cent of clients initially refused or resisted engagement in the imaginal confrontation intervention (Paivio and Nieuwenhuis, 2001). Nevertheless, contrary to expectations, there was no evidence that individuals with more severe trauma-related factors had more difficulties with the imaginal confrontation intervention.

Focusing

Focusing is a therapeutic method in which individuals are invited to attend to, and 'carry forward', their bodily felt experiencing. It was developed by Eugene Gendlin, a colleague of Carl Rogers, in the 1950s and 1960s, and is incorporated into a range of therapeutic practices (in particular process-experiential therapy – Elliott, Watson et al., 2004), as well as forming the centrepiece of its own therapeutic orientation ('focusing-oriented psychotherapy', Gendlin, 1996). As discussed above, focusing has been shown to help clients deepen their level of experiencing; and one study has suggested that 'good' person-centred/experiential therapy sessions are characterised by a greater use of focusing – either client- or therapist-initiated – with 75 per cent of positive sessions containing focusing, compared with 33 per cent of negative sessions (Hendricks, 2002). Consistent with this, there is also evidence to indicate that clients who receive focusing instructions have better outcomes than those in client-centred therapy alone (though, again, there is the potential problem of allegiance effects – Sachse et al., 1992 cited in Hendricks, 2002).

RECOMMENDED READING

Cain, D. J. and Seeman, J. (eds) (2002) *Humanistic Psychotherapies: Handbook of Research and Practice.* Washington, DC: American Psychological Association. Comprehensive summary of the research on the efficacy of techniques and orientations within the humanistic field.

Generic Techniques and Practices

Contracting and Boundaries

Research indicates that the particular contractual arrangements made by therapist and client prior to the commencement of therapy – such as whether the therapy is time-limited or unlimited, and whether the client pays a normal or reduced fee – are not strongly related to outcomes (Orlinsky et al., 1994).

With respect to the relationship between boundaries and outcomes, research is relatively sparse. One interesting study that throws some light on this question, however, is a recent survey of factors associated with perceived benefits in therapy by 600 lesbian, gay and bisexual clients (Jones et al., 2003). As might be expected, the presence of sexual boundary violations (for instance, a therapist attempting to fondle a client) was strongly associated with negative experiences in therapy. However, the presence of social boundary violations (in which the client was invited to do something social with the therapist or in which the therapist accepted the client's invitation to a social event) was unrelated to perceived outcomes. What is more, the presence of 'boundary extensions' (in which the therapist attended an event of special significance to the client or visited or phoned the client at home or in the hospital when the client was sick) was *positively* associated with perceived benefits of therapy. Such findings are consistent with the research discussed in Box 6.2, which suggests that a therapist's willingness to 'go the extra mile' may be an important predictor of positive therapeutic outcomes.

Therapist 'Response Modes'

Listening

Correlational research suggests that listening – in the sense of providing clients with a space to talk, and actively attending to their verbal and non-verbal expressions – is experienced by many clients as one of the most facilitative aspects of therapy. When asked what helped them overcome their suicidal behaviour and thinking, for instance, a sample of 35 previously suicidal clients gave 'being listened to' one of the highest ratings: 4.4 on a 1–5 scale (1 = *not important* to 5 = *extremely important*) (Paulson and Worth, 2002). Similarly, 'being a good listener' is often rated as one of the most helpful therapist characteristics (Glass and Arnkoff, 2000); while a recent study found that 'the counsellor not really listening' was rated as *the* most unhelpful or hindering thing that a therapist could do out of eighty items (Paulson et al., 2001). One reason why listening may be helpful in therapy is because it serves to deepen the therapeutic relationship. When asking about critical incidents that served to form or strengthen the therapeutic alliance, for instance, Bedi and colleagues (2005: 318) found that 'active listening' was the third most commonly cited type of experience: for instance, 'The therapist remembered and repeated back to me things that I had said in previous sessions.'

At the same time, research into directivity and non-directivity (see above) suggests that listening, alone, can be experienced by some clients as frustrating, withholding or uncaring; and there is also some evidence to indicate that better outcomes in therapy are associated with greater, rather than less, therapist verbal activity (Orlinsky et al., 1994). Moreover, as Maluccio (1979) found in his qualitative interviews, although clients do often appreciate being listened to, they may be surprised by such a non-interventionist therapeutic stance, or be puzzled as to how it is supposed to help them. Maluccio (1979: 74) writes: 'While talking and listening are … taken for granted by practitioners, they may make little sense to clients. It seems therefore that workers have a responsibility to explain helping methods and techniques to clients, particularly those that clash with the client's expectations or conceptions.'

Paraphrasing

Paraphrasing can be defined as restating the meaning of another person's verbal (or non-verbal) disclosures in one's own words. Within the counselling and psychotherapy research field, it has been used to refer to four related interventions:

- *restatements*: a simple rephrasing or repeating of what a client has said
- *reflections of feelings*: a restatement including an explicit reference to the client's feelings and emotions
- *non-verbal referents*: addressing an aspect of the client's non-verbal behaviour, for instance, 'you smiled when you said how angry you were'
- *summaries*: tying together different ideas and themes.
  (Hill et al., 1988; Williams, 2002)

Aside from listening, paraphrasing is possibly the most frequently used technique by counsellors, constituting some 10 to 30 per cent of all therapist interventions (Williams, 2002). Subjectively, it seems to be fairly well evaluated by participants in therapy. Hill and colleagues (1988), for instance, found that paraphrasing statements were rated by both clients and therapists as one of the more helpful response modes (means of 6.71 and 6.46 on a 9-point scale, respectively, 1 = *extremely hindering* to 9 = *extremely helpful*), and were associated with increased feelings of being supported as well as deepened levels of experiencing (see below). They also found that negative reactions to paraphrasing statements were rare. Paraphrasing has also been associated with higher levels of client collaboration (Allen et al., 1996). However, studies of the relationship between the frequency of paraphrasing statements and therapeutic outcomes – as with other therapist response modes (Stiles and Shapiro, 1994) – have yet to show a direct relationship between the former and the latter (Orlinsky et al., 2004).

Encouragement

Given the relationship between clients' expectations of change and the actual outcomes of therapy (see Chapter 4), it would be reasonable to assume that therapist interventions that can encourage and mobilise hope will have a positive effect; and, indeed, there is evidence that this may be the case. Conte and colleagues (1995), for instance, found a strong positive correlation between clients' satisfaction with their therapists and their experiences of their therapists as 'encouraging'; similarly, Glass and colleagues (2001: 459) report research indicating that around three-quarters of successful clients 'rate their therapist's confidence that they would improve as either very or extremely important'. Heightening a client's sense of hope may be particularly important in initial sessions or in very brief therapy, mobilising his or her motivation and capacity to engage in the therapeutic process (Larsen et al., 2007). As with listening, encouragement and positive comments also seem to be helpful in establishing and strengthening the therapeutic alliance (Bedi et al., 2005). One client, for instance, described as critical to the formation of the relationship a moment when 'The therapist congratulated me for the things I was doing and had done to help myself' (Bedi et al., 2005: 318).

Asking Questions

Although questions are used quite frequently as a counsellor technique (Williams, 2002), clients tend to rate both closed questions (which typically require a one- or two-word response) and open questions (which encourage the client to expand on a topic) as one of the least helpful therapist responses (Elliott et al., 1982; Hill et al., 1988). However, they are still rated, on average, as moderately helpful rather than actively hindering (Williams, 2002). Closed questions, in particular, have been given a low helpfulness rating (Hill et al., 1988), and have been found to produce a lack of reaction in clients. Open questions, by contrast, tend to evoke in clients a feeling of being challenged or a negative reaction, but at the same time did lead to a deepening of experiencing (Hill et al., 1988). Williams concludes that questions may be helpful to some extent, and may enable clients to express greater levels of affect, but writes that 'it is important not to overuse questions as a therapeutic technique' (Williams, 2002: 242).

Guidance and Advice

A review of the research on the relationship between therapeutic outcomes and prescriptiveness, guidance and advice suggests that such interventions are often experienced as unhelpful (Orlinsky et al., 2004). Hill and colleagues (1988), for instance, found that they were given one of the lowest ratings on helpfulness by clients and therapists, and led to relatively low levels of client experiencing. There is also evidence that they are related to lower ratings of therapist empathy (Barkham and Shapiro, 1986), lower compliance with the therapist (Patterson and Forgatch, 1985), and less successful counselling sessions (Friedlander et al., 1985). However, several other studies have indicated that clients *can* experience advice and guidance – particularly when it is 'good advice' – as helpful (e.g. Elliott, 1985; Elliott et al., 1982). Burckell and Goldfried (2006), for instance, found that clients rated 'someone who gives me advice' as a beneficial therapist characteristic; while

Conte and colleagues (1995) found that clients were both more satisfied and had better outcomes with therapists who were described as giving good advice. Similarly, 'Supershrink' (Ricks et al., 1974: 288, see Chapter 4) 'often expressed opinions on how problems might be handled'; and Maluccio (1979) found that some clients experienced advice-giving as an indication of the therapist's sensitivity and acceptance, and felt uncared for and rejected when it was withheld. While in general, then, the offering of advice does not tend to be experienced as particularly helpful, the research evidence does not support its total prohibition. Indeed, Jones and colleagues (1988) found that giving explicit advice and guidance was one of the best predictors of positive outcomes for clients high in psychological distress, and this suggests that it may be particularly helpful for highly disturbed clients for whom insight-orientated practices may be more 'risky' (Orlinsky et al., 2004).

RECOMMENDED READING

Williams, E.N. (2002) 'Therapist techniques', in G.S. Tryon (ed.), *Counselling Based on Process Research: Applying What we Know.* Boston: Allyn & Bacon, pp. 232–264. Excellent summary of research evidence for a range of verbal and non-verbal 'response modes' that are used across different orientations.

Touch

Research into the effects of physical contact in therapy is only in its infancy, but the preliminary evidence suggests that it can be experienced as both helpful and unhelpful by clients, depending on its context and the manner in which it emerges (this section only discusses non-erotic touch (i.e. touch which is clearly not sexual in intent or content); sexual contact is clearly prohibited by professional codes of ethics; see, for instance, the BACP (2007) *Ethical Framework for Good Practice in Counselling and Psychotherapy*). Based on qualitative interviews with ten female clients who had been in therapy with men, Geib (1996) found that six of the clients had experienced touch as unambivalently positive, while four reported mixed experience and said that, ultimately, it had been counter-therapeutic. Factors associated with a positive, rather than negative, experience, were:

1 The therapist provided an environment where the client felt that she, rather than the therapist, was in control.
2 The therapist was clearly responding to the client's needs, rather than his own.
3 The therapist encouraged open discussion of the contact, rather than avoiding the topic.
4 The therapist made sure that physical and emotional intimacy developed at the same pace, rather than being insensitive to this issue of timing.
  (Geib, 1996: 114)

When such factors are in place, research indicates that touch may help clients feel more connected with their therapists and can communicate a sense of acceptance and care (Geib, 1996; Horton, 1996) – helping clients to feel supported and safe enough to 'move into threatening material or a deeper level' (Horton, 1996: 132). Research also suggests that touch can provide clients with a link to external reality and prevent them from becoming lost in their pain, as well as allowing clients to experience new modes of relating (Geib, 1996). By contrast, in instances of counter-therapeutic touch, clients can come to perceive their therapists as more needy and vulnerable; can lead to the repetition, rather than the resolution, of family-of-origin dynamics; and can make clients more reluctant to bring up negative feelings towards their therapists because of the enhanced sense of being loved (Geib, 1996). Surprisingly, perhaps, research has also found that sexual abuse survivors give more positive evaluations of touch in therapy than those not disclosing sexual abuse (Horton, 1996), with indications that it can help to restore trust, a sense of agency, and an understanding that nurturing need not be sexual. However, given that touch also has the potential to re-stimulate family-of-origin dynamics (see above), it may be that particular caution is needed in making physical contact with clients who have a history of abuse.

Box 7.3 Therapists who touch

A small-scale survey suggests that therapists who have physical contact with their clients are more likely to:

- be female
- have been sexually abused
- subscribe to a humanistic, rather than psychodynamic, orientation
- have tried more body-oriented therapies
- have had therapists who touched them
- have had teachers and supervisors who advocated touch as legitimate practice.
  (Milakovich, 1996: 89)

RECOMMENDED READING

Smith, E. W. L., Clance, P. R. and Imes, S. (eds) (1996) *Touch in Psychotherapy: Theory, Research and Practice*. New York: Guilford Press.

Homework Assignments

Homework assignments can be defined as therapeutic tasks that clients are invited to undertake between sessions, and were first recommended as part of therapy in the 1930s (Burns and

Spangler, 2000). Assignments may include practising relaxation exercises, confronting feared situations, keeping a journal, or practising interpersonal skills (Burns and Spangler, 2000).

Although homework assignments have the potential to be incorporated into a wide variety of therapeutic practices (see Kazantzis and L'Abate, 2006), the vast majority of research has been conducted on the use of homework in CBT – the therapeutic orientation with which it is most closely associated (e.g. Beck et al., 1979). Here, research indicates that compliance with homework is generally associated with positive therapeutic outcomes, with effect sizes that are in the small to medium range (Burns and Spangler, 2000; Kazantzis et al., 2000). Recent research, however, suggests that it may be the quality of homework that is the key predictor of outcomes, rather than its quantity (Schmidt and Woolaway-Bickel, 2000). Also, what is not clear is the direction of causality: is it, for instance, that doing homework makes people feel better, or is it that clients who feel better are more likely to comply with homework requests? In a complex quantitative analysis of various different possibilities, Burns and Spangler (2000) came to the conclusion that it *did* seem to be the homework bringing about reductions in levels of distress rather than alternative mechanisms. Consistent with this finding, a meta-analysis of studies which compared the use of homework assignments with controls found a significant positive effect in the medium to large range (Kazantzis et al., 2000), with greater effects for depression in comparison with anxiety; and for social skills, video tape and a range of assignments over relaxation and exposure tasks. Whether or not these findings are generalisable to other therapeutic orientations, however, has yet to be established. Also, there are likely to be individual differences in how well clients respond to homework. For instance, clients' acceptance of the therapist's rationale for using homework would seem to be related to outcomes, and Beutler and colleagues (2004) infer from this that clients who are more reactant and resistant to the therapeutic process may experience the assignment of homework as less helpful than clients who are more compliant.

Box 7.4   Self-help materials as an adjunct to therapy

A study of American counselling and clinical psychologists found that around 85 per cent had recommended a self-help book to a client in the past year and 46 per cent had recommend a film (Norcross, 2005). Given the evidence for the efficacy of self-help activities (see den Boer et al., 2004) as well as for homework (see above), such recommendations would seem to have the potential to be a useful part of the therapeutic process. The following self-help resources were rated as the most useful to clients in a survey of over 3,000 American psychologists:

Self-help books

- *Skills Training Manual for Treating Borderline Personality Disorder* (Marsha Linehan, Guilford, 1993) – borderline personality disorder
- *Becoming Orgasmic: A Sexual and Personal Growth Programme for Women* (Julia Heiman and Joseph LoPiccolo, *Piatkus, 2008*) – sexual dysfunction
- *Why Marriages Succeed or Fail* (John Gottman, Bloomsburg, 2007) – marriage

(Continued)

(Continued)

Self-help autobiographies

- *Letting Go* (Morrie Schwartz, Pan, 1998) – terminal illness and dying
- *Breaking Free from Compulsive Eating* (Geneen Roth, Penguin, 2002) – compulsive eating
- *A Grief Observed* (C. S. Lewis, Zondervan, 2001) – grieving

Self-help films

- *Iris* – dementia/Alzheimer's disease
- *Ordinary People* – suicide/death and grieving
- *I Never Sang for my Father* – men's issues
- *On Golden Pond* – ageing
- *Billy Elliott* – men's issues

(Norcross, 2005)

Recommended reading

Norcross, J.C. (2006) 'Integrating self-help into psychotherapy: 16 practical suggestions', *Professional Psychology: Research and Practice*, 37 (6): 683–93. Very valuable set of guidelines on how to use self-help resources in counselling and psychotherapy.

Norcross, J.C., Santrock, J.W., Campbell, L.F., Smith, T.P., Sommer, R. and Zuckerman, E.L. (2003) *Authoritative Guide to Self-help Resources in Mental Health* (2nd edn). New York: Guilford Press.

One form of homework that clients might be invited to undertake is to write about their experiences, and recent years have seen the emergence of a large body of research findings supporting the value of written emotional expression. In the basic research design, participants are randomly distributed to one of two writing conditions: one in which they are asked to spend fifteen to thirty minutes per day, for three to five days, writing about their deepest thoughts and feelings and about an extremely important emotional issue that has affected them; and a control condition in which they are instructed to spend the same amount of time writing about something more superficial (Pennebaker, 1997). Such studies find that writing about emotional topics brings about significant reductions in psychological distress – as well as improvements in physiological functioning, such as antibody levels against Hepatitis B (Petrie et al., 1995) – with a mean effect size equivalent to a Cohen's *d* of about 0.15 (Frattaroli, 2006). Although this would be classed as a small effect size, it should be borne in mind that many of these interventions are very brief, and longer periods of disclosure or studies with more instances of disclosure demonstrate significantly larger effect sizes. Interestingly, studies which compare writing versus talking to a therapist or a tape recorder find comparable biological, mood or cognitive effects; and receiving feedback from others does not seem to enhance the effectiveness of the procedure (Pennebaker, 1997). Also, disclosure about positive events seems to be as beneficial as disclosure about negative events (Frattaroli, 2006).

RECOMMENDED READING

Pennebaker, J.W. (1997) 'Writing about emotional experiences as a therapeutic process', *Psychological Science*, 8 (3): 162–6.

Feedback on Client Progress

Within the counselling and psychotherapy research field, one of the most interesting and potentially important innovations in recent years has been the development of systems that track, and provide feedback on, client progress (Lambert, 2007; Miller et al., 2005). In these systems, clients complete a brief outcome measure every time they attend counselling or psychotherapy (Lambert and colleagues, who have led research in this field, use the 'Outcome Questionnaire-45' ['OQ-45']; while Miller and colleagues use the four-item 'Outcome Rating Scale'). The scores are then processed (generally by computer), and fed back to the therapist prior to the following session. If the client is found to be 'not-on-track' – i.e. their outcome scores are deviating significantly in a negative direction from what would be expected for clients at their initial levels of distress – then the feedback to the therapist is accompanied by an 'alarm signal' (such as a red sticker on the client's notes) which warns the therapist that there is a high chance of negative outcomes. Therapists are also advised to carefully review the case and to consider possible strategies for addressing the problem, such as working on the therapeutic alliance. In the Lambert system, a red signal alarm is used for clients whose trajectory is in the lowest 10 per cent of what would be expected. If the scores indicate *some* possibility of negative outcomes, the therapist is given a yellow signal alarm. Green signals are reserved for clients who are on-track.

The underlying premise for these systems is that deterioration as a result of therapy – which occurs in 5–10 per cent of clients (see Chapter 2) – can be most powerfully predicted by knowing a client's initial levels of distress and their response after one or more sessions of counselling or psychotherapy. Hence, if a client starts to get worse, there is a good chance that this will continue (see Chapter 2), and Lambert and colleagues (2007) calculate that their system can identify almost nine out of ten clients who would be likely to deteriorate – far higher than what therapists, alone, can predict.

As might be expected, this signal alarm system does not seem to have a strong effect on clients who are on-track (Lambert, 2007). However, for clients who are not on-track (i.e. red or yellow alarm signals), the system appears to produce dramatic benefits. Lambert (2007), for instance, reports effect sizes of between 0.34 to 0.92 (in the medium to large range) against treatment-as-usual controls (Lambert, 2007); while Miller and colleagues (2005) found a doubling of overall effectiveness across clients. Moreover, use of progress feedback systems seems to reduce drop-out, with not-on-track clients attending for an average of two or three sessions more when the system was used. In terms of reliable and/or clinically significant change for not-on-track clients, Lambert and colleagues found that this improved from 22 per cent to 33 per cent when progress feedback was used; and further increased to 45 per cent when therapists were also provided with a set of 'Clinical Support Tools' to help them make decisions about how to address the problems (Whipple et al., 2003). Providing progress feedback to clients as well as to therapists – for instance, 'Compared with the majority of patients, it does not appear that you are experiencing the expected levels of progress that most patients have experienced ...' (Hawkins et al., 2004: 323) – was also found, in one study, to bring about significant improvements in outcomes over therapist feedback alone, though this has not been replicated.

IMPLICATIONS FOR PRACTICE

A growing body of evidence indicates that the routine monitoring of client progress – through inviting clients to regularly complete outcome evaluation forms and through addressing difficulties that might become evident – is one of the most useful things that therapists can do to enhance the effectiveness of their work. For a simple guide to evaluating your practice, see Box 8.2.

RECOMMENDED READING

Lambert, M.J. (2007) Presidential address: 'What we have learned from a decade of research aimed at improving psychotherapy outcome in routine care', *Psychotherapy Research*, 17 (1): 1–14.

Duncan, B.L., Miller, S.D. and Sparks, J.A. (2004) Chapter 3, 'Becoming outcome informed', in *The Heroic Client*. San Francisco: Jossey-Bass. See also http://www.talkingcure.com.

Manualisation

Since the publication of Beck and colleagues' *Cognitive Therapy of Depression* in 1979, treatment manuals have proliferated within the psychotherapy field. Although the term 'manual' may conjure up images of minute-by-minute sets of instructions, in fact, most therapy manuals are broader guides to treatment (Crits-Christoph and Gibbons, 2002), intended to give definitive descriptions of the principles and techniques of a particular therapeutic approach and a clear statement of how therapists should deliver it, with concrete examples (Wampold, 2001).

Although such manuals emerged primarily for research purposes (and are now a required element of most funded and published efficacy research programmes), there is considerable debate as to whether counsellors and psychotherapists, more generally, should be practising according to manualised guidelines. Here, research suggests that practitioners' attitudes are equally likely to be positive or negative towards their use (Addis and Krasnow, 2000).

In general, the research seems to indicate that the use of treatment manuals neither enhances, nor detracts from, therapeutic effectiveness (Beutler et al., 2004; Chambless and Ollendick, 2001; Wampold, 2001). Meta-analyses of efficacy studies, for instance, indicate that levels of change in highly structured experimental environments (where manuals are nearly always used) are relatively similar to those in clinically representative conditions (where the use of manuals is much less frequent – Lipsey and Wilson, 1993; Shadish et al., 2000). Similarly, while some studies directly comparing standardised and more flexible practices have found the former to be more effective (e.g. Schulte et al., 1992), others have found no difference, or a modest positive advantage for the non-manualised therapy (Beutler et al., 2004). Furthermore, while some studies have indicated that competence in specific manualised therapy techniques predicts the outcome of psychotherapy (e.g. Shaw et al., 1999), others have found that use of particular manualised techniques is associated with poorer outcomes (Castonguay et al., 1996), or leads to therapists being experienced as less warm and friendly (Henry et al., 1993).

Telephone- and Internet-Based Interventions

Given that non-verbal communication is rated as one of the most important elements in the formation and strengthening of the therapeutic alliance (Bedi et al., 2005), it might be assumed that non-face-to-face therapeutic interventions are likely to be severely limited in their effectiveness. However, in recent years, there has been a growing interest in conducting therapy by telephone or internet, partly in recognition that these modes of communication have some distinct advantages: for instance, greater ease of access for people living in remote areas or with mobility problems, lower costs of providing therapeutic services, and the greater immediacy with which help can be provided (Leach and Christensen, 2006). In addition, research has suggested that many clients are quite satisfied with these therapeutic modalities, with no consistent evidence to demonstrate that they lead to a poorer therapeutic alliance than a face-to-face approach (e.g. Barak et al., in press). In fact, there is some evidence that individuals may actually be more disclosing of personal information via computer-mediated communication (Mallen, 2003).

In terms of effectiveness, a growing body of research suggests that therapeutic programmes based primarily on non-face-to-face modes of delivery can be highly efficacious, with outcomes that are not significantly different from those found in face-to-face practices (e.g. Barak et al., in press; Leach and Christensen, 2006). A meta-analysis of the efficacy of telephone-based interventions (generally CBT and practised in conjunction with homework tasks, workbooks or diaries), for instance, found that it was significantly more effective than controls in the treatment of depression, anxiety, eating disorders, substance use and re-hospitalisation for schizophrenia (Leach and Christensen, 2006), with evidence that gains were maintained at follow-up (e.g. Mohr et al., 2005). Similarly, research has indicated that web-based therapeutic programmes (with or without minimal therapeutic contact) can be effective with a range of psychological difficulties, with particularly large effect sizes for panic and anxiety disorders (Barak et al., in press). From pre-internet therapy to post-internet therapy, for instance, Carlbring and colleagues (2005) found effect sizes of between 1.45 and 0.37 for clients with panic disorder; slightly less than those who had face-to-face therapy (2.14 to 0.48), but not significantly different overall, and about equivalent levels of satisfaction across the two approaches.

RECOMMENDED READING

Barak, A., Hen, L., Boniel-Nissim, M. and Shapira, N. (in press) 'A comprehensive review and a meta-analysis of the effectiveness of internet-based psychotherapeutic interventions', *Journal of Technology in Human Services*.

Leach, L.S. and Christensen, H. (2006) 'A systematic review of telephone-based interventions for mental disorders', *Journal of Telemedicine and Telecare*, 12 (3): 122–9.

Summary of Key Findings

- A range of bona fide therapeutic techniques has been shown to have a positive impact on clients, when compared with a non-therapeutic or placebo control.
- There is little evidence to demonstrate that certain techniques are more effective than other bona fide techniques or practices.
- Cognitive-behavioural techniques, particularly exposure-based interventions, are most strongly supported by the evidence, demonstrating especially good results for anxiety problems.
- Interpretations, particularly when they are accurate, tentatively worded and embedded in a strong therapeutic alliance, have consistently been related to positive therapeutic outcomes.
- Humanistic techniques, based on deepening levels of experiencing and emotional processing, have been shown to lead to positive therapeutic outcomes.
- There is evidence to support both directive and non-directive practices, though the data suggests that, in general, both extremes should be avoided.
- Listening, paraphrasing and encouraging all seem to be experienced by clients as helpful, with more mixed responses to asking questions and guidance and advice.

- Providing therapists with feedback on client progress seems to bring about dramatic improvements for clients who are at risk of negative outcomes.
- For many forms of psychological distress, telephone- and internet-administered interventions appear to be as effective as face-to-face interventions.

QUESTIONS FOR REFLECTION

1 In your own work as a client or therapist, what techniques or practices have you experienced as helpful? Is this consistent with the research evidence?
2 How would you account for the lack of evidence that any one technique is more effective than another?
3 Given the evidence base, do you think that clients who specifically want to overcome phobias should be referred to therapists with a training in exposure techniques? What are the arguments for and against this practice?
4 Based on the evidence presented in this chapter, do you feel that you are more drawn to a directive, or non-directive, way of working? Why?
5 Which of the evidence-based techniques discussed in this chapter might you integrate into your own work?

8

Conclusion

This chapter discusses:

- What the evidence tells us, in summary, about the practice of counselling and psychotherapy.
- Some of the key questions that still need answering.
- How readers can stay up to date with the latest research.
- Some suggestions for conducting your own research.

What Do We Know so Far (with Some Certainty)?

Given the evidence reviewed in this book, there are a number of things about the practice of counselling and psychotherapy that we can say with some confidence:

- Counselling and psychotherapy helps: in general, people who have therapy end up less distressed than those who do not.
- For many forms of psychological distress, therapy is as effective as medication, and possibly more so in the long term.
- Psychological therapies are cost-effective forms of treatment.
- There is particularly strong evidence that cognitive-behavioural therapies are effective in treating a wide range of psychological difficulties.
- In general, there are only small differences in the effectiveness of different bona fide therapies.
- Clients' levels of involvement in therapy and their capacity to make use of the therapeutic relationship are among the strongest predictors of outcomes.
- Therapists' ways of relating to their clients are more important to the outcomes of therapy than their personal, demographic or professional characteristics.
- Positive outcomes are associated with a collaborative, caring, empathic, skilled way of relating.
- Therapeutic techniques can be a useful part of the counselling and psychotherapy process.

Box 8.1 Choosing (and using) a therapist: a research-informed guide

- If you are experiencing a specific form of psychological distress (see Box 3.1), you may want to consider seeing a therapist who is trained in one of the empirically supported treatments for that difficulty.
- Think about seeing a therapist who can help you capitalise on your strengths: for instance, if you are good at understanding why you do the things you do, an insight-orientated therapist (such as a psychodynamic practitioner) may be more suited to you than a behaviourally orientated one.
- If you are from a marginalised social group, you may find it particularly helpful to work with a therapist from a similar grouping; but whatever therapist you choose, make sure that they are fully accepting and valuing of who you are.
- Ask potential therapists what thoughts they might have on why you are facing the difficulties you are and what they think might help. If these are radically different from your own understandings, it may be more difficult to establish a good working relationship.
- If you find that things are getting worse after a few sessions, try to address this with your therapist and talk about ways in which the therapy might be more helpful to you. Given the tendency for clients to defer to their therapists (Chapter 7), this can be difficult to do, but addressing difficulties early on in therapy can make a significant difference to the eventual outcomes.
- And remember, probably the best predictor of the outcomes of therapy will be the extent to which you actively involve yourself in the process: 'clients, not therapists, make therapy work' (Duncan et al., 2004: 12).

Drawing these findings together, it seems reasonable to propose that, at the heart of most successful therapies, is a client who is willing and able to become involved in making changes to her or his life. If that client then encounters a therapist whom she or he trusts, likes and feels able to collaborate with, the client can make use of a wide range of techniques and practices to move closer towards her or his goals. For different clients, different kinds of therapist input may be more or less helpful; and there may be certain kinds of input that are particularly helpful for clients with specific psychological difficulties; but the evidence suggests that the key predictor of outcomes remains the extent to which the client is willing and able to make use of whatever the therapist provides (see Box 8.1). The old joke, then, would seem to have got it right:

'How many therapists does it take to change a lightbulb?'

'One, but the lightbulb has really got to want to change.'

What Don't We Know (and Would be Good to Find out About)?

There is much, then, we can be relatively certain of, but reviewing the research on counselling and psychotherapy seems to throw up as many questions as it answers. Perhaps

the most fundamental question that still needs addressing is whether particular therapeutic orientations, or particular therapeutic techniques, really *are* more effective for
particular psychological problems than others, or whether the dodo bird verdict holds
sway at both the general and disorder-specific level. Up until now, probably the biggest
problem with research that tries to answer this question is that so many of the findings
can be accounted for simply in terms of allegiance effects: when the developers of a therapy show that their therapy is more effective than another therapy, you do not need to
be a hardened sceptic to wonder about the validity of the findings (particularly when
the developers of the other therapy 'find' the opposite results). What seems crucial, then,
is more studies that are conducted by genuinely independent bodies (e.g. Elkin et al.,
1989), or by teams of researchers who are allied to each of the different orientations
being trialled (e.g. Watson et al., 2003).

For non-CBT practitioners – as well as clients who may benefit from non-CBT therapies –
what is also urgently needed is randomised controlled trials evaluating the efficacy of
non-CBT forms of therapy for particular psychological difficulties: for instance, gestalt
therapy for depression or psychodynamic therapy for social anxiety. If the dodo bird
verdict is correct, most therapies should be found to be efficacious for most psychological problems, but without such concrete proof, such practices are increasingly likely to
fall by the wayside. This may particularly be the case in healthcare settings, in which a
prioritising of randomised controlled trial evidence and a diagnostic understanding of
psychological distress is unlikely to lessen in the foreseeable future.

At the same time, given the wealth of evidence indicating that relational, therapist,
and particularly client factors are all strongly predictive of therapeutic outcomes, it
would not make sense to focus future research efforts exclusively at the orientation-
specific level. Rather, there are numerous further questions in each of these areas that
need asking, most basically, perhaps: 'What kind of relational/therapist/client factors are
most helpful (and unhelpful) for clients with depressive/anxiety/substance abuse/etc.
difficulties?' Given the importance of client factors, there is also the key question of how
we can help clients maximise their involvement and engagement in therapy, and which
kinds of clients will do best in which kinds of therapies. However, what will also be
important when researching these client, therapist and relational factors is to try to
move beyond statements of association (for instance, that positive outcomes are *correlated* with positive alliances) to try to identify *causal* relationships: i.e. the extent to
which empathy, or client involvement actually *contributes towards* positive outcomes.

Keeping Yourself Updated

If you are interested in trying to keep up to date with the latest findings in the counselling and psychotherapy field, here are some suggestions for what you can do:

- Go to the web pages of the main counselling and psychotherapy research journals and
sign up for email alerts – you will then be emailed details of new research articles every
time an issue of the journal comes out. Leading journals in the field include: *Journal of*

Clinical Psychology; *Journal of Consulting and Clinical Psychology*; *Journal of Counselling Psychology*; *Psychotherapy Research*; *Psychotherapy: Theory, Research, Practice*.

- Subscribe to some of the more accessible counselling and psychotherapy journals, such as *Counselling and Psychotherapy Research* (and don't forget to read it when it arrives!).
- Check out research updates in professional magazines like *Therapy Today* and the *Psychotherapy Networker*.
- Check the latest reviews of evidence-based treatments for specific psychological difficulties:

  - Cochrane Library (depression, anxiety and neurosis): http://www.cochrane.org
  - NICE (Mental Health and Behaviour Conditions): http://www.nice.org.uk
  - American Psychological Association (Division 12) Empirically Supported Treatments: http://www.apa.org/divisions/div12/rev_est/

- Keep an eye out for new editions of the 'bibles' of psychotherapy research findings, in particular: *The Handbook of Psychotherapy and Behavior Change* (ed. Lambert), *What Works for Whom?* (Roth and Fonagy), *A Guide to Treatments that Work* (ed. Nathan and Gorman) and *Psychotherapy Relationships that Work* (ed. Norcross).
- If you are interested in particular areas or research question, just try Googling them or search on Google Scholar (http://scholar.google.co.uk) – chances are, something of interest will come up. If you have access to electronic databases (for instance, through a university library), ISI Web of Knowledge and PsycINFO are two of the best search engines for finding the latest studies.
- If you are struggling to make sense of much of the material presented, it may be useful to familiarise yourself with some of the basic principles of counselling and psychotherapy research. See, for instance, textbooks by McLeod (2003) and Barker et al. (2002) or, for an excellent new introduction to counselling and psychotherapy research with numerous illustrations from the field, see Ladislav Timulak's *Research in Psychotherapy and Counselling* (2008b).

Doing Your Own Research

While some of the research discussed in this book comes from studies that require a level of resourcing well beyond the capacity of most practitioners (in particular, randomised controlled trials, which can cost hundreds of thousands of pounds to run), it is also true to say that 'research can be far simpler and more user-friendly than most therapists realize' (Lebow, 2006: 211). Research and evaluation can give therapists an opportunity to find out more about their practice – for instance, what their clients experience as helpful and unhelpful – and it is also an opportunity for therapists to demonstrate the value of what they do (Lebow, 2006). Through undertaking research and disseminating findings, therapists also have an opportunity to contribute to the wider body of knowledge on the process and outcomes of counselling and psychotherapy.

In terms of what practitioners can do, perhaps the most basic level of research is simply to keep systematic records of their work: for instance, how many clients they see, what their demographic backgrounds are, and which of their clients appear to do best (Lebow, 2006). At the next level up, therapists can start to evaluate systematically the effectiveness of their work using outcome evaluation forms (see Box 8.2). Therapists might also want to evaluate their practice by inviting clients to complete service satisfaction forms (see, for instance, Attkisson and Greenfield, 1994); or 'target complaint' forms, which ask clients to rate their degree of change on individualised questionnaire items (see, for instance, Elliott's Simplified Personal Questionnaire at www.experiential-researchers.org). If therapists then pool their data with other practitioners (bearing in mind, of course, issues of confidentiality and ethics), it becomes possible to start developing data-sets that can be used to test specific hypotheses: for instance, the general effectiveness of psychosynthesis or the effectiveness of psychosynthesis with particular client groups (see www.coreims.co.uk for details of how to share your data via CORE Net). Even working alone, there is still much that practitioners can do: for instance, recent years have seen a burgeoning interest in case study research (see, for instance, the online journal *Pragmatic Case Studies in Psychotherapy* (http://pcsp.libraries.rutgers.edu/index.php/pcsp) whereby individual practitioners can write up and share in-depth, systematic reports of their work with clients.

Box 8.2   How to evaluate your practice using CORE-OM

1   Go to www.coreims.co.uk and download one of the outcome measures for free.
2   Invite clients to complete a CORE outcome measure at the beginning of their first and last sessions or even at the beginning of each session (to make sure that you are using the forms correctly, obtain the relevant User Guide from the CORE website or through contacting services in your locality that use CORE – email admin@coreims.co.uk for details).
3   Instructions for scoring are on the forms themselves or you can purchase software to do it (CORE PC) from the CORE website; to compare your outcomes against UK benchmarks, see *Counselling and Psychotherapy Research*, 6 (1) (March, 2006).

Several other easy-to-use counselling and psychotherapy evaluation systems are available via the internet, including the US-based OQ Measures (www.oqmeasures.com), the Outcome Rating Scale (www.talkingcure.com), and the Strengths and Difficulties Questionnaire for children and young people (www.sdqinfo.com).

RECOMMENDED READING

Lebow, J. (2006) *Research for the Psychotherapist: From Science to Practice*, Part IV. London: Routledge.

Increasingly, students on counselling and psychotherapy training courses are also being supported – or required – to carry out their own empirical research projects. Here,

I would make one particularly strong plea. When I first started supervising Masters projects, I vehemently believed that students should follow their own passions, and research whatever questions were of most interest and importance to them. Now I am not so sure. Obviously, it is essential that students are energised about their work, but the problem is, if everyone follows their own personal interests, what can emerge is a hotchpotch of findings that do not really contribute to a coherent and evolving body of knowledge. Now, I am much more inclined to encourage students to start by looking at what questions are out there in the field. What have other people done? How could you build on their research? What different angle or different approach could you take to develop our understandings? And if students are keen to do qualitative research, one of the most valuable things they can do is simply to carry out in-depth interviews with clients (within specific groups, or contexts, or therapies) about what they found helpful and unhelpful in therapy (see Clarke et al., 2004, for an excellent example of this). Here, by starting with questions that emerge from the field, students have much more of an opportunity to become engaged with the wider counselling and psychotherapy research community, to dialogue with others asking similar questions, and to produce results that can really help to take the field forward.

And Finally...

Today, it is becoming increasingly difficult for counsellors and psychotherapists to evade the call to become research-informed, but it is my hope that therapists can be so much more than that: 'research-inspired', 'research-invigorated', or 'research-revitalised'. Research findings in counselling and psychotherapy can help counsellors and psychotherapists be the best practitioners that they can be for their clients, and what better sorts of friends would we want to have around?

QUESTIONS FOR REFLECTION

1   How would you summarise for yourself what we know so far about what makes therapy effective?
2   What questions in this book are you particularly interested in? How could you find out more?
3   What questions do you have about the outcomes or process of therapy that are not answered in this book? How could you find some answers?
4   Are the facts really friendly?

Appendix: The Efficacy and Effectiveness of Different Therapeutic Orientations

The following sections review the evidence for a range of therapeutic approaches. It focuses on those orientations for which there is, at least, a moderate amount of relevant evidence. This means that some of the more popular, but under-researched, orientations, such as existential therapy or psychosynthesis, are not reviewed here. Definitions of the specific orientations are given in the Glossary.

Humanistic Therapies

Humanistic approaches to therapy are well-supported by the findings presented in Chapter 6, which indicate that positive therapeutic outcomes are closely associated with empathic, accepting, collaborative and genuine therapeutic relationships; the findings in Chapter 4, which support the humanistic assumption that clients are the principal drivers of therapeutic change; and the findings in Chapter 7 on the efficacy of specific humanistic techniques.

Meta-analyses of humanistic therapies, as a whole, support the hypothesis that they are efficacious and effective forms of therapy, with a large average pre–post effect size of 0.99, reducing down to 0.89 when compared against wait-list or no-therapy controls (Elliott, Greenberg et al., 2004). This is similar to the overall effect sizes of other orientations, such as CBT and psychodynamic therapy, with evidence indicating that they may be efficacious for clients with depressive, traumatic, schizophrenic and health-related problems (although, as with the psychodynamic therapies, there is less evidence for their impact with anxiety disorders) (Elliott, Greenberg et al., 2004).

Person-Centred (Client-Centred) Therapies

Meta-analysis of outcome data from fifty-two studies of 'pure' person-centred therapy suggest that it is, in general, as effective and efficacious as other humanistic and non-humanistic therapy, with an average effect size against controls of 0.78, maintained at follow-up (Elliott, 2007). This is slightly less than the average effect size for the humanistic therapies overall; and significantly but 'trivially' smaller than the average effect size for CBT (a difference of –0.19), but these differences disappear when researcher allegiance is controlled for (Elliott, 2007). As discussed in Chapter 3, 'real-world' data from UK primary care settings also suggests that person-centred therapy is as effective as CBT and psychodynamic therapy for a range of psychological difficulties (Stiles et al., 2008; Stiles et al., 2006). With respect to *specific* psychological problems, evidence is strongest that person-centred therapy is efficacious for clients with mild and/or moderate depression, in adults and in children and young people (e.g. King et al., 2000).

Gestalt Therapy

A recent meta-analysis indicates a respectable average effect size of 1.23 from pre- to post-therapy, and 0.64 against controls (on the basis of three studies) (Elliott, Greenberg et al., 2004). A review of the evidence also suggests that gestalt therapy can be as effective as cognitive and client-centred therapies in the treatment of depression, simple phobias and other psychological difficulties (Strümpfel and Goldman, 2002).

Process-Experiential/Emotion-Focused Therapy

Process-experiential therapy is one of the most rigorously researched forms of humanistic practice (see Elliott, Greenberg et al., 2004), and has been shown to be efficacious in the treatment of depression and trauma and abuse, with an average pre- to post-therapy effect size across all client groups of 1.2, and 0.89 against controls (Elliott, Greenberg et al., 2004). Compared with CBT, process-experiential therapy has shown some superiority: Watson and colleagues (2003), for instance, found that it brought about significantly greater improvements in the interpersonal domain for depressed clients, though these differences disappear when allegiance factors are controlled for (Elliott, Greenberg et al., 2004). Similarly, studies which compare process-experiential therapy against a more classical form of person-centred therapy have shown the former to be significantly more effective, but this may also be due to allegiance effects (Elliott, Greenberg et al., 2004).

'Counselling'

Although the term 'counselling' is commonly used – as in this book – to refer to a wide range of therapeutic practices, it is also used – mainly in healthcare settings – to refer to a primarily supportive, non-directive, short-term form of talking therapy (e.g. Department of Health, 2001; Sainsbury Centre for Mental Health, 2006). Drawing on evidence from rigorously controlled trials, the UK's Department of Health (2001: 36) suggest that such a practice may be beneficial to clients who 'are having difficulty adjusting to life events, illnesses, disabilities or losses (including childbirth and bereavement)'. The Department of Health guidelines go on to state that 'There is evidence of effectiveness with mixed anxiety/depression and generic psychological distress presenting in primary care. Specific client groups (e.g. bereavement reactions, mild post-natal depression) may also benefit from counselling and other brief therapies.'

Psychodynamic Therapies

Psychodynamic therapies are well-supported by the evidence on the importance of the therapeutic alliance, as well as research linking the use of interpretations to positive outcomes (see Chapters 6 and 7). However, frequent use of transference interpretations tends to be contraindicated by the research.

As with most other non-cognitive-behavioural therapies, the evidence base for psychodynamic therapies is weak relative to the number of therapists in practice (Fonagy et al., 2005) though this is beginning to change.

Short-Term Psychodynamic Psychotherapy

Meta-analyses of the most rigorously controlled studies indicate that short-term psychodynamic psychotherapy (generally of less than forty weeks) 'appears effective for a broad range of common mental disorders, with evidence of modest to moderate benefits which generally persist in the medium and longer term' (Abbass et al., 2006: 10). From pre- to post-therapy, Leichsenring and colleagues (2004) found large effect sizes of 1.39 for target problems, 0.90 for general psychiatric symptoms, and 0.80 for social functioning, all of which increased somewhat at follow-up.

Consistent with the dodo bird verdict, meta-analyses of comparative trials indicate that, overall, short-term psychodynamic psychotherapies and other forms of psychological therapy (primarily CBT) do not differ significantly concerning their outcomes at end of therapy or follow-up (Anderson and Lambert, 1995; Leichsenring et al., 2004). Such an equivalence of outcomes is also evident in the two large-scale studies of therapeutic effectiveness by Stiles and colleagues (2006; 2008).

With respect to the efficacy of short-term psychodynamic psychotherapy with specific psychological difficulties, there is evidence to suggest that it is an efficacious treatment for clients with depression (Leichsenring, 2001), with large pre–post effect sizes on depressive symptoms of between 0.94 and 2.49 – equivalent to the outcomes of cognitive-behavioural and behavioural therapeutic practices. Anorexia nervosa is another psychological difficulty for which short-term psychodynamic therapies appear to be of benefit (Fonagy et al., 2005; Sainsbury Centre for Mental Health, 2006), with particularly good evidence for cognitive analytic therapy (Treasure et al., 1995). There is also some evidence that short-term psychodynamic psychotherapy is efficacious for clients who abuse opiates but, interestingly, not cocaine (Fonagy et al., 2005). Despite its centrality to psychoanalytic theory, however, there is very little evidence to suggest that psychodynamic therapies help clients deal with *anxiety* difficulties, and there are many other psychological problems for which the efficacy of psychodynamic therapy has yet to be demonstrated (Fonagy et al., 2005).

Psychoanalysis

Here, evidence of efficacy is particularly 'patchy' (Fonagy et al., 2005); indeed, in a comprehensive survey of all the available evidence, the Research Committee of the International Psychoanalytic Association came to the conclusion that, 'There are no definitive studies which show psychoanalysis to be unequivocally effective relative to an active placebo or an alternative method of treatment' (Fonagy, 2002: 287). Nevertheless, pre- to post-therapy effectiveness studies suggest that psychoanalysis is consistently helpful for clients with milder, 'neurotic' difficulties, and may produce long-lasting, increasing alleviation across a range of symptoms (Fonagy et al., 2005). Furthermore, a growing body of carefully controlled research suggests that a psychoanalytically orientated, partial hospitalisation programme can bring about impressive improvements for clients diagnosed with borderline personality disorder, with dramatic drops in the number of suicide attempts, self-mutilations and inpatient stays after six months of treatment (as compared with controls), and continued improvements for as long as three years post-admission (Bateman and Fonagy, 1999; 2001). Indeed, a recent meta-analysis of psychodynamic treatments (both short- and long-term) for clients with personality disorders – primarily borderline personality disorder – found a large average pre–post effect size of 1.46 (compared with 1.00 for CBT), and a mean recovery rate of 59 per cent (Leichsenring and Leibing, 2003).

Aptitude-Treatment Interactions

There is some evidence to suggest that psychodynamic therapies may be particularly appropriate for high-functioning clients, and 'less appropriate for more disturbed patients' (Mohr, 1995: 19) – particularly when the disturbances are in the relational and interpersonal field. As we have seen in Chapter 6, transference interpretations – a mainstay of much psychodynamic practice – are generally contraindicated for clients with higher levels of relational difficulties; and studies which compare the effectiveness of 'interpretative' therapies (i.e. insight-oriented, anxiety-provoking and 'expressive') against the effectiveness of 'supportive' therapies (i.e. externally oriented and anxiety-suppressive) tend to find that clients with mature styles of relating do better in the former than in the latter, while the reverse is true for clients with more dysfunctional relational patterns (e.g. Piper et al., 2001). At the same time, it is important to note that a number of studies have shown that psychodynamic therapies can be very effective with highly distressed clients, including those diagnosed with personality disorders (Bateman and Fonagy, 2001; Leichsenring and Leibing, 2003). There is also some research to suggest that clients who are 'self-reflective, introverted, and/or introspective' may tend to benefit more from insight-oriented procedures, such as psychodynamic therapy (Beutler et al., 2004: 262). Such a finding is highly consistent with the capitalisation model of therapeutic change discussed in Chapter 4.

Cognitive-Behavioural Therapies

Overall, as we saw in Chapter 3, cognitive and behavioural therapies have been shown to be efficacious for a wide range of psychological difficulties – far more so than for any other therapeutic orientation. A range of CBT techniques has also been shown to be highly efficacious (Chapter 7). Meta-analyses of specific forms of CBT, such as rational emotive behaviour therapy and personal construct psychotherapy, have demonstrated moderate to large effect sizes (Metcalfe et al., 2007; Smith and Glass, 1977). Cognitive and behavioural therapies have been found, in most instances, to be as effective, or more effective, than pharmacological treatments (Emmelkemp, 2004); and researchers in the CBT field have also claimed that it is significantly more effective than other therapeutic approaches for certain psychological problems, particularly anxiety disorders (e.g. Gloaguen et al., 1998; Hunsley and Di Giulio, 2002). However, as we saw in Chapter 3, allegiance effects and other confounding factors makes such conclusions debatable, and studies which compare the efficacy of CBT practices with other bona fide therapies tend to find only negligible differences (Wampold, 2001). Nevertheless, where differences do emerge (e.g. Shapiro and Shapiro, 1982), they *do* tend to favour CBT.

Cognitive Therapy

In general, research indicates that clients respond well to cognitively based therapies, with around half of all outpatients achieving complete remission, large effect sizes against minimal treatment controls, and outcomes that are at least as good as those of other psychosocial and pharmacological practices (Hollon and Beck, 2004). With respect to specific difficulties (see Chapter 3), cognitive therapies have been shown to be efficacious with a wide range of psychological and physical problems, with particularly robust evidence to support their use in the treatment of depression (Gloaguen et al., 1998) and certain anxiety disorders (Hollon and Beck, 2004). However, it should be noted that there remain many psychological problems, such as anorexia, for which effective cognitive therapies have yet to be developed (Hollon and Beck, 2004).

Skills Training Programmes

Social Skills and Communication Training

Social skills training is most commonly delivered to individuals diagnosed with schizophrenia (Dilk and Bond, 1996). A meta-analysis of the effectiveness of these, and related, programmes for individuals with severe mental illness found an effect size that was in the medium range (Dilk and Bond, 1996), though change was greater on the acquisition of specific skills than on symptom reduction. Assertiveness training programmes were significantly more effective than general interpersonal skills programmes (Dilk and Bond, 1996); and this also appears to be true in the treatment of substance abuse, where social skills training has an average effect size of 0.78 against alternative treatments (Roth and Fonagy, 2005). Social skills training programmes, such as 'Personal Effectiveness Training' and 'Social Effectiveness Therapy', have also been shown to be effective with socially phobic individuals (Emmelkemp, 2004; Turner et al., 1995); although recent research suggests that this may be less to do with skills acquisition, and more a consequence of *in vivo* exposure (i.e. practising certain behaviours in social settings to the point that anxiety subsides, Emmelkemp, 2004; Woody and Ollendick, 2006). With respect to depression, there is some evidence that assertiveness training may be of value (Sanchez et al., 1980), but 'the relationship between improved social performance and reduction in depressed moods remains unclear' (Emmelkemp, 2004: 412). For alcohol dependence, communication skills training was more effective than an alcohol education control (Rohsenow et al., 2001).

Coping Skills Training

Tarrier and colleagues (1993) showed that a 'coping strategy enhancement' method brought about significant reductions in psychotic symptoms as compared with a waiting period control, with some indications that it was more effective than a 'problem-solving' form of CBT (see below). Coping skills training programmes have also been developed for substance abusers, to help them deal more effectively with the desire to take drugs and with negative moods. These have been shown to bring about significant improvements, with some evidence to indicate that such programmes may be particularly effective for clients with more severe levels of sociopathy or psychopathy, as compared with more interpersonal therapeutic approaches (Kadden et al., 1989). 'Self-control training', in which problem drinkers are taught to consume alcohol in more measured ways (for instance, by learning to extend the amount of time between drinks) has been shown to reduce alcohol consumption as compared with no-treatment controls, with some indications that such a controlled drinking approach may be more effective than an abstinence-based treatment (Walters, 2000). Overall, however, there is no evidence to indicate that a cognitive-behavioural coping skills approach is more effective than any other treatment programme (Longabaugh and Morgenstern, 1999).

Relapse Prevention

Like problem-solving therapy, relapse prevention has been found to lead to significant reductions in obesity as compared with a no-treatment control, though to a somewhat lesser extent than the problem-solving approach (Perri et al., 2001). Relapse prevention has also been shown to be effective in the treatment of substance abuse problems over no-treatment controls, with evidence strongest for smoking and then alcohol abuse (Carroll, 1996). As with coping skills training, however, there is no evidence that relapse prevention is more effective than other therapeutic practices, although it was associated with significantly better outcomes for clients with higher levels of psychosocial impairment.

Problem-Solving Therapy

Problem-solving therapy has been shown to be helpful in the treatment of depression (National Institute for Health and Clinical Excellence, 2007b); and, as stated above, there is some evidence that this approach may lead to a reduction in psychotic symptoms for clients with schizophrenia (Tarrier et al., 1993). It has also been shown to lead to significantly greater weight loss among clients with obesity than a no-treatment control (Perri et al., 2001), with over a third of clients losing 10 per cent of body weight or more following a year-long programme. A meta-analysis of problem-solving therapy across different client groups found a large overall effect size of 1.37 against waiting-list or no-treatment controls, with no significant differences in outcomes from other bona fide therapies (Malouff et al., 2007).

Relaxation Training

Probably the most widely evaluated relaxation programme is 'applied relaxation', which was developed for the treatment of phobic clients (Öst, 1987). Here, clients are initially taught to monitor and identify signs of anxiety, and then to relax themselves through a 'progressive relaxation' procedure, in which they tense, and then relax, specific groups of muscles. In the 'application' stage of the relaxation programme, they are then helped to generalise these skills out to real-life anxiety-inducing situations. Research suggests that this comprehensive applied relaxation procedure is more effective than just the progressive relaxation component, *per se* (Öst, 1988).

Applied relaxation has been found to be effective in the treatment of generalised anxiety disorder, at a level equivalent to that of cognitive therapy (Siev and Chambless, 2007). Öst and Breiholtz (2000), for instance, found that cognitive therapy and applied relaxation brought about clinical improvement rates of 53 per cent and 56 per cent respectively. By contrast, while research indicates that applied relaxation is efficacious in the treatment of panic disorders (e.g. Öst and Westling, 1995), most studies have found it to be less effective than a combined cognitive-behavioural programme (e.g. Clark et al., 1994; Siev and Chambless, 2007). Applied relaxation has also been found to yield significantly better results than no-treatment controls for a range of other problems, such as specific and social phobias, headaches and back pain (Öst, 1987).

'Third-Generation' Cognitive-Behaviour Therapies

Dialectical Behaviour Therapy (DBT)

Compared with treatment as usual, DBT has been found to reduce rates of self-harm and parasuicidal behaviours in clients diagnosed with borderline personality disorder (see Chapter 3) (Binks et al., 2006); and it has also been shown to reduce levels of drug dependency (Linehan et al., 1999), hospital utilisation and drop-out from therapy (Koerner and Linehan, 2000) in this client group, though not the diagnosis of borderline personality disorder, *per se* (Binks et al., 2006). There is also evidence that DBT can bring about significant reductions in binge-eating behaviour as compared with a wait-list control (Telch et al., 2001).

Mindfulness-Based Cognitive Therapy

Compared with treatment as usual, Ma and Teasdale (2004) showed that mindfulness-based cognitive therapy reduced rates of relapse by more than half. This was most obvious in clients who had experienced four or more episodes of depression (38 per cent of clients relapsing compared with 100 per cent in treatment as usual). By contrast, clients with just two previous episodes of depression did not do better with this approach; and other research has also indicated that mindfulness-based cognitive therapy is most effective with the more severely depressed (Kenny and Williams, 2007). Consistent with their hypothesised mechanism of change, mindfulness-based cognitive therapy was also not found to be effective for clients whose recurrence of depression was triggered by specific life events, as opposed to internal cognitive processes (Ma and Teasdale, 2004).

Acceptance and Commitment Therapy (ACT)

Preliminary controlled research indicates that ACT is significantly more effective than treatment as usual or wait-list controls for a range of psychological problems, such as rehospitalisation for psychosis (Bach and Hayes, 2002) and opiate addiction (Hayes et al., 2004). Of more interest, however, are claims that ACT may have superior outcomes to traditional CBT, with a meta-analysis of preliminary comparative studies giving an effect size of 0.73 in favour of ACT (Hayes et al., 2006). In support of this finding, a number of 'micro-studies' (in which researchers have focused on the impact of specific components of ACT) have suggested that ACT strategies – in particular, the acceptance of 'negative' thoughts and feelings – may be more effective than traditional CBT 'control-based' practices (Hayes et al., 2006). Given, however, that nearly all of the above studies have been conducted by researchers associated with ACT, it may be that these differences are primarily a consequence of allegiance effects.

Aptitude-Treatment Interactions

Consistent with the capitalisation hypothesis, data from the NIMH TDCRP project (see Box 3.3) indicate that clients with higher levels of cognitive functioning tend to be more responsive to CBT (Sotsky et al., 1991). Similarly, there is some evidence to indicate that cognitive and behavioural therapies may be more effective with clients who have an awareness of their problems and have the capacity to identify and apply practical solutions, as compared with clients whose principal difficulties may be inaccessible to consciousness or actively avoided (Stiles et al., 1997). There is also some evidence that clients with externalising coping styles (i.e. those who tend to deal with their problems by 'acting out') may do particularly well with this approach (Beutler et al., 2004).

Creative Therapies

Art Therapy

While a small number of case studies and pre- to post-therapy studies indicate that participation in art therapy is associated with significant improvements on a range of measures for both adults and children (Gilroy, 2006; Saunders and Saunders, 2000), controlled studies – both randomised and non-randomised – give a more mixed picture (Reynolds et al., 2000). Here, clients in art therapy sometimes (e.g. Gussak, 2006), but not always, do significantly better than clients in control conditions (e.g. Odell-Miller et al., 2006). Along these lines, a Cochrane Review of art therapy for schizophrenia and schizophrenia-like illnesses found a small but significant difference in favour of art therapy in one of the two controlled studies identified, but concluded that further evaluation is needed (Ruddy and Milnes, 2005).

Dramatherapy

The website of the British Association of Dramatherapists (http://www.badth.org.uk/Research/compresear.htm) indexes a range of uncontrolled studies demonstrating an association between participation in dramatherapy and positive psychological change. Particularly good evidence for this association exists for clients diagnosed with schizophrenia (Yotis, 2006). However, a Cochrane Review of randomised controlled trials evaluating the efficacy of dramatherapy for schizophrenia or schizophrenia-like illnesses concluded that the benefits or harms of this practice were, as yet, unclear, because of difficulties interpreting the findings of the few controlled trials in this area (Ruddy and Dent-Brown, 2007).

Psychodrama

Controlled studies indicate that psychodrama can have a positive effect on clients' behaviours (Kellermann, 1987). More specifically, a meta-analysis of the efficacy of psychodrama techniques found a mean effect size of 0.95 against controls, with 'doubling' (in which a member of the group enacts the 'protagonist' – i.e. the principal person doing the therapeutic work – alongside himself or herself) having the largest mean effect size of 1.36, followed by 'role reversal' (in which the protagonist plays the role of someone else in their lives) with a mean effect size of 0.93 (Kipper and Ritchie, 2003).

Music Therapy

Four out of five randomised controlled trials in a recent Cochrane Review found that music therapy significantly reduced symptoms of depression (Maratos et al., 2008). A Cochrane Review of music therapy for schizophrenia or schizophrenia-like illnesses also found that it led to significantly better outcomes over standard care alone on measures of global state, with some indications that it also led to significant improvements on mental state, negative symptoms (effect size = 0.86) and social functioning (effect size = 0.78), when sufficient numbers of music therapy sessions were provided (Gold et al., 2005). In addition, it has been found to have an effect size against controls (both pre-therapy and no-treatment) of 0.61 for children and young people with a range of psychological problems (Gold et al., 2004), with larger changes for eclectic forms of music therapy as compared with behavioural ones (Gold et al., 2004). For children with autistic spectrum disorders, music therapy has also been found to lead to significant improvements in communicative skills as compared with a placebo control, with effect sizes in the medium range (0.50 for gestural and 0.36 for verbal communicative skills).

Dance Movement Therapy

A meta-analysis of the efficacy and effectiveness of dance movement therapy for a range of adult and child populations obtained a medium effect size against controls – equivalent to a d of about 0.63. This was greater for adults and adolescents than for children, and greatest on measures of anxiety as compared with anger and self-concept (Ritter and Graff, 1996). Along these lines, a recent German randomised controlled trial has indicated that dance movement therapy may be effective in reducing stress (Bräuninger, cited in Koch and Bräuninger, 2005). Changes in body awareness as a result of participating in dance movement therapy have been widely studied, with research suggesting that individuals come to see their bodies as more graceful, fast, active, strong and beautiful (Ritter and Graff, 1996). Closely related to this, qualitative research suggests that clients with body-centred problems, such as anorexia or breast cancer, benefit particularly from participation in dance movement therapy (Ritter and Graff, 1996).

Contemporary and Integrative Practices

Transactional Analysis (TA)

Although little controlled research on TA has been conducted in recent years, Smith and Glass's (1977) meta-analysis of psychotherapy outcome studies found that it had a respectable medium effect size of 0.58 against controls – equivalent to most other therapies. In terms of comparative effectiveness, a replication of the Consumer Reports survey (1995, see Chapter 2) with just transactional analysis clients reported significantly greater improvements than in the original study: for instance, 69 per cent of those who started out feeling very poor said the transactional analysis had made things a lot better, compared with 54 per cent across the other therapies (Novey, 1999). However, these findings may be a result of differences in the methods of the two studies (in particular, clients in the Novey study handed their questionnaires back via their therapists).

Neurolinguistic Programming (NLP)

Despite claims it performs 'therapeutic magic', a review of the experimental research found that 'The basic tenets of NLP have failed to be reliably verified in almost 86 per cent of the controlled studies' (Sharpley, 1987: 105).

Interpersonal Therapy (IPT)

Although interpersonal therapy is not a widely practised approach to therapy, it is one of the best validated forms of counselling and psychotherapy, with convincing evidence that it is an efficacious therapy for depression, at a level generally equivalent to CBT and anti-depressant treatment (de Mello et al., 2005; Elkin et al., 1989). There is also some evidence to indicate that it may be effective in the treatment of bulimia, though evidence here is more equivocal (Fairburn et al., 1993). Consistent with the capitalisation hypothesis, data from the NIMH TDCRP suggests that good outcomes in interpersonal therapy, particularly for males, are associated with higher pre-therapy levels of social functioning, higher interpersonal sensitivity, and higher satisfaction with social relationships (Sotsky et al., 1991).

Motivational Interviewing

Like interpersonal therapy, motivational interviewing has been intensively evaluated in a number of large-scale randomised controlled trials. Research findings suggest that it is particularly effective for alcohol problems, with more sustained effects than counselling as usual (Ball et al., 2007); and there is also evidence that it can be effective for substance abuse and diet and exercise problems, with an overall effect size against controls of around 0.5, sustained as long as four years post-therapy (Burke et al., 2003). Motivational interviewing has been found to be as effective as other bona fide therapies, such as CBT and twelve-step facilitation, but with interventions that are briefer by an average of three hours (Burke et al., 2003). Consistent with the principles underpinning motivational interviewing, research also indicates that greater confrontation of problem drinkers – such as challenging, disagreeing, head-on disputes, incredulity, sarcasm and emphasising negative client characteristics – is associated with greater amounts of drinking (Miller et al., 1993). However, as with cognitive therapies and the cognitive theory of change (see Box 7.1), there is no direct support for the theory that motivational interviewing works by enhancing clients' motivations to change (Burke et al., 2003).

Solution-Focused Brief Therapy

Meta-analyses of the efficacy of solution-focused brief therapy with adults and children and young people suggest that it has a small to moderate effect size over controls (0.13 to 0.26), with no indications that it is more effective (or less effective) than other, more problem-orientated approaches (Gingerich and Eisengart, 2000; Kim, 2008). One meta-analysis *has* suggested that it has a positive effect in less time than more traditional psychotherapies (Stams et al., 2006 cited in Bannink, 2007); but there is also evidence that the average length of therapy in solution-focused brief therapy is about the same as in other orientations (Stalker et al., 1999).

Eye-Movement Desensitisation and Reprocessing (EMDR)

Rigorously controlled research suggests that EMDR is efficacious for clients experiencing post-traumatic stress disorder, but not more so than CBT or other exposure-based treatment (Davidson and Parker, 2001). Considerable controversy exists as to whether eye movements are an essential, or even helpful, element of the EMDR process (EMDR Institute, 2004), with a recent meta-analysis of the published data indicating 'no significant incremental benefit because of eye movements' (Davidson and Parker, 2001: 310).

Hypnotherapy

A meta-analysis of controlled studies with adults and children that compared hypnotic interventions with untreated controls obtained a mean effect size of 0.56, with evidence of efficacy for smoking cessation, anxiety (particularly test anxiety), psychosocial aspects of medical procedures (for instance, quality of life following bypass surgery), psychosocial aspects of the treatment of cancer (such as pain and nausea following chemotherapy) and somatic complaints (such as headaches and asthma) (Bongartz et al., 2002; Flammer and Bongartz, 2003). With respect to this latter category, a systematic review of the effectiveness of hypnotherapy in the management of irritable bowel syndrome found encouraging results (Wilson et al., 2006), with hypnotherapy identified in the list of empirically supported psychological interventions as a 'probably efficacious' treatment for this problem (Chambless and Ollendick, 2001). In addition, hypnotic procedures have been shown to significantly enhance the efficacy of CBT, particularly in the treatment of obesity (Kirsch et al., 1995). Consistent with the above research, a study of the comparative effect of hypnotherapy on different psychological symptoms indicated that it may be most effective in reducing levels of anxiety, and particularly anxiety as manifested through bodily symptoms (Gould and Krynicki, 1989).

Religion-Accommodative Practices

Given that as many as 92 per cent of people in a country like the United States are affiliated with a religion (McCullough, 1999), that many people experience distress from religious or spiritual problems (about one in four of a sample of US college students, Wade et al., 2007), and that as many as 50 per cent of clients may want to discuss religious or spiritual issues in counselling (particularly individuals with higher levels of past spiritual experiences) (Rose et al., 2001), it is understandable that recent years have seen various attempts to develop religion-accommodative, or 'religiously tailored' therapies. Religious and spiritual components that are common across these practices include teaching spiritual-religious principles, client prayer, reading sacred texts, and religious imagery or spiritual meditation (Smith et al., 2007).

   A recent meta-analysis of religious and spiritually adapted psychotherapies found an overall medium effect size of 0.56 (Smith et al., 2007). A meta-analysis of studies comparing religious-accommodative counselling with standard treatments found no overall differences (McCullough, 1999), though studies in which significant differences have emerged have favoured the religiously accommodative approaches (Worthington and Sandage, 2002). However, as with the research findings regarding matching on religious values (see Chapter 5), there is some research to indicate that clients with strong religious commitments respond particularly well to therapists who use specific religious interventions (Wade et al., 2007). Interestingly, there is also research to suggest that, while religious therapists may not do any better with religious clients when a religiously tailored approach is used, non-religious therapists may be significantly more helpful to religious clients when working in a religiously accommodative way (Propst et al., 1992). Much of the above research has been conducted using Christian clients and Christian-accommodative therapy, but Malaysian research on Muslim-acommodative therapies suggests that it is also as effective, and possibly more effective, than an alternative secular approach (Worthington and Sandage, 2002).

Glossary

Acceptance and commitment therapy (ACT)

A third-generation CBT which aims to help clients make fuller contact with the present moment through both acceptance and mindfulness of private experiences, and a commitment to behavioural change.

Activity scheduling

A cognitive-behavioural technique in which clients are encouraged to plan and monitor their daily activities.

Agoraphobia

An anxiety disorder characterised by a fear of being in situations from which escape might be difficult or embarrassing.

Alliance rupture

A tension or breakdown in the collaborative relationship between client and therapist.

Anorexia nervosa

An eating disorder characterised by low body-weight, body-image distortion, and an intense fear of gaining weight.

Anxiety disorders

A group of psychological difficulties characterised by persistent feelings of apprehension, tension or uneasiness, which disrupt daily functioning.

Anxiety management

A therapeutic programme for generalised anxiety disorder which incorporates a range of cognitive and behavioural elements, such as relaxation, education about anxiety and acquisition of coping strategies.

Applied muscle tension

A specific behavioural intervention for blood-injury phobias, in which the person is taught a muscle-tensing procedure to reverse a drop in blood pressure and prevent fainting.

Applied relaxation

A behavioural therapy programme in which clients are taught to identify signs of anxiety, relax themselves through a sequence of tensing and relaxing muscles ('progressive relaxation'), and then to apply these skills to real-life situations.

Aptitude-treatment interaction (ATI)

A phenomenon in which clients with particular qualities and characteristics do better in a particular form of therapy than others.

Art therapy

A form of psychotherapeutic practice that uses such media as paintings, drawings, crayons and clay for therapeutic purposes.

Attachment style

Individuals' particular patterns of behaving, thinking and feeling in close relationships.

Axis I disorder (*DSM*)

A clinical syndrome, such as social phobia or major depressive disorder.

Axis II disorder (*DSM*)

A personality or developmental disorder, such as borderline personality disorder or autism.

Bibliotherapy

A form of self-help therapy based around the use of written materials.

Bipolar disorder

A category of mood disorders characterised by the presence of extremely elevated moods, often alternating with depressive episodes.

Bulimia nervosa

An eating disorder characterised by binge eating followed by problematic compensatory behaviours to prevent weight gain, such as self-induced vomiting.

Clinically significant improvement

Movement from within the range of scores for a clinical population to the range of scores for a non-clinical population.

Cochrane Review

A UK-based series of systematic reviews evaluating the efficacy of healthcare interventions (see http://cochrane.org).

Cognitive-analytic therapy

A brief psychotherapy developed by Anthony Ryle, which integrates a range of cognitive and analytical concepts and practices to help clients understand maladaptive patterns and their origins, and develop alternative strategies for living.

Cognitive-behavioural therapy (CBT)

A range of techniques and therapies that try to produce change by directly influencing thinking, behaviour, or both.

Cognitive restructuring

See cognitive therapy.

Cognitive therapy

A range of therapeutic practices that try to produce change by directly influencing thinking.

Cohen's *d*

A commonly used effect size measure, indicating the amount of difference between two groups relative to 'background' variation: a *d* of 0.2 can be considered 'small', a *d* of 0.5 'medium,' and a *d* of 0.8 'large'.

Coital alignment technique

A sexual position which is designed to improve a woman's chance of orgasm during genital intercourse.

Communication training

See social skills training.

Community reinforcement approaches

A therapeutic programme for substance-abuse problems which uses a range of behavioural strategies to increase individual and social rewards for sobriety, while reducing rewards for drinking.

Comorbidity

The presence of more than one form of severe psychological distress in an individual at the same time.

Complicated grief (aka pathological grief)

A grief response that is of greater intensity than normal, has a longer duration, is associated with more complications, and interferes more with daily functioning.

Component studies

Studies which look at the efficacy of particular aspects of therapeutic practice: 'additive' designs look at the effect of adding a particular practice, while 'dismantling' designs look at the effect of taking away a particular practice.

Congruence

Being freely and deeply oneself in a relationship, with one's experiences accurately represented in awareness.

Contingency management

A behavioural therapeutic approach which uses positive rewards to reinforce the achievement of positive changes.

Control group

A group of individuals with characteristics similar to those in the 'experimental group', but who do not participate in the procedure being tested.

Coping skills training

A range of techniques and therapeutic programmes that aim to help clients develop their abilities to cope with particular stressors or difficult situations.

Correlation

The degree of association between two variables, ranging from 1 (total positive association) to −1 (total negative association), with 0 indicating no relationship between the two variables.

Countertransference

Therapists' reactions to clients that are based on therapists' unresolved conflicts.

Cue exposure

A form of behavioural therapy for substance-use problems, in which clients are exposed to stimuli associated with the problematic behaviour (for instance, a syringe or a wine glass) until the desire to use subsides.

Dance movement therapy

A form of psychotherapeutic practice based around the use of movement and dance.

Debriefing

A single-session early intervention in which traumatised individuals are encouraged to process their experience emotionally through recollection or reworking of the traumatic event.

Depression (aka major depression/depressive disorder, unipolar depression)

A mood disorder characterised by the existence of one or more depressive episodes (in the absence of manic episodes), in which the person experiences low mood or loss of interest, accompanied by such symptoms as low energy, changes in appetite, poor concentration, feelings of guilt or worthlessness, and suicidal ideation.

Dialectical behaviour therapy (DBT)

A third-generation CBT developed by Marsha Linehan and colleagues for the treatment of borderline personality disorder, which emphasises behavioural change, self-acceptance and emotional regulation.

Dramatherapy

A psychotherapeutic practice that incorporates such media as performance, drama games and improvisational exercises.

Drop-out

Generally defined as failure to attend a last scheduled visit, or as withdrawing from therapy before a therapist thinks it is advisable.

DSM

One of the most widely used systems of diagnosis: *The Diagnostic and Statistical Manual of Mental Disorders* of the American Psychiatric Association; now in its 4th edition ('*DSM-IV*').

Duluth model

A feminist-informed, psycho-educational group intervention for male perpetrators of domestic violence.

Eating disorders

A group of psychological difficulties characterised by compulsions to eat, or to not eat, in ways which disturb physical and psychological wellbeing.

Effect size

A measure of the strength of relationship between two variables (for the purposes of this book, used synonymously with Cohen's *d*).

Effectiveness

The extent to which an intervention, when used under ordinary circumstances, brings about a desired effect.

Efficacy

The potential to bring about a desired effect.

Emotion-focused therapy

See process-experiential therapy.

Empathy

Entering the private perceptual world of another and having an accurate, felt understanding of their experiencing.

Empirical

Based on concrete experiences or observations as opposed to purely theoretical conjecture: not to be confused with 'empiricism', a branch of philosophy that considers experiences or observations as the only true source of knowledge.

Experiential therapies

See humanistic therapies.

Exposure

A set of behavioural therapeutic techniques in which anxiety is purposefully evoked through confrontation with a situation that produces fear.

Exposure and response-prevention treatment

Confrontation with feared situation while being encouraged to desist from engaging in ritual or compulsive behaviours.

Eye-movement desensitisation and reprocessing (EMDR)

A psychological treatment aimed to help clients overcome distress associated with traumatic experiences, in which clients are invited to focus on an external stimulus, such as a moving object in front of their eyes, while attending to emotionally disturbing material.

Family therapy

A set of therapeutic practices which focus on 'treating' the family rather than any one specific individual.

Feedback

Information provided to a person, from an external source, about the person's behaviour or the effects of that behaviour.

Generalised anxiety disorder

An anxiety disorder characterised by excessive and uncontrollable worry over everyday things, such that daily functioning is impeded.

Gestalt therapy

A humanistic, relationally orientated psychotherapy which invites clients to participate in a range of creative 'experiments' (such as two-chair dialogue) to help them develop their here-and-now awareness and live more fully in the moment.

Grief

Distress resulting from a bereavement.

Hierarchy of evidence

A means of grading the strength of evidence, based on the presumed susceptibility of research findings to bias. The following hierarchy (in descending order of importance), outlined by Eccles et al. (1998), is used as the basis for the UK Department of Health's (2001: 18) clinical practice guidelines for psychological therapies and counselling, and is the approximate order of weighting for the present text:

Ia   Evidence from meta-analysis of randomised controlled trials
Ib   Evidence from at least one randomised controlled trial
IIa   Evidence from at least one study without randomisation
IIb   Evidence from at least one other type of quasi-experimental study
III   Evidence from descriptive studies, such as comparative studies, correlation studies, and case-control studies
IV   Evidence from expert committee reports or opinions, or clinical experience of respected authority or both.

Humanistic therapies

A family of psychological therapies which place particular emphasis on drawing on clients' strengths and resources, and which tend to adopt a strongly relational stance.

Hypnosis

A method used to induce a trance-like state of heightened suggestibility.

Hypnotherapy

Any therapy that uses hypnosis as a main technique.

Hypothesis

A tentative explanation of certain observations or facts.

Imaginal exposure

Therapeutic confrontation with a visualised image of the situation that produces fear.

***In vivo* exposure**

Therapeutic confrontation with the actual situation that produces fear.

Inpatient

A patient who resides at the institute in which he or she is being treated.

Interoceptive exposure

Therapeutic confrontation with the bodily symptoms that produce fear.

Interpersonal therapy (IPT)

A structured therapy that evolved, primarily for research purposes, to put into practice the basic principles of an interpersonal approach to psychodynamic therapy.

Interpretations

Therapist statements which go beyond what the client has overtly recognised to suggest new understandings of experiences.

Masturbation training

A treatment approach in which women (or men) are encouraged to learn about their bodies and relax to the point that they can experience orgasm.

Mean

The mathematic average of a set of scores, calculated by summing the scores and dividing by the number of scores.

Mediating variable

A factor that accounts for the relationship between two variables.

Meta-analysis

A statistical procedure which pools findings from different studies to estimate overall effects.

Mindfulness-based cognitive therapy

A third-generation CBT programme for clients with 'treatment-resistant' depression, which teaches them meditation skills to help them disengage from dysfunctional thought patterns.

Moderating variable

A factor that affects the relationship between two variables.

Motivational enhancement therapy

A time-limited, four-session adaptation of motivational interviewing, in which clients are given feedback based on individual results from standardised assessment measures.

Motivational interviewing

A client-centred but semi-directive therapeutic style that works to enhance clients' intrinsic motivations to change.

Music therapy

A form of psychotherapy in which practitioners interact with their clients through a variety of musical media, such as music-making, singing and listening to music.

National Institute of Mental Health Treatment of Depression Collaborative Research Program (NIMH TDCRP)

One of the largest and most discussed randomised controlled trials in the counselling and psychotherapy field, conducted in the 1980s, which compared the efficacy of CBT, interpersonal therapy, anti-depressant treatment and a placebo control for the treatment of depression.

Neurolinguistic programming (NLP)

A contemporary therapeutic approach emphasising, among other things, modelling individuals who achieve excellence, and matching therapists' communications to clients' 'preferred representational system'.

Non-directive counselling

See person-centred therapy.

Non-directivity

A therapeutic stance in which the practitioner tries to refrain from directing his or her client in any particular way.

Obesity

An eating disorder in which there is a high body-weight due to an excessive accumulation of fat.

Obsessive–compulsive disorder

An anxiety disorder characterised by intense, recurrent, unwanted thoughts and rituals.

Outpatient

A patient who does not reside at the institute in which he or she is being treated.

p-value

The probability that a particular difference between groups has come about by chance.

Panic control treatment

A therapeutic treatment for panic disorder which uses a range of cognitive and behavioural strategies.

Panic disorder

An anxiety disorder characterised by episodes of intense fear or anxiety, often accompanied by physical symptoms, such as rapid heartbeat and dizziness: the frequent co-existence of panic disorder with agoraphobia (the fear of being in public places from which escape might be difficult) means that panic disorders are sometimes categorised in terms of being with, or without, agoraphobia.

Paradoxical interventions

Therapeutic interventions in which therapists seem to take an 'anti-therapeutic' stance *vis-à-vis* the client's problems.

Person-centred therapy (aka client-centred therapy)

A humanistic therapy characterised by a relatively non-directive therapeutic stance, with a strong emphasis on the provision of an empathic, accepting and honest therapeutic relationship.

Personality disorders

Constellations of relatively enduring, maladaptive traits that can result in significant subjective distress and functional impairment: see Table 4.1 for the *DSM-IV* taxonomy of personality disorders.

Positive regard

A warm acceptance of the other and their experiences without conditions.

Post-traumatic stress disorder

An anxiety disorder that follows from the experiencing of a traumatic or highly stressful event, characterised by intrusive and distressing memories of the event, jumpiness, numbness, and attempts to avoid anything associated with memories of the event.

Predilection

Clients' beliefs about the origins of their distress and what they expect will be helpful to them.

Premature ejaculation

A sexual dysfunction characterised by the inability to delay ejaculation for as long as would be wanted.

Problem-solving therapy

A behavioural therapeutic programme in which clients are taught a set of skills that can be used to address problems and difficulties effectively.

Process-experiential therapy (aka **emotion-focused therapy**)

A relatively new form of humanistic therapy, which incorporates a range of gestalt and related techniques into a person-centred, relational foundation.

Project MATCH

The largest randomised trial of verbal therapies to date, conducted in the 1990s, which examined the effectiveness of CBT, motivational enhancement therapy and twelve-step facilitation for alcohol problems, finding equivalence across the therapies and little evidence of aptitude-treatment interactions.

Psychoanalysis

A form of psychodynamic psychotherapy that adheres closely to Freud's original formulations, with two or more sessions per week and treatment duration of a year or more.

Psychodrama

A form of dramatherapy in which participants have an opportunity to explore, through enactment in a group, problems and issues in their lives.

Psychodynamic therapy

A family of psychological therapies which aim to help clients develop a greater awareness and understanding of the unconscious forces determining their thoughts, feelings and behaviours.

Psycho-education

A range of educational strategies used to inform people about their problems and how to overcome them.

Psychological mindedness

A person's ability to understand people and their problems in psychological terms.

Qualitative research

Language-based research, in which experiences, perceptions, observations, etc. are not reduced to numerical form.

Quantitative research

Number-based research, generally incorporating statistical analysis.

Randomisation

The process of assigning research participants to treatment or control conditions by chance, to minimise the likelihood of systematic differences between groups.

Randomised controlled trial (RCT) (aka randomised clinical trial)

An experimental study in which participants are randomly assigned to two or more groups, such that the efficacy of the different interventions can be identified.

Rational emotive behaviour therapy (REBT)

An early form of cognitive-behavioural therapy which puts particular emphasis on the disputation of irrational or dysfunctional beliefs.

Relapse

A term drawn from the medical field, indicating a return to psychological ill-health following a period of improvement.

Relapse prevention

Therapeutic programmes incorporating a range of behavioural and cognitive strategies to try to help clients refrain from relapsing into problematic patterns of behaving, thinking or feeling.

Relaxation training

See applied relaxation.

Reliable improvement

Positive change on an indicator of psychological distress that cannot be attributed to random measurement error.

Research

A systematic process of inquiry that leads to the development of new knowledge.

Researcher allegiance effects

The tendency for researchers to 'find' results that support their own beliefs, expectations or preferences.

Resistance

Client behaviour that exhibits a reluctance to participate in the tasks of therapy.

Schizophrenia

A severe form of psychological distress characterised by 'positive symptoms' (such as hallucinations) and 'negative symptoms' (such as emotional withdrawal).

Self-disclosure

Therapist statements that reveal something personal about the therapist.

Self-harm (aka self-injury)

Deliberate injury or hurt inflicted by a person upon her or his own body.

Self-involving statements

A form of self-disclosure, in which the therapist expresses a personal response to the client in the here-and-now.

Sensate focus exercises

A series of exercises aimed to address sexual difficulties, which encourage partners to take turns paying attention to their own sensations.

Significant difference

A meaningful and important difference between two or more groups that is unlikely to be due to chance variations.

Social phobia (aka 'social anxiety')

An intense and persistent fear of being evaluated negatively by others.

Social skills training

An individual or group behaviour therapy practice, in which individuals are taught to communicate and relate more effectively.

Solution-focused brief therapy

A contemporary therapeutic approach that uses a range of strategies to help clients focus on strengths and solutions rather than problems.

Specific phobias (aka 'simple phobias')

A group of anxiety disorders characterised by an excessive fear of specific objects or situations, such as chickens ('alektorophobia').

Squeeze technique

A technique commonly employed for premature ejaculation, in which pressure is applied to the penis to retard ejaculation.

Standard deviation

A measure of the spread of a set of data, larger standard deviations meaning that the scores are more dispersed.

Substance abuse

Excessive use of, and dependence on, a psychoactive substance, leading to detrimental effects on an individual's mental or physical wellbeing.

Supportive-expressive therapy

A short-term, psychodynamically derived therapy that combines interpretative interventions with supportive, alliance-fostering techniques.

Systematic desensitisation

Gradual exposure to a feared stimulus, generally in imagination, while in a state of deep muscle relaxation.

Therapeutic alliance

The quality and the strength of the collaborative relationship between therapist and client.

Therapeutic technique

A well-defined procedure implemented to accomplish a particular task or goal.

Third-generation cognitive-behaviour therapies (aka third-generation behaviour therapies)

A new wave of cognitive-behavioural therapies which, although highly structured and focused on behaviour change, tend to emphasise an acceptance, and mindfulness, of cognitions and experiences, as opposed to the suppression or control of 'negative' thoughts.

Transactional analysis

A therapeutic orientation based around a number of specific psychological concepts developed by Eric Berne and colleagues in the mid-twentieth century, incorporating psychodynamic, humanistic and cognitive-behavioural elements.

Transference

The process of transferring to and repeating early patterns of behaviour with present-day partners.

Transference interpretations

Interpretations that help the patient to understand the link between their interactions with the therapist and the interactions they experience with others.

Twelve-step facilitation

A brief, structured approach to facilitating recovery from substance-use problems based on the principles of twelve-step programmes.

Vaginismus

A psychological problem in which the muscles around the vagina tighten involuntarily.

Virtual reality exposure

Confrontation with a simulated version of a feared object or situation: for instance, simulated flying.

Research Quiz Answers

1   A (see 'How much effect does counselling and psychotherapy have?', Chapter 2).
    If you are a trainee and you said C or D, you may be on the wrong course!
2   C (from Hansen et al., 2002). See 'How much therapy do clients need?', Chapter 2.
3   C (see Beutler and Castonguay, 2006; Castonguay et al., 2006). See 'Age and
    experience', Chapter 5.
4   B. This finding comes from a major study by King and colleagues (2000), which
    is discussed throughout the book.
5   B – in general, therapy tends to be better at helping clients capitalise on
    strengths rather than compensate for deficiencies. See 'Psychosocial functioning',
    Chapter 4.
6   C (Orlinsky et al., 1994). It can be tempting to assume that what therapists do, or
    how they relate to their clients, is the principal determinant of outcomes; but
    reviews of the research suggest that clients' active involvement in therapy is the
    best predictor of the effectiveness of therapy (see 'Motivation and involvement',
    Chapter 4).
7   A (see, for instance, Beutler et al., 2004; Mohr et al., 1991). This is known as an
    'aptitude-treatment' interaction (ATI), whereby different kinds of clients seem
    to do better in different kinds of therapies. See 'Aptitude-treatment interac-
    tions', Chapter 3, and 'Non-directivity', Chapter 7.
8   A (see Bedi et al., 2005). Surprising perhaps, but it shows that technical and
    relaional processes are often much more interlinked than we might imagine.
    See the introduction to Chapter 7.
9   A (see Gabbard et al., 1997). This would seem to be primarily due to the reduced
    inpatient costs, which is the primary cost-saving that psychological therapies
    bring about. See 'Cost-effectiveness', Chapter 2.
10 B (see Beutler et al., 2004) – many studies indicate that the sex of the therapist
    makes no difference to the outcomes of therapy, but where differences do exist,
    they generally favour female therapists. See 'Gender', Chapter 4.

QUESTIONS FOR REFLECTION

Having found out the correct answers to these questions, which of the answers, if any, surprised you?

- What had you expected the research to indicate?
- What might this say about your assumptions/biases?

References

Abbass, A., Hancock, J., Henderson, J. and Kisley, S. (2006) 'Short-term psychodynamic psychotherapies for common mental disorders', *Cochrane Database of Systematic Reviews* (4).

Ablon, J.S. and Jones, E.E. (1999) 'Psychotherapy process in the National Institute of Mental Health Treatment of Depression Collaborative Research Program', *Journal of Consulting and Clinical Psychology*, 67 (1): 64–75.

Abramowitz, J.S. (1996) 'Variants of exposure and response prevention in the treatment of obsessive–compulsive disorder: a meta-analysis', *Behavior Therapy*, 27 (4): 583–600.

Addis, M.E. and Jacobson, N.S. (1996) 'Reasons for depression and the process and outcome of cognitive-behavioral psychotherapies', *Journal of Consulting and Clinical Psychology*, 64 (6): 1417–24.

Addis, M.E. and Krasnow, A.D. (2000) 'A national survey of practicing psychologists' attitudes toward psychotherapy treatment manuals', *Journal of Consulting and Clinical Psychology*, 68 (2): 331–9.

Ahn, H.N. and Wampold, B.E. (2001) 'Where oh where are the specific ingredients? A meta-analysis of component studies in counseling and psychotherapy', *Journal of Counseling Psychology*, 48 (3): 251–7.

Ainsworth, M.D.S., Blehar, M.C., Waters, E. and Wall, S. (1978) *Patterns of Attachment: A Psychological Study of the Strange Situation*. Hillsdale, NJ: Lawrence Erlbaum.

Allen, J.G., Coyne, L., Colson, D.B., Horwitz, L., Gabbard, G.O., Frieswyk, S.H. et al. (1996) 'Pattern of therapist interventions associated with patient collaboration', *Psychotherapy*, 33 (2): 254–61.

Allumbaugh, D.L. and Hoyt, W.T. (1999) 'Effectiveness of grief therapy: a metaanalysis', *Journal of Counseling Psychology*, 46 (3): 370–80.

Andersen, B. and Anderson, W. (1985) 'Client perceptions of counselors using positive and negative self-involving statements', *Journal of Counseling Psychology*, 32 (3): 462–5.

Anderson, E.M. and Lambert, M.J. (1995) 'Short-term dynamically oriented psychotherapy: a review and meta-analysis', *Clinical Psychology Review*, 15 (6): 503–14.

Andrusyna, T.P., Luborsky, L., Pham, T. and Tang, T.Z. (2006) 'The mechanisms of sudden gains in Supportive-Expressive therapy for depression', *Psychotherapy Research*, 16 (5): 526–35.

Antonuccio, D.O., Lewinsohn, P.M. and Steinmetz, J.L. (1982) 'Identification of therapist differences in a group treatment for depression', *Journal of Consulting and Clinical Psychology*, 50 (3): 433–5.

Antony, M.M. and Roemer, L. (2003) 'Behavior therapy', in A.S. Gurman and S.B. Messer (eds), *Essential Psychotherapies: Theory and Practice* (2nd edn). New York: Guilford Press, pp. 182–223.

APA (2006) 'Evidence-based practice in psychology', *American Psychologist*, 61 (4): 271–85.

Aronson, E., Wilson, T.D. and Akert, R.M. (1999) *Social Psychology*. New York: Longman.

Asay, T.P. and Lambert, M.J. (1999) 'The empirical case for the common factors in therapy: quantitative findings', in M. Hubble, B.L. Duncan and S.D. Miller (eds), *The Heart and Soul of Change: What Works in Therapy*. Washington, DC: American Psychological Association, pp. 33–55.

Asay, T.P. and Lambert, M.J. (2002) 'Therapist relational variables', in D.J. Cain and J. Seeman (eds), *Humanistic Psychotherapies: Handbook of Theory and Practice*. Washington, DC: American Psychological Association, pp. 531–57.

Atkinson, D.R., Worthington, R.L., Dana, D.M. and Good, G.E. (1991) 'Etiology beliefs, preferences for counseling orientations, and counseling effectiveness', *Journal of Counseling Psychology*, 38 (3): 258–64.

Attkisson, C.C. and Greenfield, T.K. (1994) 'Client Satisfaction Questionnaire–8 and Service Satisfaction Scale–30', in M.E. Maruish (ed.), *The Use of Psychological Testing for Treatment Planning and Outcome Assessment*. Hillsdale, NJ: Lawrence Erlbaum, pp. 402–20.

Babcock, J.C., Green, C.E. and Robie, C. (2004) 'Does batterers' treatment work? A meta-analytic review of domestic violence treatment', *Clinical Psychology Review*, 23 (8): 1023–53.

Bacaltchuk, J., Hay, P. and Trefiglio, R. (2001) 'Antidepressants versus psychological treatments and their combination for bulimia nervosa (Review)', *Cochrane Database of Systematic Reviews* (4).

Bach, P. and Hayes, S.C. (2002) 'The use of acceptance and commitment therapy to prevent the rehospitalization of psychotic patients: a randomized controlled trial', *Journal of Consulting and Clinical Psychology*, 70 (5): 1129–39.

Bachelor, A. (1988) 'How clients perceive therapist empathy: a content analysis of "received" empathy', *Psychotherapy: Theory, Research, Practice, Training*, 25(2): 227–40.

Bachelor, A. (1991) 'Comparison and relationship to outcome of diverse dimensions of the helping alliance as seen by client and therapist', *Psychotherapy: Theory, Research, Practice, Training*, 28 (4): 534–49.

Bachelor, A. and Hovarth, A. (1999) 'The therapeutic relationship', in M. Hubble, B.L. Duncan and S.D. Miller (eds), *The Heart and Soul of Change: What Works in Therapy*. Washington, DC: American Psychological Association, pp. 133–78.

Bakker, A., Spinhoven, P., van Balkom, A., Vleugel, L. and van Dyck, R. (2000) 'Cognitive therapy by allocation versus cognitive therapy by preference in the treatment of panic disorder', *Psychotherapy and Psychosomatics*, 69 (5): 240–43.

Baldwin, S.A., Wampold, B.E. and Imel, Z.E. (2007) 'Untangling the alliance-outcome correlation: exploring the relative importance of therapist and patient variability in the alliance', *Journal of Consulting and Clinical Psychology*, 75 (6): 842–52.

Balestrieri, M., Willams, P. and Wilkinson, G. (1988) 'Specialist mental health treatment in general practice: a meta-analysis', *Psychological Medicine*, 18: 711–17.

Ball, S.A., Martino, S., Nich, C., Frankforter, T.L., Van Horn, D., Crits-Christoph, P. et al. (2007) 'Site matters: multisite randomized trial of motivational enhancement therapy in community drug abuse clinics', *Journal of Consulting and Clinical Psychology*, 75 (4): 556–67.

Balmforth, J. (2006) 'Clients' experiences of how perceived differences in social class between counsellor and client affect the therapeutic relationship', in G. Proctor, M. Cooper, P. Sanders and B. Malcolm (eds), *Politicising the Person-Centred Approach: An Agenda for Social Change*. Ross-on-Wye: PCCS Books, pp. 215–24.

Bambling, M., King, R., Raue, P., Schweitzer, R. and Lambert, W. (2006) 'Clinical supervision: its influence on client-rated working alliance and client symptom reduction in the brief treatment of major depression', *Psychotherapy Research*, 16 (3): 317–31.

Bannink, F.P. (2007) 'Solution-focused brief therapy', *Journal of Contemporary Psychotherapy*, 37 (2): 87–94.

Barak, A., Hen, L., Boniel-Nissim, M. and Shapira, N. (in press) 'A comprehensive review and a meta-analysis of the effectiveness of internet-based psychotherapeutic interventions', *Journal of Technology in Human Services*.

Barker, C.B., Pistrang, N. and Elliott, R. (2002) *Research Methods in Clinical Psychology: An Introduction for Students and Practitioners* (2nd edn). Chichester: John Wiley.

Barkham, M. and Shapiro, D.A. (1986) 'Counselor verbal response-modes and experienced empathy', *Journal of Counseling Psychology*, 33 (1): 3–10.

Barkham, M., Rees, A., Stiles, W.B., Shapiro, D.A., Hardy, G.E. and Reynolds, S. (1996) 'Dose-effect relations in time-limited psychotherapy for depression', *Journal of Consulting and Clinical Psychology*, 64 (5): 927–35.

Barrett, M.S. and Berman, J.S. (2001) 'Is psychotherapy more effective when therapists disclose information about themselves?' *Journal of Consulting and Clinical Psychology*, 69 (4): 597–603.

Barrett-Lennard, G.T. (1986) 'The relationship inventory now: issues and advances in theory, method and use', in L.S. Greenberg and W.M. Pinsof (eds), *The Psychotherapeutic Process: A Research Handbook*. New York: Guilford Press, pp. 439–76.

Barrett-Lennard, G.T. (2003) 'Measuring experienced relationship: an odyssey (1957–2003)', in *Steps on a Mindful Journey*. Ross-on-Wye: PCCS Books, Chapter 8.

Bateman, A. and Fonagy, P. (1999) 'Effectiveness of partial hospitalization in the treatment of borderline personality disorder: a randomized controlled trial', *American Journal of Psychiatry*, 156 (10): 1563–9.

Bateman, A. and Fonagy, P. (2001) 'Treatment of borderline personality disorder with psychoanalytically oriented partial hospitalization: an 18-month follow-up', *American Journal of Psychiatry*, 158 (1): 36–42.

Bates, Y. (ed.) (2006) *Shouldn't I be Feeling Better by Now?* London: Palgrave.

Baucom, D.H., Shoham, V., Meuser, K.T., Daiuto, A.D. and Stickle, T.R. (1998) 'Empirically supported couple and family interventions for marital distress and adult mental health problems', *Journal of Consulting and Clinical Psychology*, 66 (1): 53–88.

Baumeister, R.F. (1991) *Meanings of Life*. New York: Guilford Press.

Beck, A.T., John, R.A., Shaw, B.F. and Emery, G. (1979) *Cognitive Therapy of Depression*. New York: Guilford Press.

Bedi, R.P., Davis, M.D. and Williams, M. (2005) 'Critical incidents in the formation of the therapeutic alliance from the client's perspective', *Psychotherapy: Theory, Research, Practice, Training*, 42 (3): 311–23.

Bednar, R.L., Melnick, J. and Kaul, T.J. (1974) 'Risk, responsibility, and structure: a conceptual framework for initiating group counseling and psychotherapy', *Journal of Counseling Psychology*, 21 (1): 31–7.

Bende, B. and Crossley, D. (2000) 'Psychotherapy patients' views of treatment: on learning from the patient', *Psychiatric Bulletin*, 24 (12): 453–6.

Berman, J.S. and Norton, N.C. (1985) 'Does professional training make a therapist more effective?' *Psychological Bulletin*, 98 (2): 401–7.

Beutler, L.E. and Castonguay, L.G. (2006) 'The task force on empirically based principles of change', in L.G. Castonguay and L.E. Beutler (eds), *Principles of Therapeutic Change that Work*. New York: Oxford University Press, pp. 3–10.

Beutler, L.E., Castonguay, L.G. and Follette, W.C. (2006) 'Integration of therapeutic factors in dysphoric disorders', in L.G. Castonguay and L.E. Beutler (eds), *Principles of Therapeutic Change that Work*. New York: Oxford University Press, pp. 111–7.

Beutler, L.E., Blatt, S.J., Alimohamed, S., Levy, K.N. and Angtuaco, L. (2006) 'Participant factors in treating dysphoric disorders', in L.G. Castonguay and L.E. Beutler (eds), *Principles of Therapeutic Change that Work*. New York: Oxford University Press, pp. 13–63.

Beutler, L.E., Machado, P.P.P., Engle, D. and Mohr, D. (1993) 'Differential patient × treatment maintenance among cognitive, experiential, and self-directed psychotherapies', *Journal of Psychotherapy Integration*, 3 (1): 15–31.

Beutler, L.E., Malik, M., Alimohamed, S., Harwood, M.T., Talebi, H., Noble, S. et al. (2004) 'Therapist variables', in M.J. Lambert (ed.), *Bergin and Garfield's Handbook of Psychotherapy and Behavior Change* (5th edn). Chicago: John Wiley & Sons, pp. 227–306.

Beutler, L.E., Mohr, D.C., Grawe, K., Engle, D. and MacDonald, R. (1991) 'Looking for differential treatment effects: cross-cultural predictors of differential psychotherapy efficacy', *Journal of Psychotherapy Integration*, 1 (2): 121–41.

Beutler, L.E., Engle, D., Mohr, D., Daldrup, R.J., Bergan, J., Meredith, K. et al. (1991) 'Predictors of differential response to cognitive, experiential, and self-directed psychotherapeutic procedures', *Journal of Consulting and Clinical Psychology*, 59 (2): 333–40.

Binks, C.A., Fenton, M., McCarthy, L., Lee, T., Adams, C.E. and Duggan, C. (2006) 'Psychological therapies for people with borderline personality disorder', *Cochrane Database of Systematic Reviews* (1).

Birmaher, B., Brent, D.A., Kolko, D., Baugher, M., Bridge, J., Holder, D. et al. (2000) 'Clinical outcome after short-term psychotherapy for adolescents with major depressive disorder', *Archives of General Psychiatry*, 57 (1): 29–36.

Bischoff, M.M. and Tracey, T.J.G. (1995) 'Client resistance as predicted by therapist behavior: a study of sequential dependence', *Journal of Counseling Psychology*, 42 (4): 487–95.

Bisson, J.I., Jenkins, P.L., Alexander, J. and Bannister, C. (1997) 'Randomised controlled trial of psychological debriefing for victims of acute burn trauma', *British Journal of Psychiatry*, 171 (1): 78–81.

Blatt, S.J., Quinlan, D.M., Pilkonis, P.A. and Shea, M.T. (1995) 'Impact of perfectionism and need for approval on the brief treatment of depression – the National Institute of Mental Health Treatment of Depression Collaborative Research Program Revisited', *Journal of Consulting and Clinical Psychology*, 63 (1): 125–32.

Blatt, S.J., Sanislow, C.A., Zuroff, D.C. and Pilkonis, P.A. (1996) 'Characteristics of effective therapists: further analyses of data from the National Institute of Mental Health Treatment of Depression Collaborative Research Program', *Journal of Consulting and Clinical Psychology*, 64 (6): 1276–84.

Blatt, S.J., Zuroff, D.C., Bondi, C.M., Sanislow, C.A. and Pilkonis, P.A. (1998) 'When and how perfectionism impedes the brief treatment of depression: further analyses of the National Institute of Mental Health Treatment of Depression Collaborative Research Program', *Journal of Consulting and Clinical Psychology*, 66 (2): 423–8.

Blowers, C., Cobb, J. and Mathews, A. (1987) 'Generalised anxiety: a controlled treatment study', *Behaviour Research and Therapy*, 25 (6): 493–502.

Boelen, P.A., de Keijser, J., van den Hout, M.A. and van den Bout, J. (2007) 'Treatment of complicated grief: a comparison between cognitive-behavioral therapy and supportive counseling', *Journal of Consulting and Clinical Psychology*, 75 (2): 277–84.

Bohart, A.C. (1980) 'Toward a cognitive theory of catharsis', *Psychotherapy: Theory, Research, Practice, Training*, 17 (2): 192–201.

Bohart, A.C. and Greenberg, L.S. (eds) (1997) *Empathy Reconsidered: New Directions in Psychotherapy*. Washington, DC: American Psychological Association.

Bohart, A.C. and Tallman, K. (1999) *How Clients Make Therapy Work: The Process of Active Self-Healing*. Washington: American Psychological Association.

Bohart, A.C., Elliott, R., Greenberg, L.S. and Watson, J.C. (2002) 'Empathy', in J.C. Norcross (ed.), *Psychotherapy Relationships that Work: Therapist Contributions and Responsiveness to Patients*. New York: Oxford University Press, pp. 89–108.

Boisvert, C.M. and Faust, D. (2006) 'Practicing psychologists' knowledge of general psychotherapy research findings: implications for science–practice relations', *Professional Psychology: Research and Practice*, 37 (6): 708–16.

Bond, M., Banon, E. and Grenier, M. (1998) 'Differential effects of interventions on the therapeutic alliance with patients with personality disorders', *Journal of Psychotherapy Practice and Research*, 7 (4): 301–18.

Bongartz, W., Flammer, E. and Schwonke, R. (2002) 'Efficiency of hypnosis. A meta-analytic study', *Psychotherapeut*, 47 (2): 67–76.

Booth, R. and Rachman, S. (1992) 'The reduction of claustrophobia – I', *Behaviour Research and Therapy*, 30 (3): 207–21.

Bordin, E.S. (1979) 'The generalizability of the psychoanalytic concept of the working alliance', *Psychotherapy: Theory, Research, Practice, Training*, 16 (3): 252–60.

Bowers, A.M.V. and Bieschke, K.J. (2005) 'Psychologists' clinical evaluations and attitudes: an examination of the influence of gender and sexual orientation', *Professional Psychology: Research and Practice*, 36 (1): 97–103.

Bowlby, J. (1979) 'The making and breaking of affectional bonds', in *The Making and Breaking of Affectional Bonds*. London: Routledge, pp. 150–201.

Bradley, R., Greene, J., Russ, E., Dutra, L. and Westen, D. (2005) 'A multidimensional meta-analysis of psychotherapy for PTSD', *American Journal of Psychiatry*, 162 (2): 214–27.

Bratton, S.C., Ray, D., Rhine, T. and Jones, L. (2005) 'The efficacy of play therapy with children: a meta-analytic review of treatment outcomes', *Professional Psychology: Research and Practice*, 36 (4): 376–90.

British Association for Counselling and Psychotherapy (2007) *Ethical Framework for Good Practice in Counselling and Psychotherapy*. Rugby: BACP.

Brogan, M.M., Prochaska, J.O. and Prochaska, J.M. (1999) 'Predicting termination and continuation status in psychotherapy using the transtheoretical model', *Psychotherapy: Theory, Research, Practice, Training*, 36 (2): 105–13.

Burckell, L.A. and Goldfried, M.R. (2006) 'Therapist qualities preferred by sexual-minority individuals', *Psychotherapy: Theory, Research, Practice, Training*, 43 (1): 32–49.

Burke, B.L., Arkowitz, H. and Menchola, M. (2003) 'The efficacy of motivational interviewing: a meta-analysis of controlled clinical trials', *Journal of Consulting and Clinical Psychology*, 71 (5): 843–61.

Burlingame, G.M., Fuhriman, A. and Johnson, J.E. (2002) 'Cohesion in group psychotherapy', in J.C. Norcross (ed.), *Psychotherapy Relationships that Work: Therapist Contributions and Responsiveness to Patients*. New York: Oxford University Press, pp. 71–87.

Burns, D.D. and Spangler, D.L. (2000) 'Does psychotherapy homework lead to improvements in depression in cognitive-behavioral therapy or does improvement lead to increased homework compliance?' *Journal of Consulting and Clinical Psychology*, 68 (1): 46–56.

Burns, D.D. and Spangler, D.L. (2001) 'Do changes in dysfunctional attitudes mediate changes in depression and anxiety in cognitive behavioral therapy?' *Behavior Therapy*, 32 (2): 337–69.

Bury, C., Raval, H. and Lyon, L. (2007) 'Young people's experiences of individual psychoanalytic psychotherapy', *Psychology and Psychotherapy: Theory, Research and Practice*, 80 (1): 79–96.

Campbell, T.A. (2007) 'Psychological assessment, diagnosis, and treatment of torture survivors: a review', *Clinical Psychology Review*, 27 (5): 628–41.

Carey, T., Carey, M., Stalker, K., Mullan, R., Murray, L. and Spratt, M. (2007) 'Psychological change from the inside looking out: a qualitative investigation', *Counselling and Psychotherapy Research*, 7 (3): 178–87.

Carlbring, P., Gunnarsdottir, M., Hedensjo, L., Andersson, G., Ekselius, L. and Furmark, T. (2007) 'Treatment of social phobia: randomised trial of internet-delivered cognitive-behavioural therapy with telephone support', *British Journal of Psychiatry*, 190 (2): 123–8.

Carlbring, P., Nilsson-Ihrfelt, E., Waara, J., Kollenstam, C., Buhrman, M., Kaldo, V. et al. (2005) 'Treatment of panic disorder: live therapy vs. self-help via the Internet', *Behaviour Research and Therapy*, 43 (10): 1321–33.

Carr, A. (2007) *The Effectiveness of Psychotherapy: A Review of Research*. Dublin: Irish Council for Psychotherapy.

Carroll, K.M. (1996) 'Relapse prevention as a psychosocial treatment: a review of controlled clinical trials', *Experimental and Clinical Psychopharmacology*, 4 (1): 46–54.

Castonguay, L.G. and Beutler, L.E. (2006a) 'Common and unique principles of therapeutic change: What do we know and what do we need to know?' in L.G. Castonguay and L.E. Beutler (eds), *Principles of Therapeutic Change that Work*. New York: Oxford University Press, pp. 353–69.

Castonguay, L.G. and Beutler, L.E. (eds) (2006b) *Principles of Therapeutic Change that Work*. New York: Oxford University Press.

Castonguay, L.G., Goldfried, M.R., Wiser, S., Raue, P.J. and Hayes, A.M. (1996) 'Predicting the effect of cognitive therapy for depression: a study of unique and common factors', *Journal of Consulting and Clinical Psychology*, 64 (3): 497–504.

Castonguay, L.G., Gross Holtforth, M., Coombs, M.M., Beberman, R.A., Kakouros, A.A., Boswell, J.F. et al. (2006) 'Relationship factors in treating dysphoric disorders', in L.G. Castonguay and L.E. Beutler (eds), *Principles of Therapeutic Change that Work*. Oxford: Oxford University Press, pp. 65–81.

Chambless, D.L. (2002) 'Beware the Dodo bird: the dangers of overgeneralization', *Clinical Psychology: Science and Practice*, 9 (1): 13–6.

Chambless, D.L. and Hollon, S.D. (1998) 'Defining empirically supported therapies', *Journal of Consulting and Clinical Psychology*, 66 (1): 7–18.

Chambless, D.L. and Ollendick, T.H. (2001) 'Empirically supported psychological interventions: controversies and evidence', *Annual Review of Psychology*, 52: 685–716.

Chambless, D.L., Sanderson, W.C., Shoham, V., Bennett Johnson, S., Pope, K.S. et al. (1996) 'An update on empirically validated therapies', *The Clinical Psychologist*, 49 (4): 5–18.

Chiles, J.A., Lambert, M.J. and Hatch, A.L. (1999) 'The impact of psychological interventions on medical cost offset: a meta-analytic review', *Clinical Psychology: Science and Practice*, 6 (2): 204–20.

Chilvers, C., Dewey, M., Fielding, K., Gretton, V., Miller, P., Palmer, B. et al. (2001) 'Antidepressant drugs and generic counselling for treatment of major depression in primary care: randomised trial with patient preference arms', *British Medical Journal*, 322 (7289): 772–5.

Choy, Y., Fyer, A.J. and Lipsitz, J.D. (2007) 'Treatment of specific phobia in adults', *Clinical Psychology Review*, 27 (3): 266–86.

Christensen, A. and Jacobson, N.S. (1994) 'Who (or what) can do psychotherapy: the status and challenge of nonprofessional therapies', *Psychological Science*, 5 (1): 8–14.

Christensen, L.B. (1997) *Experimental Methodology* (7th edn). London: Allyn & Bacon.

Claiborn, C.D., Goodyear, R.K. and Horner, P.A. (2002) 'Feedback', in J.C. Norcross (ed.), *Psychotherapy Relationships that Work: Therapist Contributions and Responsiveness to Patients*. New York: Oxford University Press, pp. 217–33.

Clark, D.M., Salkovskis, P.M., Hackmann, A., Middleton, H., Anastasiades, P. and Gelder, M. (1994) 'A comparison of cognitive therapy, applied relaxation and Imipramine in the treatment of panic disorder', *British Journal of Psychiatry*, 164 (6): 759–69.

Clarke, H., Rees, A. and Hardy, G.E. (2004) 'The big idea: clients' perspectives of change processes in cognitive therapy', *Psychology and Psychotherapy: Theory, Research and Practice*, 77 (1): 67–89.

Clarkin, J.F. and Levy, K.N. (2004) 'The influence of client variables on psychotherapy', in M.J. Lambert (ed.), *Bergin and Garfield's Handbook of Psychotherapy and Behavior Change* (5th edn). Chicago: John Wiley & Sons, pp. 194–226.

Compas, B.E., Haaga, D.A.F., Keefe, F.J., Leitenberg, H. and Williams, D.A. (1998) 'Sampling of empirically supported psychological treatments from health psychology: smoking, chronic pain, cancer, and bulimia nervosa', *Journal of Consulting and Clinical Psychology*, 66 (1): 89–112.

Connell, J., Barkham, M., Cahill, J., Gilbody, S. and Madill, A. (2006) *Counselling in Higher and Further Education: A Systematic Scoping Review*. Rugby: BACP.

Connolly, M.B., Crits-Christoph, P., Shappell, S., Barber, J.P., Luborsky, L. and Shaffer, C. (1999) 'Relation of transference interpretations to outcome in the early sessions of brief supportive-expressive psychotherapy', *Psychotherapy Research*, 9 (4): 485–95.

Consumer Reports (1995, November) 'Mental health: does therapy help?', 734–9.

Conte, H.R., Ratto, R., Clutz, K. and Karasu, T.B. (1995) 'Determinants of outpatients' satisfaction with therapists – relation to outcome', *Journal of Psychotherapy Practice and Research*, 4 (1): 43–51.

Cooper, M. (2001) 'Embodied empathy', in S. Haugh and T. Merry (eds), *Empathy*. Ross-on-Wye: PCCS Books, pp. 218–29.

Cooper, M. (2003) *Existential Therapies*. London: Sage.

Cooper, M. (2004) 'Viagra for the brain: psychotherapy research and the challenge of existential therapeutic practice', *Existential Analysis*, 15 (1): 2–14.

Cooper, M. (2006a) *Counselling in Schools Project Phase II: Evaluation Report*. Glasgow: Counselling Unit, University of Strathclyde.

Cooper, M. (2006b) 'Socialist humanism: a progressive politics for the twenty-first century', in G. Proctor, M. Cooper, P. Sanders and B. Malcolm (eds), *Politicising the Person-Centred Approach: An Agenda for Social Change*. Ross-on-Wye: PCCS Books, pp. 80–94.

Cooper, M. and McLeod, J. (2007) 'A pluralistic framework for counselling and psychotherapy: implications for research', *Counselling and Psychotherapy Research*, 7 (3): 135–43.

Cooper, M., Schmid, P., O'Hara, M. and Wyatt, G. (eds) (2007) *The Handbook of Person-Centred Psychotherapy and Counselling*. Basingstoke: Palgrave.

Craske, M.G., Maidenberg, E. and Bystritsky, A. (1995) 'Brief cognitive-behavioral versus nondirective therapy for panic disorder', *Journal of Behaviour Therapy and Experimental Psychiatry*, 26 (2): 113–20.

Craske, M.G., Rowe, M., Lewin, M. and Noriega-Dimitri, R. (1997) 'Interoceptive exposure versus breathing retraining within cognitive-behavioural therapy for panic disorder with agoraphobia', *British Journal of Clinical Psychology*, 36 (1): 85–99.

Crits-Christoph, P. and Gibbons, M.B.C. (2002) 'Relational interpretations', in J.C. Norcross (ed.), *Psychotherapy Relationships that Work: Therapist Contributions and Responsiveness to Patients*. New York: Oxford University Press, pp. 285–300.

Crits-Christoph, P., Barber, J.P. and Kurcias, J.S. (1993) 'The accuracy of therapists' interpretations and the development of the therapeutic alliance', *Psychotherapy Research*, 3 (1): 25–35.

Crits-Christoph, P., Cooper, A. and Luborsky, L. (1988) 'The accuracy of therapists' interpretations and the outcome of dynamic psychotherapy', *Journal of Consulting and Clinical Psychology*, 56 (4): 490–95.

Crits-Christoph, P., Baranackie, K., Kurcias, J.S., Carroll, K.M., Perry, K., Luborsky, L. et al. (1991) 'Meta-analysis of therapist effects in psychotherapy outcome studies', *Psychotherapy Research*, 1 (2): 81–91.

Crits-Christoph, P., Gibbons, M.B.C., Crits-Christoph, K., Narducci, J., Schamberger, M. and Gallop, R. (2006) 'Can therapists be trained to improve their alliances? A preliminary study of alliance-fostering psychotherapy', *Psychotherapy Research*, 16 (3): 268–81.

Crits-Christoph, P., Siqueland, L., Blaine, J., Frank, A., Luborsky, L., Onken, L.S. et al. (1999) 'Psychosocial treatments for cocaine dependence: National Institute on Drug Abuse Collaborative Cocaine Treatment Study', *Archives of General Psychiatry*, 56 (6): 493–502.

Cutler, R.L. (1958) 'Countertransference effects in psychotherapy', *Journal of Consulting Psychology*, 22 (5): 349–56.

Dance, K.A. and Neufeld, R.W. (1988) 'Aptitude-treatment interaction research in the clinical setting: a review of attempts to dispel the "patient uniformity" myth', *Psychological Bulletin*, 104 (2): 192–213.

Dare, C., Eisler, I., Russell, G., Treasure, J. and Dodge, L. (2001) 'Psychological therapies for adults with anorexia nervosa', *British Journal of Psychiatry*, 178 (3): 216–21.

Davidson, P.R. and Parker, K.C.H. (2001) 'Eye movement desensitization and reprocessing (EMDR): a meta-analysis', *Journal of Consulting and Clinical Psychology*, 69 (2): 305–16.

Dawe, S., Powell, J., Richards, D., Gossop, M., Marks, I., Strang, J. et al. (1993) 'Does post-withdrawal cue exposure improve outcome in opiate addiction – a controlled trial', *Addiction*, 88 (9): 1233–45.

Dawe, S., Rees, V.W., Mattick, R., Sitharthan, T. and Heather, N. (2002) 'Efficacy of moderation-oriented cue exposure for problem drinkers: a randomized controlled trial', *Journal of Consulting and Clinical Psychology*, 70 (4): 1045–50.

De Maat, S., Dekker, J., Schoevers, R. and De Jonghe, F. (2006) 'Relative efficacy of psychotherapy and pharmacotherapy in the treatment of depression: a meta-analysis', *Psychotherapy Research*, 16 (5): 562–72.

de Mello, M.F., Mari, J.D., Bacaltchuk, J., Verdeli, H. and Neugebauer, R. (2005) 'A systematic review of research findings on the efficacy of interpersonal therapy for depressive disorders', *European Archives of Psychiatry and Clinical Neuroscience*, 255 (2): 75–82.

Dembo, R., Ikle, D.N. and Ciarlo, J.A. (1983) 'The influence of client–clinician demographic match on client treatment outcomes', *Journal of Psychiatric Treatment and Evaluation*, 5 (1): 45–53.

den Boer, P., Wiersma, D., Russo, S. and van den Bosch, R.J. (2005) 'Paraprofessionals for anxiety and depressive disorders', *Cochrane Database of Systematic Reviews* (2).

den Boer, P., Wiersma, D. and van den Bosch, R.J. (2004) 'Why is self-help neglected in the treatment of emotional disorders? A meta-analysis', *Psychological Medicine*, 34 (6): 959–71.

Denis, C., Lavie, E., Fatséas, M. and Auriacombe, M. (2004) *Psychotherapeutic Interventions for Cannabis Abuse and/or Dependence in Outpatient Ssettings. Cochrane Database of Systematic Reviews* (3).

Department of Health (2001) *Treatment Choices in Psychological Therapies and Counselling.* London: Department of Health.

DeRubeis, R.J. and Feeley, M. (1990) 'Determinants of change in cognitive therapy for depression', *Cognitive Therapy and Research*, 14 (5): 469–82.

Devine, D.A. and Fernald, P.S. (1973) 'Outcome effects of receiving a preferred, randomly assigned, or nonpreferred therapy', *Journal of Consulting and Clinical Psychology*, 41 (1): 104–7.

Dickerson, F.B. (2000) 'Cognitive behavioral psychotherapy for schizophrenia: a review of recent empirical studies', *Schizophrenia Research*, 43 (2–3): 71–90.

Dickerson, F.B. and Lehman, A.F. (2006) 'Evidence-based psychotherapy for schizophrenia', *Journal of Nervous and Mental Disease*, 194 (1): 3–9.

DiGiuseppe, R. and Tafrate, R.C. (2003) 'Anger treatment for adults: a meta-analytic review', *Clinical Psychology: Science and Practice*, 10 (1): 70–84.

Dilk, M.N. and Bond, G.R. (1996) 'Meta-analytic evaluation of skills training research for individuals with severe mental illness', *Journal of Consulting and Clinical Psychology*, 64 (6): 1337–46.

Dormaar, M., Dijkman, C.I.M. and de Vries, M.W. (1989) 'Consensus in patient–therapist interactions. A measure of the therapeutic relationship related to outcome', *Psychotherapy and Psychosomatics*, 51 (2): 69–76.

Dowd, E.T. and Boroto, D.R. (1982) 'Differential effects of counselor self-disclosure, self-involving statements, and interpretation', *Journal of Counseling Psychology*, 29 (1): 8–13.

Duncan, B.L., Miller, S.D. and Sparks, J.A. (2004) *The Heroic Client: A Revolutionary Way to Improve Effectiveness through Client-directed, Outcome-informed Therapy.* San Francisco: Jossey-Bass.

Dunnett, A., Cooper, M., Wheeler, S., Balamoutsou, S., Wilson, C., Hill, A. et al. (2007) *Towards Regulation: The Standards, Benchmarks and Training Requirements for Counselling and Psychotherapy.* Rugby: BACP.

Durlak, J.A. (1979) 'Comparative effectiveness of paraprofessional and professional helpers', *Psychological Bulletin*, 86 (1): 80–92.

Eames, V. and Roth, A. (2000) 'Patient attachment orientation and the early working alliance – a study of patient and therapist reports of alliance quality and ruptures', *Psychotherapy Research*, 10 (4): 421–34.

Eccles, M., Freemantle, N. and Mason, J. (1998) 'North of England evidence based guidelines development project: methods of developing guidelines for efficient drug use in primary care', *British Medical Journal*, 316 (7139): 1232–5.

Edwards, C.E. and Murdock, N.L. (1994) 'Characteristics of therapist self-disclosure in the counseling process', *Journal of Counseling and Development*, 72 (March/April): 384–9.

Eisler, I., Dare, C., Hodes, M., Russell, G., Dodge, E. and le Grange, D. (2000) 'Family therapy for adolescent anorexia nervosa: the results of a controlled comparison of two family interventions', *Journal of Child Psychology and Psychiatry*, 41 (6): 727–36.

Elkin, I., Falconnier, L., Martinovich, Z. and Mahoney, C. (2006) 'Therapist effects in the National Institute of Mental Health Treatment of Depression Collaborative Research Program', *Psychotherapy Research*, 16 (2): 144–60.

Elkin, I., Gibbons, R.D., Shea, M.T., Sotsky, S.M., Watkins, J.T., Pilkonis, P.A. et al. (1995) 'Initial severity and differential treatment outcome in the National Institute of Mental Health Treatment of Depression Collaborative Research Program', *Journal of Consulting and Clinical Psychology*, 63 (5): 841–7.

Elkin, I., Shea, M.T., Watkins, J.T., Imber, S.D., Sotsky, S.M., Collins, J.F. et al. (1989) 'National Institute of Mental Health Treatment of Depression Collaborative Research Program – general effectiveness of treatments', *Archives of General Psychiatry*, 46 (11): 971–82.

Elkin, I., Yamaguchi, J.L., Arnkoff, D.B., Glass, C.R., Sotsky, S.M. and Krupnick, J.L. (1999) '"Patient-treatment fit" and early engagement in therapy', *Psychotherapy Research*, 9 (4): 437–51.

Elliott, R. (1985) 'Helpful and nonhelpful events in brief counseling interviews – an empirical taxonomy', *Journal of Counseling Psychology*, 32 (3): 307–22.

Elliott, R. (2007) 'Person-centred approaches to research', in M. Cooper, P. Schmid, M. O'Hara and G. Wyatt (eds), *The Handbook of Person-Centred Psychotherapy and Counselling*. Basingstoke: Palgrave, pp. 327–40.

Elliott, R., Barker, C.B., Caskey, N. and Pistrang, N. (1982) 'Differential helpfulness of counselor verbal response-modes', *Journal of Counseling Psychology*, 29 (4): 354–61.

Elliott, R., Greenberg, L.S. and Lietaer, G. (2004) 'Research on experiential therapies', in M.J. Lambert (ed.), *Bergin and Garfield's Handbook of Psychotherapy and Behavior Change* (5th edn). Chicago: John Wiley & Sons, pp. 493–539.

Elliott, R., Watson, J.C., Goldman, R. and Greenberg, L.S. (2004) *Learning Emotion-Focused Therapy: The Process-Experiential Approach to Change*. Washington, DC: American Psychological Association.

EMDR Institute, I (2004) *What is EMDR?* Retrieved 25 Jan. 2007, from http://www.emdr.com/q&a.htm.

Emmelkemp, P.M.G. (2004) 'Behavior therapy with adults', in M.J. Lambert (ed.), *Bergin and Garfield's Handbook of Psychotherapy and Behavior Change* (5th edn). Chicago: John Wiley & Sons, pp. 393–446.

Eysenck, H.J. (1957) 'The effects of psychotherapy: an evaluation', *Journal of Consulting Psychology*, 16 (5): 319–24.

Eysenck, H.J. (1978) 'An exercise in mega-silliness', *American Psychologist*, 33 (5): 517.

Fahy, T.A. and Russell, G.F.M. (1993) 'Outcome and prognostic variables in bulimia-nervosa', *International Journal of Eating Disorders*, 14 (2): 135–45.

Fairburn, C.G., Jones, R., Peveler, R.C., Hope, R.A. and O'Connor, M. (1993) 'Psychotherapy and bulimia-nervosa – longer-term effects of interpersonal psy-chotherapy, behavior-therapy, and cognitive-behavior therapy', *Archives of General Psychiatry*, 50 (6):419–28.

Farber, B.A. and Lane, J.S. (2002) 'Positive regard', in J.C. Norcross (ed.), *Psychotherapy Relationships that Work: Therapist Contributions and Responsiveness to Patients*. New York: Oxford University Press, pp. 175–94.

Farsimadan, F., Draghi-Lorenz, R. and Ellis, J. (2007) 'Process and outcome of therapy in ethnically similar and dissimilar therapeutic dyads', *Psychotherapy Research*, 17 (5): 567–75.

Fava, G., Rafanelli, C., Grandi, S., Conti, S., Ruini, C., Mangelli, L. et al. (2001) 'Long-term outcome of panic disorder with agoraphobia treated by exposure', *Psychological Medicine*, 31 (5): 891–8.

Feeley, M., DeRubeis, R.J. and Gelfand, L.A. (1999) 'The temporal relation of adherence and alliance to symptom change in cognitive therapy for depression', *Journal of Consulting and Clinical Psychology*, 67 (4): 578–82.

Feifel, H. and Eells, J. (1963) 'Patients and therapists assess the same psychotherapy', *Journal of Consulting Psychology*, 27 (4): 310–18.

Finn, S.E. and Tonsager, M.E. (1997) 'Information-gathering and therapeutic models of assessment: complementary paradigms', *Psychological Assessment*, 9 (4): 374–85.

Flammer, E. and Bongartz, W. (2003) 'On the efficacy of hypnotherapy: a meta-analytic study', *Contemporary Hypnosis*, 20 (4): 179–97.

Foa, E.B., Rothbaum, B.O., Riggs, D.S. and Murdock, T.B. (1991) 'Treatment of post-traumatic stress disorder in rape victims: a comparison between cognitive-behavioural procedures and counselling', *Journal of Consulting and Clinical Psychology*, 59 (5): 715–23.

Follette, W.C. and Greenberg, L.S. (2006) 'Technique factors in treating dysphoric disorders', in L.G. Castonguay and L.E. Beutler (eds), *Principles of Therapeutic Change that Work*. New York: Oxford University Press, pp. 83–109.

Fonagy, P. (ed.) (2002) *An Open Door Review of Outcome Studies in Psychoanalysis* (2nd rev. edn). London: International Psychoanalytical Association.

Fonagy, P., Roth, A. and Higgitt, A. (2005) 'The outcome of psychodynamic psychotherapy for psychological disorders', *Clinical Neuroscience Research*, 4 (5–6): 367–77.

Fonagy, P., Leigh, T., Steele, M., Steele, H., Kennedy, R., Mattoon, G. et al. (1996) 'The relation of attachment status, psychiatric classification, and response to psychotherapy', *Journal of Consulting and Clinical Psychology*, 64 (1): 22–31.

Foreman, D.M. (1990) 'The ethical use of paradoxical interventions in psychotherapy', *Journal of Medical Ethics*, 16 (4): 200–5.

Foreman, S.A. and Marmar, C.R. (1985) 'Therapist actions that address initially poor therapeutic alliances in psychotherapy', *American Journal of Psychiatry*, 142 (8): 922–6.

Frank, J.D. and Frank, J.B. (1993) *Persuasion and Healing* (3rd edn). Baltimore: Johns Hopkins University.

Frankl, V.E. (1986) *The Doctor and the Soul: From Psychotherapy to Logotherapy* (from German trans. R. Winston and C. Winston, 3rd edn). New York: Vintage Books.

Frattaroli, J. (2006) 'Experimental disclosure and its moderators: a meta-analysis', *Psychological Bulletin*, 132 (6): 823–65.

Friedlander, M.L., Thibodeau, J.R. and Ward, L.G. (1985) 'Discriminating the good from the bad therapy hour – a study of dyadic interaction', *Psychotherapy*, 22 (3): 631–42.

Friedman, S.M. and Gelso, C.J. (2000) 'The development of the inventory of countertransference behavior', *Journal of Clinical Psychology*, 56 (9): 1221–35.

Gabbard, G.O., Lazar, S.G., Hornberger, J. and Spiegel, D. (1997) 'The economic impact of psychotherapy: a review', *American Journal of Psychiatry*, 154 (2): 147–55.

Gaffan, E.A., Tsaousis, J. and Kemp-Wheeler, S.M. (1995) 'Researcher allegiance and meta-analysis: the case of cognitive therapy for depression', *Journal of Consulting and Clinical Psychology*, 63 (6): 966–80.

Gaston, L., Marmar, C.R., Gallagher, D. and Thompson, L.W. (1989) 'Impact of confirming patient expectations of change processes in behavioral, cognitive, and brief dynamic psychotherapy', *Psychotherapy*, 26 (3): 296–302.

Geib, P. (1996) 'The experience of nonerotic physical contact in traditional psychotherapy', in E.W.L. Smith, P.R. Clance and S. Imes (eds), *Touch in Psychotherapy: Theory, Research and Practice*. New York: Guilford Press, pp. 109–26.

Gelso, C.J. and Carter, J.A. (1985) 'The relationship in counseling and psychotherapy: components, consequences, and theoretical antecedents', *The Counselling Psychologist*, 13 (2): 155–243.

Gelso, C.J. and Hayes, J.A. (2002) 'The management of countertransference', in J.C. Norcross (ed.), *Psychotherapy Relationships that Work: Therapist Contributions and Responsiveness to Patients*. New York: Oxford University Press, pp. 267–83.

Gelso, C.J., Latts, M.G., Gomez, M.J. and Fassinger, R.E. (2002) 'Countertransference management and therapy outcome: an initial evaluation', *Journal of Clinical Psychology*, 58 (7): 861–7.

Gelso, C.J., Hill, C.E., Mohr, J.J., Rochlen, A.B. and Zack, J. (1999) 'Describing the face of transference: psychodynamic therapists' recollections about transference in cases of successful long-term therapy', *Journal of Counseling Psychology*, 46 (2): 257–67.

Gendlin, E.T. (1996) *Focusing-Oriented Psychotherapy: A Manual of the Experiential Method*. New York: Guilford Press.

Gilroy, A. (2006) *Art Therapy, Research and Evidence-Based Practice*. London: Sage.

Gingerich, W.J. and Eisengart, S. (2000) 'Solution-focused brief therapy: a review of the outcome research', *Family Process*, 39 (4): 477–98.

Gladstein, G.A. and Associates (1987) *Empathy and Counselling: Explorations in Theory and Research*. NewYork: Springer-Verlag.

Glass, C.R. and Arnkoff, D.B. (2000) 'Consumers' perspectives on helpful and hindering factors in mental health treatment', *Journal of Clinical Psychology*, 56 (11): 1467–80.

Glass, C.R., Arnkoff, D.B. and Shapiro, S.J. (2001) 'Expectations and preferences', *Psychotherapy*, 38 (4): 455–61.

Gloaguen, V., Cottraux, J., Cucherat, M. and Blackburn, I.-M. (1998) 'A meta-analysis of the effects of cognitive therapy in depressed patients', *Journal of Affective Disorders*, 49 (1): 59–72.

Gold, C., Voracek, M. and Wigram, T. (2004) 'Effects of music therapy for children and adolescents with psychopathology: a meta-analysis', *Journal of Child Psychology and Psychiatry*, 45 (6): 1054–63.

Gold, C., Heldal, T.O., Dahle, T. and Wigram, T. (2005) 'Music therapy for schizophrenia or schizophrenia-like illnesses', *Cochrane Database of Systematic Reviews* (2).

Goldfried, M.R., Castonguay, L.G., Hayes, A.M., Drozd, J.F. and Shapiro, D.A. (1997) 'A comparative analysis of the therapeutic focus in cognitive-behavioral and psychodynamic-interpersonal sessions', *Journal of Consulting and Clinical Psychology*, 65 (5): 740–48.

Goldman, R.N., Greenberg, L.S. and Pos, A.E. (2005) 'Depth of emotional experience and outcome', *Psychotherapy Research*, 15 (3): 248–60.

Goodyear, R.K. (1990) 'Research of the effects of test interpretation: a review', *Counselling Psychologist*, 18 (2): 240–57.

Goss, S. and Mearns, D. (1997) 'A call for a pluralist epistemological understanding in the assessment and evaluation of counselling', *British Journal of Guidance and Counselling*, 25 (2): 189–98.

Gould, R.A. and Clum, G.A. (1993) 'A meta-analysis of self-help treatment approaches', *Clinical Psychology Review*, 13 (2): 169–86.

Gould, R.A., Otto, M.W. and Pollack, M.H. (1995) 'A meta-analysis of treatment outcome for panic disorder', *Clinical Psychology Review*, 15 (8): 819–44.

Gould, R.A., Otto, M.W., Pollack, M.H. and Yap, L. (1997) 'Cognitive behavioral and pharmacological treatment of generalized anxiety disorder: a preliminary meta-analysis', *Behavior Therapy*, 28 (2): 285–305.

Gould, R.C. and Krynicki, V.E. (1989) 'Comparative effectiveness of hypnotherapy on different psychological symptoms', *American Journal of Clinical Hypnosis*, 32 (2): 110–17.

Grant, B. (2002) 'Principled and instrumental non-directiveness in person-centered and client-centered therapy', in D.J. Cain (ed.), *Classics in the Person-Centered Approach*. Ross-on-Wye: PCCS Books, pp. 371–7.

Greenberg, L.S. (1980) 'The intensive analysis of recurring events from the practice of Gestalt-therapy', *Psychotherapy: Theory, Research, Practice, Training*, 17 (2): 143–52.

Greenberg, L.S. and Dompierre, L.M. (1981) 'Specific effects of Gestalt 2-chair dialog on intrapsychic conflict in counseling', *Journal of Counseling Psychology*, 28 (4): 288–94.

Greenberg, L.S. and Rice, L.N. (1981) 'The specific effects of a Gestalt intervention', *Psychotherapy: Theory, Research, Practice, Training*, 18 (1): 31–7.

Greenberg, L.S. and Watson, J. (1998) 'Experiential therapy of depression: differential effects of client-centered relationship conditions and process experiential interventions', *Psychotherapy Research*, 8 (2): 210–24.

Greenberg, L.S., Korman, L.M. and Paivio, S.C. (2002) 'Emotions in humanistic psychotherapy', in D.J. Cain and J. Seeman (eds), *Humanistic Psychotherapies: Handbook of Research and Practice*. Washington, DC: American Psychological Association, pp. 499–530.

Grissom, R.J. (1996) 'The magical number .7+/−.2: Meta-meta-analysis of the probability of superior outcome in comparisons involving therapy, placebo, and control', *Journal of Consulting and Clinical Psychology*, 64 (5): 973–82.

Guajardo, J.M.F. and Anderson, T. (2007) 'An investigation of psychoeducational interventions about therapy', *Psychotherapy Research*, 17 (1): 120–27.

Gurman, A.S. (1977) 'The patient's perception of the therapeutic relationship', *Effective Psychotherapy: A Handbook of Research* (chap. 19): 503–43.

Gussak, D. (2006) 'Effects of art therapy with prison inmates: a follow-up study', *Arts in Psychotherapy*, 33 (3): 188–98.

Gutierrez, M.J. and Scott, J. (2004) 'Psychological treatment for bipolar disorders – a review of randomised controlled trials', *European Archives of Psychiatry and Clinical Neuroscience*, 254 (2): 92–8.

Haddock, G., Lewis, S., Bentall, R., Dunn, G., Drake, R. and Tarrier, N. (2006) 'Influence of age on outcome of psychological treatments in first-episode psychosis', *British Journal of Psychiatry*, 188 (3): 250–54.

Hansen, N.B., Lambert, M.J. and Forman, E.M. (2002) 'The psychotherapy dose-response effect and its implications for treatment delivery services', *Clinical Psychology: Science and Practice*, 9 (3): 329–43.

Hanson, J. (2005) 'Should your lips be zipped? How therapist self-disclosure and non-disclosure affects clients', *Counselling and Psychotherapy Research*, 5 (2): 96–104.

Hardy, G.E., Barkham, M., Shapiro, D.A., Rees, A., Stiles, W.B. and Reynolds, S. (1995) 'Impact of cluster-C personality-disorders on outcomes of contrasting brief psychotherapies for depression', *Journal of Consulting and Clinical Psychology*, 63 (6): 997–1004.

Hattie, J.A., Sharpley, C.F. and Rogers, H.J. (1984) 'Comparative effectiveness of professional and paraprofessional helpers', *Psychological Bulletin*, 95 (3): 534–41.

Hawkins, E.J., Lambert, M.J., Vermeersch, D.A., Slade, K.L. and Tuttle, K.C. (2004) 'The therapeutic effects of providing patient progress information to therapists and patients', *Psychotherapy Research*, 14 (3): 308–27.

Hawton, K., Townsend, E., Arensman, E., Gunnell, D., Hazell, P., House, A. et al. (1999) 'Psychosocial and pharmacological treatments for deliberate self-harm', *Cochrane Database of Systematic Reviews* (4).

Hay, P.P.J., Bacaltchuk, J., Claudino, A.M., Yong, P.Y., Byrnes, R. and Ben-Tovim, D. (2007) 'Individual psychotherapy in the outpatient treatment of adults with anorexia nervosa', *Cochrane Database of Systematic Reviews* (1).

Hayes, J.A. and Gelso, C.J. (2001) 'Clinical implications of research on countertransference: science informing practice', *Journal of Clinical Psychology/In Session*, 57 (8): 1041–51.

Hayes, J.A., Riker, J.R. and Ingram, M.I. (1997) 'Countertransference behavior and management in brief counseling: a field study', *Psychotherapy Research*, 7 (2): 145–53.

Hayes, J.A., McCracken, J.E., McClanahan, M.K., Hill, C.E., Harp, J.S. and Carozzoni, P. (1998) 'Therapist perspectives on countertransference: qualitative data in search of a theory', *Journal of Counseling Psychology*, 45 (4): 468–82.

Hayes, S.C., Luoma, J.B., Bond, F.W., Masuda, A. and Lillis, J. (2006) 'Acceptance and commitment therapy: model, processes and outcomes', *Behaviour Research and Therapy*, 44 (1): 1–25.

Hayes, S.C., Wilson, K.G., Gifford, E.V., Bissett, R., Piasecki, M., Batten, S.V. et al. (2004) 'A preliminary trial of Twelve-Step Facilitation and acceptance and commitment therapy with polysubstance-abusing methadone-maintained opiate addicts', *Behavior Therapy*, 35 (4): 667–88.

Heine, R.W. and Trosman, H. (1960) 'Initial expectations of the doctor–patient interaction as a factor in continuance in psychotherapy', *Psychiatry*, 23: 275–8.

Hendricks, M.N. (2002) 'Focusing-oriented/experiential psychotherapy', in D.J. Cain and J. Seeman (eds), *Humanistic Psychotherapies: Handbook of Research and Practice*. Washington, DC: American Psychological Association, pp. 221–52.

Henry, W.P., Schacht, T.E. and Strupp, H.H. (1990) 'Patient and therapist introject, interpersonal process, and differential psychotherapy outcome', *Journal of Consulting and Clinical Psychology*, 58 (6): 768–74.

Henry, W.P., Strupp, H.H., Butler, S.F., Schacht, T.E. and Binder, J.L. (1993) 'Effects of training in time-limited dynamic psychotherapy – changes in therapist behavior', *Journal of Consulting and Clinical Psychology*, 61 (3): 434–40.

Heres, S., Davis, J., Maino, K., Jetzinger, E., Kissling, W. and Leucht, S. (2006) 'Why olanzapine beats risperidone, risperidone beats quetiapine, and quetiapine beats olanzapine: an exploratory analysis of head-to-head comparison studies of second-generation antipsychotics', *American Journal of Psychiatry*, 163 (2): 185–94.

Hill, A. and Brettle, A. (in press) *Counselling and Psychotherapy in Primary Care: A Systematic Review.* Rugby: BACP.

Hill, C.E. and Knox, S. (2002) 'Self-disclosure', in J.C. Norcross (ed.), *Psychotherapy Relationships that Work: Therapist Contributions and Responsiveness to Patients.* New York: Oxford University Press, pp. 255–65.

Hill, C.E., Thompson, B.J. and Corbett, M.M. (1992) 'The impact of therapist ability to perceive displayed and hidden client reactions on immediate outcome in first sessions of brief therapy', *Psychotherapy Research*, 2 (2): 143–55.

Hill, C.E., Thompson, B.J., Cogar, M.C. and Denman, D.W. (1993) 'Beneath the surface of long-term therapy: therapist and client report of their own and each other's covert processes', *Journal of Counseling Psychology*, 40 (3): 278–87.

Hill, C.E., Helms, J.E., Tichenor, V., Spiegel, S.B. et al. (1988) 'Effects of therapist response modes in brief psychotherapy', *Journal of Counseling Psychology*, 35 (3): 222–33.

Hill, K.A. (1987) 'Meta-analysis of paradoxical interventions', *Psychotherapy*, 24 (2): 266–70.

Hilsenroth, M.J., Defife, J.A., Blagys, M.D. and Ackerman, S.J. (2006) 'Effects of training in short-term psychodynamic psychotherapy: changes in graduate clinician technique', *Psychotherapy Research*, 16 (3): 293–305.

Hoehn-Saric, R., Frank, J.D., Imber, S.D., Nash, E.H., Stone, A.R. and Battle, C.C. (1964) 'Systematic preparation of patients for psychotherapy – I. Effects on therapy behavior and outcome', *Journal of Psychiatric Research*, 2: 267–81.

Høglend, P. (1993) 'Transference interpretations and long-term change after dynamic psychotherapy of brief to moderate length', *American Journal of Psychotherapy*, 47 (4): 494–507.

Høglend, P., Johansson, P., Marble, A., Bogwald, K.P. and Amlo, S. (2007) 'Moderators of the effects of transference interpretations in brief dynamic psychotherapy', *Psychotherapy Research*, 17 (2): 162–74.

Hollon, S.D. and Beck, A.T. (2004) 'Cognitive and cognitive behavioral therapies', in M.J. Lambert (ed.), *Bergin and Garfield's Handbook of Psychotherapy and Behavior Change* (5th edn). Chicago: John Wiley & Sons, pp. 447–92.

Holloway, E. and Gonzáles-Doupé, P. (2002) 'The learning alliance of supervision: research to practice', in G.S. Tryon (ed.), *Counselling Based on Process Research: Applying What we Know.* Boston: Allyn & Bacon, pp. 132–65.

Holtforth, M.G. and Grawe, K. (2002) 'Bern inventory of treatment goals: Part 1. Development and first application of a taxonomy of treatment goal themes', *Psychotherapy Research*, 12 (1): 79–99.

Holtforth, M.G., Reubi, I., Ruckstuhl, L., Berking, M. and Grawe, K. (2004) 'The value of treatment-goal themes for treatment planning and outcome evaluation of psychiatric inpatients', *International Journal of Social Psychiatry*, 50 (1): 80–91.

Hope, D.A., Heimberg, R.G. and Bruch, M.A. (1995) 'Dismantling cognitive-behavioral group therapy for social phobia', *Behaviour Research and Therapy*, 33 (6): 637–50.

Horton, J. (1996) 'Further research on the patient's experience of touch in psychotherapy', in E.W.L. Smith, P.R. Clance and S. Imes (eds), *Touch in Psychotherapy: Theory, Research and Practice*. New York: Guilford Press, pp. 127–41.

Horvath, A.O. and Bedi, R.P. (2002) 'The alliance', in J.C. Norcross (ed.), *Psychotherapy Relationships that Work: Therapist Contributions and Responsiveness to Patients*. New York: Oxford University Press, pp. 37–69.

Horvath, A.O. and Goheen, M.D. (1990) 'Factors mediating the success of defiance- and compliance-based interventions', *Journal of Counseling Psychology*, 37 (4): 363–71.

Horvath, A.O. and Greenberg, L.S. (1989) 'Development and validation of the Working Alliance Inventory', *Journal of Counseling Psychology*, 36 (2): 223–33.

Howard, K.I., Kopta, S.M., Krause, M.S. and Orlinsky, D.E. (1986) 'The dose–effect relationship in psychotherapy', *American Psychologist*, 41 (2): 159–64.

Hubble, M., Duncan, B.L. and Miller, S.D. (1999) *The Heart and Soul of Change: What Works in Therapy*. Washington, DC: American Psychological Association.

Hunsley, J. and Di Giulio, G. (2002) 'Dodo bird, phoenix, or urban legend?' *Scientific Review of Mental Health Practices*, 1 (1): 11–22.

Huppert, J.D., Bufka, L.F., Barlow, D.H., Gorman, J.M., Shear, M.K. and Woods, S.W. (2001) 'Therapists, therapist variables, and cognitive-behavioral therapy outcome in a multicenter trial for panic disorder', *Journal of Consulting and Clinical Psychology*, 69 (5): 747–55.

Iacoviello, B.M., McCarthy, K.S., Barrett, M.S., Rynn, M., Gallop, R. and Barber, J.P. (2007) 'Treatment preferences affect the therapeutic alliance: implications for randomized controlled trials', *Journal of Consulting and Clinical Psychology*, 75 (1): 194–8.

Ilardi, S.S. and Craighead, W.E. (1994) 'The role of nonspecific factors in cognitive-behavior therapy for depression', *Clinical Psychology: Science and Practice*, 1 (2): 138–56.

Jacobson, N.S. and Truax, P.A. (1991) 'Clinical significance: a statistical approach to defining meaningful change in psychotherapy research', *Journal of Consulting and Clinical Psychology*, 59 (1): 12–19.

Jacobson, N.S., Dobson, K.S., Truax, P.A., Addis, M.E., Koerner, K., Gollan, J.K. et al. (1996) 'A component analysis of cognitive-behavioral treatment for depression', *Journal of Consulting and Clinical Psychology*, 64(2): 295–304.

Jones, E.E. and Pulos, S.M. (1993) 'Comparing the process in psychodynamic and cognitive-behavioral therapies', *Journal of Consulting and Clinical Psychology*, 61 (2): 306–16.

Jones, E.E., Cumming, J.D. and Horowitz, M.J. (1988) 'Another look at the nonspecific hypothesis of therapeutic effectiveness', *Journal of Consulting and Clinical Psychology*, 56 (1): 48–55.

Jones, E.E., Krupnick, J.L. and Kerig, P.K. (1987) 'Some gender effects in a brief psychotherapy', *Psychotherapy*, 24 (3): 336–52.

Jones, E.E., Parke, L.A. and Pulos, S.M. (1992) 'How therapy is conducted in the private consulting room: a multidimensional description of brief psychodynamic treatments', *Psychotherapy Research*, 2 (1): 16–30.

Jones, M.A., Botsko, M. and Gorman, B.S. (2003) 'Predictors of psychotherapeutic benefit of lesbian, gay, and bisexual clients: the effects of sexual orientation matching and other factors', *Psychotherapy: Theory, Research, Practice, Training*, 40 (4): 289–301.

Kadden, R.M., Cooney, N.L., Getter, H. and Litt, M.D. (1989) 'Matching alcoholics to coping skills or interactional therapies: posttreatment results', *Journal of Consulting and Clinical Psychology*, 57: 698–704.

Kato, P.M. and Mann, T. (1999) 'A synthesis of psychological interventions for the bereaved', *Clinical Psychology Review*, 19 (3): 275–96.

Kazantzis, N. and L'Abate, L. (2006) *Handbook of Homework Assignments in Psychotherapy: Research, Practice, and Prevention*. New York: Springer-Verlag.

Kazantzis, N., Deane, F.P. and Ronan, K.R. (2000) 'Homework assignments in cognitive and behavioral therapy: a meta-analysis', *Clinical Psychology: Science and Practice*, 7 (2): 189–202.

Keating, A.M. and Fretz, B.R. (1990) 'Christians' anticipations about counselors in response to counselor descriptions', *Journal of Counseling Psychology*, 37 (3): 293–6.

Keijsers, G.P.J., Hoogduin, C.A.L. and Schaap, C. (1994) 'Predictors of treatment outcome in the behavioral treatment of obsessive–compulsive disorder', *British Journal of Psychiatry*, 165 (6): 781–6.

Keijsers, G.P.J., Schaap, C.P.D.R. and Hoogduin, C.A.L. (2000) 'The impact of interpersonal patient and therapist behaviour on outcome in cognitive-behavior therapy', *Behaviour Modification*, 24 (2): 264–97.

Keller, M.B., McCullough, J.P., Klein, D.N., Arnow, B., Dunner, D.L. et al. (2000) 'A comparison of nefazodone, the cognitive behavioral-analysis system of psychotherapy, and their combination for the treatment of chronic depression', *Journal of Medicine*, 342 (20): 1462–70.

Kellermann, P.F. (1987) 'Outcome research in classical psychodrama', *Small Group Behavior*, 18 (4): 459–69.

Kelly, T.A. and Strupp, H.H. (1992) 'Patient and therapist values in psychotherapy – perceived changes, assimilation, similarity, and outcome', *Journal of Consulting and Clinical Psychology*, 60 (1): 34–40.

Kenny, M.A. and Williams, J.M.G. (2007) 'Treatment-resistant depressed patients show a good response to mindfulness-based cognitive therapy', *Behaviour Research and Therapy*, 45 (3): 617–25.

Kiesler, D.B. (1966) 'Some myths of psychotherapy research and the search for a paradigm', *Psychological Bulletin*, 65 (2): 110–36.

Kim, D.M., Wampold, B.E. and Bolt, D.M. (2006) 'Therapist effects in psychotherapy: a random-effects modeling of the National Institute of Mental Health Treatment of Depression Collaborative Research Program data', *Psychotherapy Research*, 16 (2): 161–72.

Kim, J.S. (2008) 'Examining the effectiveness of solution-focused brief therapy: a meta-analysis', *Research on Social Work Practice*, 18 (2): 107–16.

King, M., Nazareth, I., Lampe, F., Bower, P., Chandler, M., Morou, M. et al. (2005) 'Impact of participant and physician intervention preferences on randomized trials – a systematic review', *Journal of the American Medical Association*, 293 (9): 1089–99.

King, M., Semylen, J., Killaspy, H., Nazareth, I. and Osborn, D. (2007) *A Systematic Review of Research on Counselling and Psychotherapy for Lesbian, Gay, Bisexual and Transgender People*. Rugby: BACP.

King, M., Sibbald, B., Ward, E., Bower, P., Lloyd, M., Gabbay, M. et al. (2000) 'Randomised controlled trial of non-directive counselling, cognitive-behaviour therapy and usual general practitioner care in the management of depression as well as mixed anxiety and depression in primary care', *Health Technology Assessment*, 4 (19).

Kipper, D.A. and Ritchie, T.D. (2003) 'The effectiveness of psychodramatic techniques: a meta-analysis', *Group Dynamics – Theory Research and Practice*, 7 (1): 13–25.

Kirsch, I., Montgomery, G. and Sapirstein, G. (1995) 'Hypnosis as an adjunct to cognitive-behavioral psychotherapy – a metaanalysis', *Journal of Consulting and Clinical Psychology*, 63 (2): 214–20.

Kivlighan, D.M. (1985) 'Feedback in group-psychotherapy – review and implications', *Small Group Behavior*, 16 (3): 373–85.

Kivlighan, D.M. and Shaughnessy, P. (2000) 'Patterns of working alliance development: a typology of client's working alliance ratings', *Journal of Counseling Psychology*, 47 (3): 362–71.

Klein, M.H., Kolden, G.G., Michels, J.L. and Chisolm-Stockard, S. (2002) 'Congruence', in J.C. Norcross (ed.), *Psychotherapy Relationships that Work: Therapist Contributions and Responsiveness to Patients*. New York: Oxford University Press, pp. 195–215.

Klein, M.J., Mathieu-Coughlan, P. and Kiesler, D.B. (1986) 'The experiencing scales', in L.S. Greenberg and W.M. Pinsof (eds), *The Psychotherapeutic Process: A Research Handbook*. New York: Guilford Press, pp. 21–71.

Knox, S., Hess, S.A., Petersen, D.A. and Hill, C.E. (1997) 'A qualitative analysis of client perceptions of the effects of helpful therapist self-disclosure in long-term therapy', *Journal of Counseling Psychology*, 44 (3): 274–83.

Koch, S.C. and Bräuninger, I. (2005) 'International dance/movement therapy research: theory, methods, and empirical findings', *American Journal of Dance Therapy*, 27 (1): 37–46.

Koerner, K. and Linehan, M.M. (2000) 'Research on dialectical behavior therapy for patients with borderline personality disorder', *Psychiatric Clinics of North America*, 23 (1): 151–67.

Kolb, D.L., Davis, C.S., Beutler, L.E., Crago, M. and Shanfield, S.B. (1985) 'Patient and therapy process variables relating to dropout and change in psychotherapy', *Psychotherapy*, 22 (4): 702–10.

Kopta, S.M., Howard, K.I., Lowry, J.L. and Beutler, L.E. (1994) 'Patterns of symptomatic recovery in psychotherapy', *Journal of Consulting and Clinical Psychology*, 62 (5): 1009–16.

Krupnick, J.L., Sotsky, S.M., Simmens, S., Moyer, J., Elkin, I., Watkins, J. et al. (1996) 'The role of the therapeutic alliance in psychotherapy and pharmacotherapy outcome: findings in the National Institute of Mental Health Treatment of Depression Collaborative Research Program', *Journal of Consulting and Clinical Psychology*, 64 (3): 532–9.

Ladany, N. and Melincoff, D.S. (1999) 'The nature of counselor supervisor nondisclosure', *Counselor Education and Supervision*, 38 (3): 161–76.

Ladany, N., Hill, C.E., Corbett, M.M. and Nutt, E.A. (1996) 'Nature, extent, and importance of what psychotherapy trainees do not disclose to their supervisors', *Journal of Counseling Psychology*, 43 (1): 10–24.

Lafferty, P., Beutler, L.E., and Crago, M. (1989) 'Differences between more and less effective psychotherapists – a study of select therapist variables', *Journal of Consulting and Clinical Psychology*, 57 (1): 76–80.

Lambert, M.J. (1986) 'Some implications of psychotherapy outcome research for eclectic psychotherapy', *International Journal of Eclectic Psychotherapy*, 5 (1): 16–45.

Lambert, M.J. (1989) 'The individual therapist's contribution to psychotherapy process and outcome', *Clinical Psychology Review*, 9 (4): 469–85.

Lambert, M.J. (1992) 'Implications of outcome research for psychotherapy integration', in J.C. Norcross and M.R. Goldstein (eds), *Handbook of Psychotherapy Integration*. New York: Basic Books, pp. 94–129.

Lambert, M.J. (2007) 'Presidential address: What we have learned from a decade of research aimed at improving psychotherapy outcome in routine care', *Psychotherapy Research*, 17 (1): 1–14.

Lambert, M.J. and Ogles, B.M. (1997) 'The effectiveness of psychotherapy supervision', in C.E. Watkins (ed.), *Handbook of Psychotherapy Supervision*. Chichester: Wiley, pp. 421–46.

Lambert, M.J. and Ogles, B.M. (2004) 'The efficacy and effectiveness of psychotherapy', in M.J. Lambert (ed.), *Bergin and Garfield's Handbook of Psychotherapy and Behavior Change* (5th edn). Chicago: John Wiley & Sons, pp. 139–93.

Larsen, D., Edey, W. and Lemay, L. (2007) 'Understanding the role of hope in counselling: exploring the intentional uses of hope', *Counselling Psychology Quarterly*, 20 (4): 401–16.

Lasky, R.G. and Salomone, P.R. (1977) 'Attraction to psychotherapy: influences of therapist status and therapist–patient age similarity', *Journal of Clinical Psychology*, 33 (2): 511–16.

Latts, M.G. and Gelso, C.J. (1995) 'Countertransference behavior and management with survivors of sexual assault', *Psychotherapy: Theory, Research, Practice, Training*, 32 (3): 405–15.

Layard, R. (2004) *Mental Health: Britain's Biggest Social Problem*. Retrieved 27 Jan. 2007, from http://www.cabinetoffice.gov.uk/strategy/downloads/files/mh_layard.pdf.

Le Grange, D. and Lock, J. (2005) 'The dearth of psychological treatment studies for anorexia nervosa', *International Journal of Eating Disorders*, 37 (2): 79–91.

Leach, L.S. and Christensen, H. (2006) 'A systematic review of telephone-based interventions for mental disorders', *Journal of Telemedicine and Telecare*, 12 (3): 122–9.

Lebow, J. (2006) *Research for the Psychotherapist: From Science to Practice*. London: Routledge.

Leichsenring, F. (2001) 'Comparative effects of short-term psychodynamic psychotherapy and cognitive-behavioral therapy in depression: a meta-analytic approach', *Clinical Psychology Review*, 21 (3): 401–19.

Leichsenring, F. and Leibing, E. (2003) 'The effectiveness of psychodynamic therapy and cognitive behavior therapy in the treatment of personality disorders: a meta-analysis', *American Journal of Psychiatry*, 160 (7): 1223–32.

Leichsenring, F., Rabung, S. and Leibing, E. (2004) 'The efficacy of short-term psychodynamic psychotherapy in specific psychiatric disorders – a meta-analysis', *Archives of General Psychiatry*, 61 (12): 1208–16.

Leitenberg, H. et al. (1975) 'Feedback and therapist praise during treatment of phobia', *Journal of Consulting and Clinical Psychology*, 43 (3): 396–404.

Levitt, J.T., Brown, T.A., Orsillo, S.M. and Barlow, D.H. (2004) 'The effects of acceptance versus suppression of emotion on subjective and psychophysiological response to carbon dioxide challenge in patients with panic disorder', *Behavior Therapy*, 35 (4): 747–66.

Levy, J.A., Glass, C.R., Arnkoff, D.B., Gershefski, J.J. and Elkin, I. (1996) 'Clients' perceptions of treatment for depression. 2. Problematic or hindering aspects', *Psychotherapy Research*, 6 (4): 249–62.

Liddle, B.J. (1996) 'Therapist sexual orientation, gender, and counseling practices as they relate to ratings on helpfulness by gay and lesbian clients', *Journal of Counseling Psychology*, 43 (4): 394–401.

Liddle, B.J. (1997) 'Gay and lesbian clients' selection of therapists and utilization of therapy', *Psychotherapy*, 34 (1): 11–18.

Lietaer, G. (1993) 'Authenticity, congruence and transparency', in D. Brazier (ed.), *Beyond Carl Rogers*. London: Constable, pp. 17–46.

Ligiéro, D.P. and Gelso, C.J. (2002) 'Countertransference, attachment, and the working alliance: the therapist's contribution', *Psychotherapy: Theory, Research, Practice, Training*, 39 (1): 3–11.

Lilienfeld, S.O. (2007) 'Psychological treatments that cause harm', *Perspectives on Psychological Science*, 2 (1): 53–70.

Lilliengren, P. and Werbart, A. (2005) 'A model of therapeutic action grounded in the patient's view of curative and hindering factors in psychoanalytic psychotherapy', *Psychotherapy*, 42 (3): 324–39.

Linehan, M.M., Dimeff, L.A., Reynolds, S.K., Comtois, K.A., Welch, S.S., Heagerty, P. et al. (2002) 'Dialectical behavior therapy versus comprehensive validation therapy plus 12-step for the treatment of opioid dependent women meeting criteria for borderline personality disorder', *Drug and Alcohol Dependence*, 67 (1): 13–26.

Linehan, M.M., Schmidt, H., Dimeff, L.A., Craft, J.C., Kanter, J. and Comtois, K.A. (1999) 'Dialectical behavior therapy for patients with borderline personality disorder and drug-dependence', *American Journal on Addictions*, 8 (4): 279–92.

Lipsey, M.W. and Wilson, D.B. (1993) 'The efficacy of psychological, educational, and behavioral treatment – confirmation from metaanalysis', *American Psychologist*, 48 (12): 1181–209.

Lipsitz, J.D., Mannuzza, S., Klein, D.F., Ross, D.C. and Fyer, A.J. (1999) 'Specific phobia 10–16 years after treatment', *Depression and Anxiety*, 10 (3): 105–11.

Longabaugh, R. and Morgenstern, J. (1999) 'Cognitive-behavioral coping-skills therapy for alcohol dependence – current status and future directions', *Alcohol Research & Health*, 23 (2): 78–85.

Lorr, M. (1965) 'Client perceptions of therapists: a study of the therapeutic relation', *Journal of Consulting Psychology*, 29 (2): 146–9.

Luborsky, L., Barber, J.P. and Crits-Christoph, P. (1990) 'Theory-based research for understanding the process of dynamic psychotherapy', *Journal of Consulting and Clinical Psychology*, 58 (3): 281–7.

Luborsky, L., Singer, B. and Luborsky, L. (1975) 'Comparative studies of psychotherapies: Is it true that "Everyone has won and all must have prizes"?' *Archive of General Psychiatry*, 32: 995–1008.

Luborsky, L., McLellan, A.T., Woody, G.E., O'Brien, C.P. and Auerbach, A. (1985) 'Therapist success and its determinants', *Archives of General Psychiatry*, 42 (6): 602–11.

Luborsky, L., Diguer, L., Seligman, D.A., Rosenthal, R., Krause, E.D., Johnson, S. et al. (1999) 'The researcher's own therapy allegiances: a "wild card" in comparisons of treatment efficacy', *Clinical Psychology: Science and Practice*, 6 (1): 95–106.

Luborsky, L., Rosenthal, R., Diguer, L., Andrusyna, T.P., Berman, J.S., Levitt, J.T. et al. (2002) 'The Dodo bird verdict is alive and well – mostly', *Clinical Psychology: Science and Practice*, 9 (1): 2–12.

Ma, S.H. and Teasdale, J.D. (2004) 'Mindfulness-based cognitive therapy for depression: replication and exploration of differential relapse prevention effects', *Journal of Consulting and Clinical Psychology*, 72 (1): 31–40.

Macran, S. and Shapiro, D.A. (1998) 'The role of personal therapy for therapists: a review', *British Journal of Medical Psychology*, 71: 13–25.

Macran, S., Stiles, W.B. and Smith, J.A. (1999) 'How does personal therapy affect therapists' practice?' *Journal of Counseling Psychology*, 46 (4): 419–31.

Mair, D. (2003) 'Gay men's experiences of therapy', *Counselling and Psychotherapy Research*, 3 (1): 33–41.

Mallen, M. (2003) 'Online counseling research', in R. Kraus, J. Zack and G. Stricker (eds), *Online Counseling: A Handbook for Mental Health Professionals*, New York: Academic Press, pp. 69–89.

Malouff, J.M., Thorsteinsson, E.B. and Schutte, N.S. (2007) 'The efficacy of problem solving therapy in reducing mental and physical health problems: a meta-analysis', *Clinical Psychology Review*, 27 (1): 46–57.

Maluccio, A.N. (1979) *Learning from Clients: Interpersonal Helping as Viewed by Clients and Social Workers*. New York: Macmillan.

Maratos, A.S., Gold, C., Wang, X. and Crawford, M.J. (2008) 'Music therapy for depression', *Cochrane Database of Systematic Reviews* (1).

Marmar, C.R., Gaston, L., Gallagher, D. and Thompson, L.W. (1989) 'Alliance and outcome in late-life depression', *Journal of Nervous and Mental Disease*, 177 (8): 464–72.

Martin, D.J., Garske, J.P. and Davis, M.K. (2000) 'Relation of the therapeutic alliance with outcome and other variables: a meta-analytic review', *Journal of Consulting and Clinical Psychology*, 68 (3): 438–50.

Martinez, F.I. (1991) 'Therapist–client convergence and similarity of religious values: their effect on client improvement', *Journal of Psychology and Christianity*, 10 (2): 137–43.

Matt, G.E. and Navarro, A.M. (1997) 'What meta-analyses have and have not taught us about psychotherapy effects: a review and future directions', *Clinical Psychology Review*, 17 (1): 1–32.

Mayet, S., Farrell, M., Ferri, M., Amato, L. and Davoli, M. (2004) *Psychosocial Treatment for Opiate Abuse and Dependency. Cochrane Database of Systematic Reviews* (4).

McCallum, M. and Piper, W.E. (1999) 'Personality disorders and response to group-oriented evening treatment', *Group Dynamics: Theory Research and Practice*, 3 (1): 3–14.

McCarthy, P.R. and Betz, N.E. (1978) 'Differential effects of self-disclosing versus self-involving counselor statements', *Journal of Counseling Psychology*, 25 (4): 251–6.

McCullough, M.E. (1999) 'Research on religion-accommodative counseling: review and meta-analysis', *Journal of Counseling Psychology*, 46 (1): 92–8.

McCullough, M.E. and Worthington, E.L. (1995) 'College-students perceptions of a psychotherapist's treatment of a religious issue – partial replication and extension', *Journal of Counseling and Development*, 73 (6): 626–34.

McGuire, H. and Hawton, K. (2001) *Interventions for vaginismus. Cochrane Database of Systematic Reviews* (2).

McIntosh, V., Jordan, J., Carter, F., Luty, S., McKenzie, J., Bulik, C. et al. (2005) 'Three psychotherapies for anorexia nervosa: a randomized, controlled trial', *American Journal of Psychiatry*, 162 (4): 741–7.

McLeod, J. (2003) *Doing Counselling Research* (2nd edn). London: Sage.

McLeod, J. (2006) 'Relational depth from the point of view of the client', Working at Relational Depth Conference, Glasgow, University of Strathclyde.

McLeod, J. (2008) *Counselling and Psychotherapy in the Workplace: A Systematic Review* (2nd edn). Rugby: BACP.

McMillan, M. and McLeod, J. (2006) 'Letting go: the client's experience of relational depth', *Person-Centered and Experiential Psychotherapies*, 5 (4): 277–92.

Mearns, D. and Cooper, M. (2005) *Working at Relational Depth in Counselling and Psychotherapy*. London: Sage.

Mergenthaler, E. (1996) 'Emotion-abstraction patterns in verbatim protocols: a new way of describing psychotherapeutic processes', *Journal of Consulting and Clinical Psychology*, 64 (6): 1306–15.

Merry, T. (2004) 'Classical client-centred therapy', in P. Sanders (ed.), *The Tribes of the Person-Centred Nation: An Introduction to the Schools of Therapy Related to the Person-Centred Approach*. Ross-on-Wye: PCCS Books, pp. 21–44.

Metcalfe, C., Winter, D. and Viney, L. (2007) 'The effectiveness of personal construct psychotherapy in clinical practice: a systematic review and meta-analysis', *Psychotherapy Research*, 17 (4): 431–42.

Meyer, B. and Pilkonis, P.A. (2002) 'Attachment style', in J.C. Norcross (ed.), *Psychotherapy Relationships that Work: Therapist Contributions and Responsiveness to Patients*. New York: Oxford University Press, pp. 367–82.

Meyer, B., Pilkonis, P.A., Proietti, J.M., Heape, C.L. and Egan, M. (2001) 'Attachment styles and personality disorders as predictors of symptom course', *Journal of Personality Disorders*, 15 (5): 371–89.

Meyer, G.J., Finn, S.E., Eyde, L.D., Kay, G.G., Moreland, K.L., Dies, R.R. et al. (2001) 'Psychological testing and psychological assessment: a review of evidence and issues', *American Psychologist*, 56 (2): 128–65.

Milakovich, J. (1996) 'Differences between therapists who touch and those who do not touch', in E.W. L. Smith, P.R. Clance and S. Imes (eds), *Touch in Psychotherapy: Theory, Research and Practice*. New York: Guilford Press, pp. 74–91.

Miller, S.D., Duncan, B.L., Sorrell, R. and Brown, G.S. (2005) 'The partners for change outcome management system', *Journal of Clinical Psychology*, 61 (2): 199–208.

Miller, W.R., Benefield, R.G. and Tonigan, J.S. (1993) 'Enhancing motivation for change in problem drinking: a controlled comparison of two therapist styles', *Journal of Consulting and Clinical Psychology*, 61 (3): 455–61.

Miller, W.R., Taylor, C.A. and West, J.C. (1980) 'Focused versus broad-spectrum behaviour therapy for problem drinkers', *Journal of Consulting and Clinical Psychology*, 48 (5): 590–601.

Miller, W.R., Walters, S.T. and Bennett, M.E. (2001) 'How effective is alcoholism treatment in the United States?' *Journal of Studies on Alcohol*, 62 (2): 211–20.

Miller, W.R., Wilbourne, P.L. and Hettema, J.E. (2002) 'What works? A summary of alcohol treatment outcome research', in R.K. Hester and W.R. Miller (eds), *Handbook of Alcoholism Treatment Approaches: Effective Alternatives* (3rd edn): London: Allyn & Bacon, pp. 13–63.

Mohr, D.C. (1995) 'Negative outcome in psychotherapy – a critical review', *Clinical Psychology: Science and Practice*, 2 (1): 1–27.

Mohr, D.C. and Beutler, L.E. (1990) 'Erectile dysfunction – a review of diagnostic and treatment procedures', *Clinical Psychology Review*, 10 (1): 123–50.

Mohr, D.C., Beutler, L.E., Engle, D., Shoham-Salomon, V., Bergan, J., Kaszniak, A.W. et al. (1990) 'Identification of patients at risk for nonresponse and negative outcome in psychotherapy', *Journal of Consulting and Clinical Psychology*, 58 (5): 622–8.

Mohr, D.C., Hart, S.L., Julian, L., Catledge, C., Honos-Webb, L., Vella, L. et al. (2005) 'Telephone-administered psychotherapy for depression', *Archives of General Psychiatry*, 62 (9): 1007–14.

Monti, P.M. and Rohsenow, D.J. (1999) 'Coping-skills training and cue-exposure therapy in the treatment of alcoholism', *Alcohol Research & Health*, 23 (2): 107–15.

Morran, D.K., Stockton, R., Cline, R.J. and Teed, C. (1998) 'Facilitating feedback exchange in groups: leader interventions', *Journal for Specialists in Group Work*, 23 (3): 257–68.

Morrow-Bradley, C. and Elliott, R. (1986) 'Utilization of psychotherapy research by practicing psychotherapists', *American Psychologist*, 41 (2): 188–97.

Moyer, A., Finney, J.W., Swearingen, C.E. and Vergun, P. (2002) 'Brief interventions for alcohol problems: a meta-analytic review of controlled investigations in treatment-seeking and non-treatment-seeking populations', *Addiction*, 97 (3): 279–92.

Mumford, E., Schlesinger, H., Glass, G., Patrick, C. and Cuerdon, T. (1984) 'A new look at evidence about reduced cost of medical utilization following mental health treatment', *American Journal of Psychiatry*, 141 (10): 1145–58.

Murphy, M.J., Faulkner, R.A. and Behrens, C. (2004) 'The effect of therapist–client racial similarity on client satisfaction and therapist evaluation of treatment', *Contemporary Family Therapy*, 26 (3): 279–92.

Najavitis, L.M. and Strupp, H.H. (1994) 'Differences in the effectiveness of psychodynamic therapists: a process-outcome study', *Psychotherapy*, 31 (1): 114–23.

Nathan, P.E. and Gorman, J.M. (2007) *A Guide to Treatments that Work* (3rd edn). New York: Oxford University Press.

National Collaborating Centre for Mental Health (2003) *Schizophrenia: Full National Clinical Guideline on Core Interventions in Primary and Secondary Care.* London: Royal College of Psychiatrists and British Psychological Society.

National Institute for Health and Clinical Excellence (2007a) *Anxiety (amended): Management of Anxiety (Panic Disorder with or without Agoraphobia, and Generalised Anxiety Disorder) in Adults in Primary, Secondary and Community Care.* London: National Institute for Health and Clinical Excellence.

National Institute for Health and Clinical Excellence (2007b) *Depression (amended): Management of Depression in Primary and Secondary Care.* London: National Institute for Health and Clinical Excellence.

National Institute for Health and Clinical Excellence (2007c) *Post-traumatic Stress Disorder: The Management of PTSD in Adults and Children in Primary and Secondary Care.* London: Royal College of Psychiatrists and British Psychological Society.

Nelson, R.A. and Borkovec, T.D. (1989) 'Relationship of client participation to psychotherapy', *Journal of Behavior Therapy and Experimental Psychiatry*, 20 (2): 155–62.

Neufeldt, S.A., Beutler, L.E. and Banchero, R. (1997) 'Research on supervisor variables in psychotherapy supervision', in C.E. Watkins (ed.), *Handbook of Psychotherapy Supervision.* Chichester: Wiley, pp. 508–24.

Newman, M.G., Crits-Christoph, P., Connolly Gibbons, M.B. and Erickson, T.M. (2006) 'Participant factors in treating anxiety disorders', in L.G. Castonguay and L.E. Beutler (eds), *Principles of Therapeutic Change that Work.* New York: Oxford University Press, pp. 121–53.

Newman, M.G., Stiles, W.B., Janeck, A. and Woody, S.R. (2006) 'Integration of therapeutic factors in anxiety disorders', in L.G. Castonguay and L.E. Beutler (eds), *Principles of Therapeutic Change that Work.* New York: Oxford University Press, pp. 187–200.

Nicholson, R.A. and Berman, J.S. (1983) 'Is follow-up necessary in evaluating psychotherapy?' *Psychological Bulletin*, 93 (2): 261–78.

Nilsson, D.E., Strassberg, D.S. and Bannon, J. (1979) 'Perceptions of counselor self-disclosure: an analogue study', *Journal of Counseling Psychology*, 26 (5): 399–404.

Norcross, J.C. (2002a) 'Empirically supported therapy relationships', in J.C. Norcross (ed.), *Psychotherapy Relationships that Work: Therapist Contributions and Responsiveness to Patients.* New York: Oxford University Press, pp. 3–16.

Norcross, J.C. (ed.) (2002b) *Psychotherapy Relationships that Work: Therapists Contributions and Responsiveness to Patients.* New York: Oxford University Press.

Norcross, J.C. (2005) 'The psychotherapist's own psychotherapy: educating and developing psychologists', *American Psychologist*, 60 (8): 840–50.

Novey, T.B. (1999) 'The effectiveness of transactional analysis', *Transactional Analysis Journal*, 29 (1): 18–30.

Ockene, J., Kristeller, J.L., Goldberg, R., Ockene, I., Merriam, P., Barrett, S. et al. (1992) 'Smoking cessation and severity of disease – the Coronary-Artery Smoking Intervention Study', *Health Psychology*, 11 (2): 119–26.

Odell-Miller, H., Hughes, P. and Westacott, M. (2006) 'An investigation into the effectiveness of the arts therapies for adults with continuing mental health problems', *Psychotherapy Research*, 16 (1): 122–39.

Oei, T.P.S. and Free, M.L. (1995) 'Do cognitive-behavior therapies validate cognitive models of mood disorders – a review of the empirical evidence', *International Journal of Psychology*, 30 (2): 145–80.

Ogles, B.M., Anderson, T. and Lunnen, K.M. (1999) 'The contribution of models and techniques to therapeutic efficacy: contradictions between professional trends and clinical research', in M. Hubble, B.L. Duncan and S.D. Miller (eds), *The Heart and Soul of Change: What Works in Therapy*. Washington, DC: American Psychological Association, pp. 201–25.

Ogrodniczuk, J.S. and Piper, W.E. (2001) 'Day treatment for personality disorders: a review of research findings', *Harvard Review of Psychiatry*, 9 (3): 105–17.

Ogrodniczuk, J.S., Piper, W.E., Joyce, A.S. and McCallum, M. (2001) 'Using DSM Axis II information to predict outcome in short-term individual psychotherapy', *Journal of Personality Disorders*, 15 (2): 110–22.

Okiishi, J., Lambert, M.J., Nielsen, S.L. and Ogles, B.M. (2003) 'Waiting for supershrink: an empirical analysis of therapist effects', *Clinical Psychology and Psychotherapy*, 10 (6): 361–73.

Orlinsky, D., Grawe, K. and Parks, B. (1994) 'Process and outcome in psychotherapy – Noch Einmal', in A.E. Bergin and S.L. Garfield (eds), *Handbook of Psychotherapy and Behavior Change*. New York: John Wiley, pp. 270–376.

Orlinsky, D.E. and Rønnestad, M.H. (eds) (2005) *How Psychotherapists Develop: A Study of Therapeutic Work and Professional Growth*. Washington, DC: American Psychological Association.

Orlinsky, D.E., Rønnestad, M.H. and Willutzki, U. (2004) 'Fifty years of psychotherapy process-outcome research: continuity and change', in M.J. Lambert (ed.), *Bergin and Garfield's Handbook of Psychotherapy and Behavior Change* (5th edn). Chicago: John Wiley & Sons, pp. 307–89.

Orne, M.T. (1962) 'On the social psychology of the psychology experiment: with particular reference to the demand characteristics and their implications', *American Psychologist*, 17 (11): 776–83.

Öst, L.G. (1987) 'Applied relaxation: description of a coping technique and review of controlled-studies', *Behaviour Research and Therapy*, 25 (5): 397–409.

Öst, L.G. (1988) 'Applied relaxation vs. progressive relaxation in the treatment of panic disorder', *Behaviour Research and Therapy*, 26 (1): 13–22.

Öst, L.G. and Breitholtz, E. (2000) 'Applied relaxation vs. cognitive therapy in the treatment of generalized anxiety disorder', *Behaviour Research and Therapy*, 38 (8): 777–90.

Öst, L.G. and Westling, B.E. (1995) 'Applied relaxation vs. cognitive-behavior therapy in the treatment of panic disorder', *Behaviour Research and Therapy*, 33 (2): 145–58.

Paivio, S.C. and Bahr, L.M. (1998) 'Interpersonal problems, working alliance, and outcome in short-term experiential therapy', *Psychotherapy Research*, 8 (4): 392–407.

Paivio, S.C. and Greenberg, L.S. (1995) 'Resolving unfinished business – efficacy of experiential therapy using empty-chair dialogue', *Journal of Consulting and Clinical Psychology*, 63 (3): 419–25.

Paivio, S.C. and Nieuwenhuis, J.A. (2001) 'Efficacy of emotion focused therapy for adult survivors of child abuse: a preliminary study', *Journal of Traumatic Stress*, 14 (1): 115–33.

Paivio, S.C., Hall, I.E., Holowaty, K.A.M., Jellis, J.B. and Tran, N. (2001) 'Imaginal confrontation for resolving child abuse issues', *Psychotherapy Research*, 11 (4): 433–53.

Pallesen, S., Mitsem, M., Kvale, G., Johnsen, B.H. and Molde, H. (2005) 'Outcome of psychological treatments of pathological gambling: a review and meta-analysis', *Addiction*, 100 (10): 1412–22.

Patterson, G.R. and Forgatch, M.S. (1985) 'Therapist behavior as a determinant for client noncompliance: a paradox for the behavior modifier', *Journal of Consulting and Clinical Psychology*, 53 (6): 846–51.

Paul, G. (1967) 'Strategy of outcome research in psychotherapy', *Journal of Consulting Psychology*, 31 (2): 109–18.

Paulson, B.L. and Worth, M. (2002) 'Counselling for suicide: client perspectives', *Journal of Counseling and Development*, 80 (1): 86–93.

Paulson, B.L., Everall, R.D. and Janice, S. (2001) 'Client perception of hindering experiences in counselling', *Counselling and Psychotherapy Research*, 1 (1): 53–61.

Pekarik, G. (1992) 'Relationship of clients' reasons for dropping out of treatment to outcome and satisfaction', *Journal of Clinical Psychology*, 48 (1): 91–8.

Pennebaker, J.W. (1997) 'Writing about emotional experiences as a therapeutic process', *Psychological Science*, 8 (3): 162–6.

Perri, M.G., Nezu, A.M., McKelvey, W.F., Shermer, R.L., Renjilian, D.A. and Viegener, B.J. (2001) 'Relapse prevention training and problem-solving therapy in the long-term management of obesity', *Journal of Consulting and Clinical Psychology*, 69 (4): 722–6.

Perry, J.C., Banon, E. and Ianni, F. (1999) 'Effectiveness of psychotherapy for personality disorders', *American Journal of Psychiatry*, 156 (9): 1312–21.

Petrie, K.J., Booth, R.J., Pennebaker, J.W., Davison, K.P. and Thomas, M.G. (1995) 'Disclosure of trauma and immune-response to a hepatitis-B vaccination program', *Journal of Consulting and Clinical Psychology*, 63 (5): 787–92.

Pilling, S., Bebbington, P., Kuipers, E., Garety, P., Geddes, J., Orbach, G. et al. (2002) 'Psychological treatments in schizophrenia: I. Meta-analysis of family intervention and cognitive behaviour therapy', *Psychological Medicine*, 32 (5): 763–82.

Piper, W.E., Azim, H.F.A., Joyce, A.S. and McCallum, M. (1991) 'Transference interpretations, therapeutic alliance, and outcome in short-term individual psychotherapy', *Archives of General Psychiatry*, 48 (10): 946–53.

Piper, W.E., Joyce, A.S., McCallum, M. and Azim, H.F. (1993) 'Concentration and correspondence of transference interpretations in short-term psychotherapy', *Journal of Consulting and Clinical Psychology*, 61 (4): 586–95.

Piper, W.E., Joyce, A.S., McCallum, M. and Azim, H.F. (1998) 'Interpretive and supportive forms of psychotherapy and patient personality variables', *Journal of Consulting and Clinical Psychology*, 66 (3): 558–67.

Piper, W.E., McCallum, M., Joyce, A.S., Rosie, J.S. and Ogrodniczuk, J.S. (2001) 'Patient personality and time-limited group psychotherapy for complicated grief', *International Journal of Group Psychotherapy*, 51 (4): 525–52.

Piper, W.E., Ogrodniczuk, J.S., Joyce, A.S., McCallum, M., Rosie, J.S., O'Kelly, J.G. et al. (1999) 'Prediction of dropping out in time-limited, interpretive individual psychotherapy', *Psychotherapy: Theory, Research, Practice, Training*, 36 (2): 114–22.

Pohlman, E. (1972) 'Should clients tell counselors what to do?' *Personnel and Guidance Journal*, 42: 456–8.

Pos, A.E., Greenberg, L.S., Goldman, R.N. and Korman, L.M. (2003) 'Emotional processing during experiential treatment of depression', *Journal of Consulting and Clinical Psychology*, 71 (6): 1007–16.

Prendergast, M.L., Podus, D., Chang, E. and Urada, D. (2002) 'The effectiveness of drug abuse treatment: a meta-analysis of comparison group studies', *Drug and Alcohol Dependence*, 67 (1): 53–72.

Prochaska, J.O. (1999) 'How do people change, and how can we change to help many more people?' in M. Hubble, B.L. Duncan and S.D. Miller (eds), *The Heart and Soul of Change: What Works in Therapy*. Washington, DC: American Psychological Association, pp. 227–55.

Prochaska, J.O., DiClemente, C.C., Velicer, W.F. and Rossi, J.S. (1993) 'Standardized, individualized, interactive, and personalized self-help programs for smoking cessation', *Health Psychology*, 12 (5): 399–405.

Prochaska, J.O., Velicer, W.F., Fava, J.L., Rossi, J.S. and Tsoh, J.Y. (2001) 'Evaluating a population-based recruitment approach and a stage-based expert system intervention for smoking cessation', *Addictive Behaviors*, 26 (4): 583–602.

Project MATCH Research Group (1997) 'Matching alcoholism treatments to client heterogeneity: Project MATCH posttreatment drinking outcomes', *Journal of Studies on Alcohol*, 58 (1): 7–29.

Project MATCH Research Group (1998) 'Therapist effects in three treatments for alcohol problems', *Psychotherapy Research*, 8 (4): 455–74.

Propst, A., Paris, J. and Rosberger, Z. (1994) 'Do therapist experience, diagnosis and functional level predict outcome in short term psychotherapy?' *Canadian Journal of Psychiatry*, 39 (3): 168–76.

Propst, L.R., Ostrom, R., Watkins, P., Dean, T. and Mashburn, D. (1992) 'Comparative efficacy of religious and nonreligious cognitive-behavioral therapy for the treatment of clinical depression in religious individuals', *Journal of Consulting and Clinical Psychology*, 60 (1): 94–103.

Rapee, R.M. and Hayman, K. (1996) 'The effects of video feedback on the self-evaluation of performance in socially anxious subjects', *Behaviour Research and Therapy*, 34 (4): 315–22.

Regan, A.M. and Hill, C.E. (1992) 'Investigation of what clients and counselors do not say in brief therapy', *Journal of Counseling Psychology*, 39 (2): 168–74.

Reid, W.J. (1997) 'Evaluating the dodo's verdict: do all interventions have equivalent outcomes?' *Social Work Research*, 21 (1): 5–16.

Rennie, D.L. (1994) 'Clients' deference in psychotherapy', *Journal of Counseling Psychology*, 41 (4): 427–37.

Rennie, D.L. (1998) *Person-Centred Counselling: An Experiential Approach*. London: Sage.

Rennie, D.L. (2004) 'Anglo-North American qualitative counselling and psychotherapy research', *Psychotherapy Research*, 14 (1): 37–55.

Reynolds, M.W., Nabors, L. and Quinlan, A. (2000) 'The effectiveness of art therapy: does it work?' *American Art Therapy*, 17 (3): 207–13.

Rhodes, R.H., Hill, C.E., Thompson, B.J. and Elliott, R. (1994) 'Client retrospective recall of resolved and unresolved misunderstanding events', *Journal of Counseling Psychology*, 41 (4): 473–83.

Ricks, D.F. (1974) 'Supershrink: methods of a therapist judged successful on the basis of adult outcomes of adolescent patients', in D.F. Ricks, M. Roff and A. Thomas (eds), *Life History Research in Psychopathology*. Minneapolis: University of Minneapolis, pp. 275–97.

Ripley, J.S., Worthington, E.L. and Berry, J.W. (2001) 'The effects of religiosity on preferences and expectations for marital therapy among married Christians', *American Journal of Family Therapy*, 29 (1): 39–58.

Ritter, M. and Graff, K. (1996) 'Effects of dance/movement therapy: a meta-analysis', *Arts in Psychotherapy*, 23 (3): 249–60.

Robbins, S.B. and Jolkovski, M.P. (1987) 'Managing countertransference feelings: an interactional model using awareness of feeling and theoretical framework', *Journal of Counseling Psychology*, 34 (3): 276–82.

Rochlin, M. (1985) 'Sexual orientation of the therapist and therapeutic effectiveness with gay clients', in J.C. Gonsiorek (ed.), *A Guide to Psychotherapy with Gay and Lesbian Clients*. New York: Harrington Park, pp. 21–9.

Rogers, C.R. (1957) 'The necessary and sufficient conditions of therapeutic personality change', *Journal of Consulting Psychology*, 21 (2): 95–103.

Rogers, C.R. (1959) 'A theory of therapy, personality and interpersonal relationships as developed in the client-centered framework', in S. Koch (ed.), *Psychology: A Study of Science* (vol. 3). New York: McGraw-Hill, pp. 184–256.

Rogers, C.R. (1961) *On Becoming a Person: A Therapist's View of Therapy*. London: Constable & Co.

Rogers, C.R. (1980a) 'Empathic: an unappreciated way of being', in *A Way of Being*. Boston: Houghton & Mifflin, pp. 137–63.

Rogers, C.R. (1980b) *A Way of Being*. Boston: Houghton & Mifflin.

Rohsenow, D.J., Monti, P.M., Rubonis, A.V., Gulliver, S.B., Colby, S.M., Binkoff, J.A. et al. (2001) 'Cue exposure with coping skills training and communication skills training for alcohol dependence: 6- and 12-month outcomes', *Addiction*, 96 (8): 1161–74.

Rønnestad, M.H. and Ladany, N. (2006) 'The impact of psychotherapy training: introduction to the special section', *Psychotherapy Research*, 16 (3): 261–7.

Rose, E.M., Westefeld, J.S. and Ansely, T.N. (2001) 'Spiritual issues in counseling: clients' beliefs and preferences', *Journal of Counseling Psychology*, 48 (1): 61–71.

Rose, S., Bisson, J., Churchill, R. and Wessely, S. (2006) 'Psychological debriefing for preventing post traumatic stress disorder (PTSD)', *Cochrane Database of Systematic Reviews* (4).

Rosenheck, R., Fontana, A. and Cottrol, C. (1995) 'Effect of clinician–veteran racial pairing in the treatment of posttraumatic stress disorder', *American Journal of Psychiatry*, 152 (4): 555–63.

Rosenthal, R. and Rosnow, R. (1991) *Essentials of Behavioural Research* (2nd edn). London: McGraw-Hill.

Rosenzweig, S. (1936) 'Some implicit common factors in diverse methods of psychotherapy: "At last the Dodo said, 'Everybody has won and all must have prizes'"', *American Journal of Orthopsychiatry*, 6: 412–15.

Roth, A. and Fonagy, P. (2005) *What Works for Whom? A Critical Review of Psychotherapy Research* (2nd edn). New York: Guilford Press.

Ruddy, R. and Dent-Brown, K. (2007) 'Drama therapy for schizophrenia or schizophrenia-like illnesses', *Cochrane Database of Systematic Reviews* (4).

Ruddy, R. and Milnes, D. (2005) 'Art therapy for schizophrenia or schizophrenia-like illnesses', *Cochrane Database of Systematic Reviews* (4).

Rude, S.S. and Rehm, L.P. (1991) 'Response to treatments for depression: the role of initial status on targeted cognitive and behavioral skills', *Clinical Psychology Review*, 11 (5): 493–514.

Ryan, V.L. and Gizynski, M.N. (1971) 'Behavior therapy in retrospect – patients' feelings about their behavior therapies', *Journal of Consulting and Clinical Psychology*, 37 (1): 1–9.

Ryle, A. and Golynkina, K. (2000) 'Effectiveness of time-limited cognitive analytic therapy of borderline personality disorder: factors associated with outcome', *British Journal of Medical Psychology*, 73: 197–210.

Saatsi, S., Hardy, G.E. and Cahill, J. (2007) 'Predictors of outcome and completion status in cognitive therapy for depression', *Psychotherapy Research*, 17 (2): 189–200.

Sachse, R. (1990) 'Concrete interventions are crucial: the influence of the therapist's processing proposals on the client's interpersonal exploration in client-centred therapy', in G. Lietaer, J. Rombauts and R. Van Balen (eds), *Client Centred and Experiential Psychotherapies in the Nineties*. Leuven: Leuven University Press, pp. 295–308.

Sachse, R. (2004) 'From client-centered to clarification-oriented psychotherapy', *Person-Centered and Experiential Psychotherapies*, 3 (1): 19–35.

Sachse, R. and Elliott, R. (2002) 'Process-outcome research on humanistic therapy variables', in D.J. Cain and J. Seeman (eds), *Humanistic Psychotherapies: Handbook of Research and Practice*. Washington, DC: American Psychological Association, pp. 83–115.

Safran, J.D. (2002) 'Brief relational psychoanalytic treatment', *Psychoanalytic Dialogues*, 12 (2): 171–95.

Safran, J.D. and Muran, J.C. (2000a) *Negotiating the Therapeutic Alliance: A Relational Treatment Guide*. New York: Guilford Press.

Safran, J.D. and Muran, J.C. (2000b) 'Resolving therapeutic alliance ruptures: diversity and integration', *Psychotherapy in Practice*, 56 (2): 233–43.

Safran, J.D. and Wallner, L.K. (1991) 'The relative predictive validity of two therapeutic alliance measures in cognitive therapy', *Psychological Assessment*, 3 (2): 188–95.

Safran, J.D., Crocker, P., McMain, S. and Murray, P. (1990) 'Therapeutic alliance rupture as a therapy event for empirical investigation', *Psychotherapy: Theory, Research, Practice, Training*, 27 (2): 154–65.

Safran, J.D., Muran, J.C., Samstag, L.W. and Stevens, C. (2002) 'Repairing alliance ruptures', in J.C. Norcross (ed.), *Psychotherapy Relationships that Work: Therapist Contributions and Responsiveness to Patients*. New York: Oxford University Press, pp. 235–54.

Sainsbury Centre for Mental Health (2006) *We Need to Talk: The Case for Psychological Therapy on the NHS*. London: Sainsbury Centre for Mental Health.

Salvio, M.-A., Beutler, L.E., Wood, J.M. and Engle, D. (1992) 'The strength of the therapeutic alliance in three treatments for depression', *Psychotherapy Research*, 2 (1): 31–6.

Sanchez, V.C., Lewinsohn, P.M. and Larson, D.W. (1980) 'Assertion training: effectiveness in the treatment of depression', *Journal of Clinical Psychology*, 36 (2): 526–9.

Sandell, R., Carlsson, J., Schubert, J., Grant, J., Lazar, A. and Broberg, J. (2006) 'Therapists' therapies: the relation between training therapy and patient change in long-term psychotherapy and psychoanalysis', *Psychotherapy Research*, 16 (3): 306–16.

Sands, A. (2000) *Falling for Therapy: Psychotherapy from a Client's Point of View*. London: Macmillan.

Saunders, E.J. and Saunders, J.A. (2000) 'Evaluating the effectiveness of art therapy through a quantitative, outcomes-focused study', *Arts in Psychotherapy*, 27 (2): 99–106.

Schmidt, N.B. and Woolaway-Bickel, K. (2000) 'The effects of treatment compliance on outcome in cognitive-behavioral therapy for panic disorder: quality versus quantity', *Journal of Consulting and Clinical Psychology*, 68 (1): 13–8.

Scholing, A. and Emmelkamp, P.M.G. (1993) 'Cognitive and behavioural treatments of fear of blushing, sweating or trembling', *Behaviour Research and Therapy*, 31 (2): 155–70.

Scholing, A. and Emmelkamp, P.M.G. (1996) 'Treatment of generalized social phobia: results at long-term follow-up', *Behaviour Research and Therapy*, 34 (5/6): 447–52.

Schulte, D., Kunzel, R., Pepping, G. and Schulte-Bahrenberg, T. (1992) 'Tailor-made versus standardized therapy of phobic patients', *Advances in Behaviour Research and Therapy*, 14 (2): 67–92.

Scottish Association for Mental Health (2006) *What's It Worth? The Social and Economic Costs of Mental Health Problems in Scotland*. Glasgow: Scottish Association for Mental Health.

Segrin, C. (2001) *Interpersonal Processes in Psychological Problems*. New York: Guilford Press.

Seligman, M.E.P. (1995) 'The effectiveness of psychotherapy – the Consumer Reports study', *American Psychologist*, 50 (12): 965–74.

Serfaty, M.A., Turkington, D., Heap, M., Ledsham, L. and Jolley, E. (1999) 'Cognitive therapy versus dietary counselling in the outpatient treatment of anorexia nervosa: effects of the treatment phase', *European Eating Disorders Review*, 7 (5): 334–50.

Shadish, W.R., Matt, G.E., Navarro, A.M. and Phillips, G. (2000) 'The effects of psychological therapies under clinically representative conditions: a meta-analysis', *Psychological Bulletin*, 126 (4): 512–29.

Shapiro, D.A. and Shapiro, D. (1982) 'Meta-analysis of comparative therapy outcome studies – a replication and refinement', *Psychological Bulletin*, 92 (3): 581–604.

Sharpley, C.F. (1987) 'Research findings on neurolinguistic programming: nonsupportive data or an untestable theory?' *Journal of Counseling Psychology*, 34 (1): 103–7.

Shaw, B.F., Elkin, I., Yamaguchi, J., Olmsted, M., Vallis, T.M., Dobson, K.S. et al. (1999) 'Therapist competence ratings in relation to clinical outcome in cognitive therapy of depression', *Journal of Consulting and Clinical Psychology*, 67 (6): 837–46.

Shear, K., Frank, E., Houck, P.R. and Reynolds, C.F. (2005) 'Treatment of complicated grief – a randomized controlled trial', *Journal of the American Medical Association*, 293 (21): 2601–8.

Sherman, J.J. (1998) 'Effects of psychotherapeutic treatments for PTSD: a meta-analysis of controlled clinical trials', *Journal of Traumatic Stress*, 11 (3): 413–35.

Shoham-Salomon, V. and Hannah, M.T. (1991) 'Client–treatment interaction in the study of differential change processes', *Journal of Consulting and Clinical Psychology*, 59 (2): 217–25.

Siev, J. and Chambless, D.L. (2007) 'Specificity of treatment effects: cognitive therapy and relaxation for generalized anxiety and panic disorders', *Journal of Consulting and Clinical Psychology*, 75 (4): 513–22.

Simpson, S., Corney, R., Fitzgerald, P. and Beecham, J. (2000) 'A randomized controlled trial to evaluate the effectiveness and cost-effectiveness of counselling patients with chronic depression', *Health Technology Assessment*, 4 (36).

Sloane, R.B., Staples, F.R., Whipple, K. and Cristol, A.H. (1977) 'Patients' attitudes toward behavior-therapy and psychotherapy', *American Journal of Psychiatry*, 134 (2): 134–7.

Smedslund, G. and Ringdal, G.I. (2004) 'Meta-analysis of the effects of psychosocial interventions on survival time in cancer patients', *Journal of Psychosomatic Research*, 57 (2): 123–31.

Smith, M.L. and Glass, G.V. (1977) 'Meta-analysis of psychotherapy outcome studies', *American Psychologist*, 32 (9): 752–60.

Smith, T.B., Bartz, J. and Richards, P.S. (2007) 'Outcomes of religious and spiritual adaptations to psychotherapy: a meta-analytic review', *Psychotherapy Research*, 17 (6): 643–55.

Snyder, C.R., Michael, S.T. and Cheavens, J.S. (1999) 'Hope as a foundation of common factors, placebos, and expectancies', in M. Hubble, B.L. Duncan and S.D. Miller (eds), *The Heart and Soul of Change: What Works in Therapy*. Washington, DC: American Psychological Association, pp. 179–200.

Soldz, S. (2006) 'Models and meanings: therapist effects and the stories we tell', *Psychotherapy Research*, 16 (2): 173–7.

Sotsky, S.M., Glass, D.R., Shea, M.T., Pilkonis, P.A., Collins, J.F., Elkin, I. et al. (1991) 'Patient predictors of response to psychotherapy and pharmacotherapy – findings in the NIMH Treatment of Depression Collaborative Research Program', *American Journal of Psychiatry*, 148 (8): 997–1008.

Spangler, D.L., Simons, A.D., Monroe, S.M. and Thase, M.E. (1997) 'Response to cognitive-behavioral therapy in depression: effects of pretreatment cognitive dysfunction and life stress', *Journal of Consulting and Clinical Psychology*, 65 (4): 568–75.

Stalker, C.A., Levene, J.E. and Coady, N.F. (1999) 'Solution-focused brief therapy – one model fits all?' *Families in Society – The Journal of Contemporary Human Services*, 80 (5): 468–77.

Steering Committee (2002) 'Empirically supported therapy relationships: conclusions and recommendations on the Division 29 Task Force', in J.C. Norcross (ed.), *Psychotherapy Relationships that Work: Therapist Contributions and Responsiveness to Patients*. New York: Oxford University Press, pp. 441–3.

Stein, D.M. and Lambert, M.J. (1995) 'Graduate training in psychotherapy – are therapy outcomes enhanced?' *Journal of Consulting and Clinical Psychology*, 63 (2): 182–96.

Stiles, W.B. and Shapiro, D.A. (1994) 'Disabuse of the drug metaphor – psychotherapy process outcome correlations', *Journal of Consulting and Clinical Psychology*, 62 (5): 942–8.

Stiles, W.B., Honos-Webb, L. and Surko, M. (1998) 'Responsiveness in psychotherapy', *Clinical Psychology: Science and Practice*, 5 (4): 439–58.

Stiles, W.B., Barkham, M., Mellor-Clark, J. and Connell, J. (2008) 'Effectiveness of cognitive-behavioural, person-centred, and psychodynamic therapies in UK primary-care routine practice: replication in a larger sample', *Psychological Medicine*, 38 (5): 677–88.

Stiles, W.B., Shankland, M.C., Wright, J. and Field, S.D. (1997) 'Aptitude-treatment interactions based on clients' assimilation of their presenting problems', *Journal of Consulting and Clinical Psychology*, 65 (5): 889–93.

Stiles, W.B., Barkham, M., Twigg, E., Mellor-Clark, J. and Cooper, M. (2006) 'Effectiveness of cognitive-behavioural, person-centred and psychodynamic therapies as practised in UK National Health Service settings', *Psychological Medicine*, 36 (4): 555–66.

Strümpfel, U. and Goldman, R. (2002) 'Contacting gestalt therapy', in D.J. Cain and J. Seeman (eds), *Humanistic Psychotherapies: Handbook of Research and Practice*. Washington, DC: American Psychological Association, pp. 189–219.

Sue, S. and Lam, A.G. (2002) 'Cultural and demographic diversity', in J.C. Norcross (ed.), *Psychotherapy Relationships that Work: Therapist Contributions and Responsiveness to Patients*. New York: Oxford University Press, pp. 401–21.

Swoboda, J.S., Dowd, E.T. and Wise, S.L. (1990) 'Reframing and restraining directives in the treatment of clinical depression', *Journal of Counseling Psychology*, 37 (3): 254–60.

Sylvain, C., Ladouceur, R. and Boisvert, J.M. (1997) 'Cognitive and behavioral treatment of pathological gambling: a controlled study', *Journal of Consulting and Clinical Psychology*, 65 (5): 727–32.

Tang, T.Z. and DeRubeis, R.J. (1999) 'Sudden gains and critical sessions in cognitive-behavioral therapy for depression', *Journal of Consulting and Clinical Psychology*, 67 (6): 894–904.

Tang, T.Z., DeRubeis, R.J., Hollon, S.D., Amsterdam, J. and Shelton, R. (2007) 'Sudden gains in cognitive therapy of depression and depression relapse/recurrence', *Journal of Consulting and Clinical Psychology*, 75 (3): 404–8.

Tarrier, N., Pilgrim, H., Sommerfield, C., Faragher, B., Reynolds, M., Graham, E. et al. (1999) 'A randomized trial of cognitive therapy and imaginal exposure in the treatment of chronic posttraumatic stress disorder', *Journal of Consulting and Clinical Psychology*, 67 (1): 13–18.

Tarrier, N., Sharpe, L., Beckett, R., Harwood, S., Baker, A. and Yusopoff, L. (1993) 'A trial of two cognitive behavioral-methods of treating drug-resistant residual psychotic symptoms in schizophrenic-patients. 2. Treatment-specific changes in coping and problem-solving skills', *Social Psychiatry and Psychiatric Epidemiology*, 28 (1): 5–10.

Task Force on Promotion and Dissemination of Psychological Procedures (1995) 'Training in and dissemination of empirically-validated psychological treatments: report and recommendations', *Clinical Psychologist*, 83 (1): 3–23.

Teasdale, J.D. (1985) 'Psychological treatments for depression – how do they work?', *Behaviour Research and Therapy*, 23 (2): 157–65.

Teasdale, J.D., Scott, J., Moore, R.G., Hayhurst, H., Pope, M. and Paykel, E.S. (2001) 'How does cognitive therapy prevent relapse in residual depression? Evidence from a controlled trial', *Journal of Consulting and Clinical Psychology*, 69 (3): 347–57.

Telch, C.F., Agras, W.S. and Linehan, M.M. (2001) 'Dialectical behavior therapy for binge eating disorder', *Journal of Consulting and Clinical Psychology*, 69 (6): 1061–5.

Thelen, M.H. and Lasoski, M.C. (1980) 'The separate and combined effects of focusing information and videotape self-confrontation feedback', *Journal of Behavior Therapy and Experimental Psychiatry*, 11 (3): 173–8.

Thompson, B.J. and Hill, C.E. (1991) 'Therapist perceptions of client reactions', *Journal of Counseling and Development*, 69 (3): 261–5.

Timulak, L. (2007) 'Identifying core categories of client-identified impact of helpful events in psychotherapy: a qualitative meta-analysis', *Psychotherapy Research*, 17 (3): 310–20.

Timulak, L. (2008a) 'Significant events in psychotherapy: an update of research findings'. Paper presented at the ScotCon/Scottish SPR Seminars, Glasgow.

Timulak, L. (2008b) *Research in Psychotherapy and Counselling*. London: Sage.

Tinsley, H.E., Bowman, S.L. and Barich, A.W. (1993) 'Counseling psychologists' perceptions of the occurrence and effects of unrealistic expectations about counseling and psychotherapy among their clients', *Journal of Counseling Psychology*, 40 (1): 46–52.

Tracey, T.J. and Dundon, M. (1988) 'Role anticipations and preferences over the course of counseling', *Journal of Counseling Psychology*, 35 (1): 3–14.

Treasure, J., Todd, G., Brolly, M., Tiller, J., Nehmed, A. and Denman, F. (1995) 'A pilot study of a randomised trial of cognitive analytical therapy vs educational behavioral therapy for adult anorexia nervosa', *Behaviour Research and Therapy*, 33 (4): 363–7.

Tryon, G.S. (2002) 'Engagement in counselling', in G.S. Tryon (ed.), *Counselling Based on Process Research: Applying What we Know*. Boston: Allyn & Bacon, pp. 1–26.

Tryon, G.S. and Winograd, G. (2002) 'Goal consensus and collaboration', in J.C. Norcross (ed.), *Psychotherapy Relationships that Work: Therapist Contributions and Responsiveness to Patients*. New York: Oxford University Press, pp. 109–25.

Tryon, G.S., Blackwell, S.C. and Hammel, E.F. (2007) 'A meta-analytic examination of client–therapist perspectives of the working alliance', *Psychotherapy Research*, 17 (6): 629–42.

Turner, S.M., Beidel, D.C. and Cooley-Quille, M.R. (1995) 'Case histories and shorter communications: two-year follow-up of social phobics with social effectiveness therapy', *Behaviour Research and Therapy*, 33 (5): 553–5.

Tyrrell, C.L., Dozier, M., Teague, G.B. and Fallot, R.D. (1999) 'Effective treatment relationships for persons with serious psychiatric disorders: the importance of attachment states of mind', *Journal of Consulting and Clinical Psychology*, 67 (5): 725–33.

Vallance, K. (2005) 'Exploring counsellor perceptions of the impact of counselling supervision on clients', *Counselling and Psychotherapy Research*, 5 (2): 107–10.

Vallejo, J., Gasto, C., Catalan, R., Bulbena, A. and Menchon, J.M. (1991) 'Predictors of antidepressant treatment outcome in melancholia: psychosocial, clinical and biological indicators', *Journal of Affective Disorders*, 21 (3): 151–62.

Van Audenhove, C. and Vertommen, H. (2000) 'A negotiation approach to intake and treatment choice', *Journal of Psychotherapy Integration*, 10 (3): 287–99.

van Balkom, A.J., van Oppen, P., Vermeulen, A.W. and van Dyck, R. (1994) 'A meta-analysis on the treatment of obsessive compulsive disorder: a comparison of antidepressants, behavior, and cognitive therapy', *Clinical Psychology Review*, 14 (5): 359–81.

van Boeijen, C.A., van Balkom, A., van Oppen, P., Blankenstein, N., Cherpanath, A. and van Dyck, R. (2005) 'Efficacy of self-help manuals for anxiety disorders in primary care: a systematic review', *Family Practice*, 22 (2): 192–6.

VandeCreek, L. and Angstadt, L. (1985) 'Client preferences and anticipations about counselor self-disclosure', *Journal of Counseling Psychology*, 32 (2): 206–14.

Wade, N.G., Worthington, E.L. and Vogel, D.L. (2007) 'Effectiveness of religiously tailored interventions in Christian therapy', *Psychotherapy Research*, 17 (1): 91–105.

Walters, G.D. (2000) 'Behavioral self-control training for problem drinkers: a meta-analysis of randomized control studies', *Behavior Therapy*, 31 (1): 135–49.

Wampold, B.E. (2001) *The Great Psychotherapy Debate: Models, Methods and Findings*. Mahwah, NJ: Erlbaum.

Wampold, B.E., Mondin, G.W., Moody, M., Stich, F., Benson, K. and Ahn, H. (1997) 'A meta-analysis of outcome studies comparing bona fide psychotherapies: empirically, "all must have prizes."', *Psychological Bulletin*, 122 (3): 203–15.

Watkins, C.E. (1990) 'The effects of counsellor self-disclosure: a research review', *Counselling Psychologist*, 18 (3): 477–500.

Watson, J.C. and Geller, S.M. (2005) 'The relation among the relationship conditions, working alliance, and outcome in both process-experiential and cognitive-behavioral psychotherapy', *Psychotherapy Research*, 15 (1–2): 25–33.

Watson, J.C., Gordon, L.B., Stermac, L., Kalogerakos, F. and Steckley, P. (2003) 'Comparing the effectiveness of process-experiential with cognitive-behavioral psychotherapy in the treatment of depression', *Journal of Consulting and Clinical Psychology*, 71 (4): 773–81.

Weaks, D. (2002) 'Unlocking the secrets of "good supervision": a phenomenological exploration of experienced counsellors' perceptions of good supervision', *Counselling and Psychotherapy Research*, 2 (1): 33–9.

Westen, D., Novotny, C.A. and Thompson-Brenner, H. (2004) 'The empirical status of empirically supported psychotherapies: assumptions, findings, and reporting in controlled clinical trials', *Psychological Bulletin*, 130 (4): 631–3.

Wheeler, S. and Richards, K. (2007) *The Impact of Clinical Supervision on Counsellors and Therapists, their Practice and their Clients: A Systematic Review of the Literature*. Lutterworth: BACP.

Whipple, J.L., Lambert, M.J., Vermeersch, D.A., Smart, D.W., Nielsen, S.L. and Hawkins, E.J. (2003) 'Improving the effects of psychotherapy: the use of early identification of treatment failure and problem-solving strategies in routine practice', *Journal of Counseling Psychology*, 50 (1): 59–68.

Wierzbicki, M. and Pekarik, G. (1993) 'A meta-analysis of psychotherapy dropout', *Professional Psychology: Research and Practice*, 24 (2): 190–5.

Wikler, M. (1989) 'The religion of the therapist: its meaning to Orthodox Jewish clients', *Hillside Journal of Clinical Psychiatry*, 11 (2): 131–46.

Williams, E.N. (2002) 'Therapist techniques', in G.S. Tryon (ed.), *Counselling Based on Process Research: Applying What we Know*. Boston: Allyn & Bacon, pp. 232–64.

Williams, K.E. and Chambless, D.L. (1990) 'The relationship between therapist characteristics and outcome of in vivo exposure treatment for agoraphobia', *Behavior Therapy*, 21 (1): 111–16.

Wilson, S., Maddison, T., Roberts, L., Greenfield, S. and Singh, S. (2006) 'Systematic review: the effectiveness of hypnotherapy in the management of irritable bowel syndrome', *Alimentary Pharmacology & Therapeutics*, 24 (5): 769–80.

Wlazlo, Z., Schroeder-Hartwig, K., Hand, I., Kaiser, G. and Munchau, N. (1990) 'Exposure in vivo vs social skills training for social phobia: long-term outcome and differential effects', *Behaviour Research and Therapy*, 28 (3): 181–93.

Woody, G.E., McLellan, A.T., Luborsky, L. and O'Brien, C.P. (1995) 'Psychotherapy in community methadone programs – a Validation Study', *American Journal of Psychiatry*, 152 (9): 1302–8.

Woody, S.R. and Ollendick, T.H. (2006) 'Technique factors in treating anxiety disorders', in L.G. Castonguay and L.E. Beutler (eds), *Principles of Therapeutic Change that Work*. New York: Oxford University Press, pp. 167–86.

Worthen, V. and McNeill, B.W. (1996) 'A phenomenological investigation of "good" supervision events', *Journal of Counseling Psychology*, 43 (1): 25–34.

Worthen, V.E. and Lambert, M.J. (2007) 'Outcome oriented supervision: advantages of adding systematic client tracking to supportive consultations', *Counselling and Psychotherapy Research*, 7 (1): 48–53.

Worthington, E.L. and Sandage, S.J. (2002) 'Religion and spirituality', in J.C. Norcross (ed.), *Psychotherapy Relationships that Work: Therapist Contributions and Responsiveness to Patients*. New York: Oxford University Press, pp. 383–99.

Worthington, E.L., Kurusu, T.A., McCullough, M.E. and Sandage, S.J. (1996) 'Empirical research on religion and psychotherapeutic processes and outcomes: a 10-year review and research prospectus', *Psychological Bulletin*, 119 (3): 448–87.

Yalom, I. (2001) *The Gift of Therapy: Reflections on Being a Therapist*. London: Piatkus.

Yotis, L. (2006) 'A review of dramatherapy research in schizophrenia: methodologies and outcomes', *Psychotherapy Research*, 16 (2): 190–200.

Zane, N., Hall, G.C. N., Sue, S., Young, K. and Nunez, J. (2004) 'Research on psychotherapy with culturally diverse populations', in M.J. Lambert (ed.), *Bergin and Garfield's Handbook of Psychotherapy and Behavior Change* (5th edn). Chicago: John Wiley & Sons, pp. 767–804.

Zlotnick, C., Elkin, I. and Shea, M.T. (1998) 'Does the gender of a patient or the gender of a therapist affect the treatment of patients with major depression?' *Journal of Consulting and Clinical Psychology*, 66 (4): 655–9.

Zlotnick, C., Shea, M.T., Pilkonis, P.A., Elkin, I. and Ryan, C. (1996) 'Gender, type of treatment, dysfunctional attitudes, social support, life events, and depressive symptoms over naturalistic follow-up', *American Journal of Psychiatry*, 153 (8): 1021–7.

Zuroff, D.C., Koestner, R., Moskowitz, D.S., McBride, C., Marshall, M. and Bagby, R.M. (2007) 'Autonomous motivation for therapy: a new common factor in brief treatments for depression', *Psychotherapy Research*, 17 (2): 137–48.

Name Index

Subject Index

Note: Page numbers in *italic* refer to the glossary.

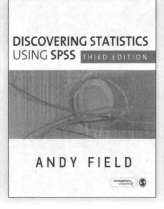
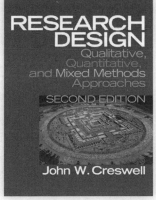

The Qualitative Research Kit

Edited by Uwe Flick

Read sample chapters online now!

Doing Ethnographic and Observational Research — Michael Angrosino — The SAGE Qualitative Research Kit — Edited by Uwe Flick

Using Visual Data in Qualitative Research — Marcus Banks — The SAGE Qualitative Research Kit — Edited by Uwe Flick

Doing Focus Groups — Rosaline Barbour — The SAGE Qualitative Research Kit — Edited by Uwe Flick

Designing Qualitative Research — Uwe Flick — The SAGE Qualitative Research Kit — Edited by Uwe Flick

Managing Quality in Qualitative Research — Uwe Flick — The SAGE Qualitative Research Kit — Edited by Uwe Flick

Analyzing Qualitative Data — Graham Gibbs — The SAGE Qualitative Research Kit — Edited by Uwe Flick

Doing Interviews — Steinar Kvale — The SAGE Qualitative Research Kit — Edited by Uwe Flick

Doing Conversation, Discourse and Document Analysis — Tim Rapley — The SAGE Qualitative Research Kit — Edited by Uwe Flick

www.sagepub.co.uk